MERCHANT OF
DEATH

MERCHANT OF
DEATH

Money, Guns, Planes, and the Man
Who Makes War Possible

DOUGLAS FARAH
AND
STEPHEN BRAUN

WILEY
John Wiley & Sons, Inc.

Published by John Wiley & Sons, Inc., Hoboken, New Jersey
Published simultaneously in Canada

Design and composition by Navta Associates. Inc.

For general information about our other products and services, please contact our Customer Care Department within the United States at (800) 762-2974, outside the United States at (317) 572-3993 or fax (317) 572-4002.

Wiley also publishes its books in a variety of electronic formats. Some content that appears in print may not be available in electronic books. For more information about Wiley products, visit our web site at www.wiley.com.

Library of Congress Cataloging-in-Publication Data:

Farah, Douglas.
    Merchant of death : money, guns, planes, and the man who makes war possible / Douglas Farah and Stephen Braun.
        p. cm.
    Includes bibliographical references and index.
    ISBN 978-0-470-04866-5 (cloth)
    ISBN 978-0-470-26196-5 (paper)
1. Bout, Viktor. 2. Transnational crime. 3. Illegal arms transfers. 4. Smuggling. 5. Security, International. I. Braun, Stephen. II. Title.
HV6252.F37 2007
364.1'33—dc22
[B]
2006037897

Printed in the United States of America

10 9 8 7 6 5 4 3 2 1

To Leslie, with love and a deep appreciation for her support,
insights, and love of a good story
—D.F.

To my wife and son, my loves and inspirations
—S.B.

CCCP   USSR

THE UNION OF SOVIET SOCIALIST REPUBLICS

PASSPORT

БУТ

ВИКТОР

АНАТОЛЬЕВИЧ

29 № 0006765

СОЮЗ СОВЕТСКИХ СОЦИАЛИСТИЧЕСКИХ РЕСПУБЛИК

29 № 0006765

Bout

Victor

Россия/Russia   г. Душанбе/ USSR

13.01.1967

м/м   28.05.1995

Посольство РФ   28.05.2000

CONTENTS

ACKNOWLEDGMENTS

From the authors:

This book is the product of the generosity and help of countless people, some named and many who cannot be. We would especially like to thank those who shared so much of their time and resources for the book and through the years, and whose help was indispensable: Lee Wolosky was a wellspring of perspective, always making himself available at a moment's notice. Johan Peleman was unstinting in forwarding history and insights. Witney Schneidman shared his memories and expertise. Kathi Austin opened her files and shared her stories. Lieutenant Colonel Chris Walker opened up the hectic world of Baghdad International Airport. Early in our project, Andreas Morgner gave us insights into the sometimes lonely efforts to keep the Bout investigation alive. Andre Verloy was extremely generous with his time and documents.

We were aided by a long list of trailblazers and guides, chief among them Phillip van Niekerk, Dirk Draulans, Robin Bhatty, Cindor Reeves, Gayle Smith, Jonathan Winer, Michael Chandler, David Biggs, Julie Sirrs, Ambassador Juan Larrain, Mohammed Eshaq, Callum Weeks, Barbara Elias, Paolo Fusi, and Paul Salopek.

A special thanks to Jeff Leen, who is one of the best editors in the business, for helping shape the manuscript. We owe a debt of gratitude to Eric Nelson at John Wiley & Sons for his insightful editing and love of the book, and Gail Ross and Howard Yoon for helping direct our efforts. Also, our thanks to Carol Guzy for her time and sharp photographer's eye.

To the many nameless who, at considerable risk, provided information, documents, and insights, our lasting appreciation. To the countless victims and survivors of a decade of war and terror caused by the flood of contraband arms, our deep and insufficient sorrow for a world that has done so little to stop the carnage.

From Douglas Farah:

My family has been extremely patient and generous with me. A heartfelt thanks for all they put up with in letting me chase stories.

A special thanks to the NEFA Foundation for its generosity in allowing me the time to write this and for vital research support. I deeply appreciate the unflagging enthusiasm of Michelle Hayes and David Draper for the project and help in times of crisis. Ron Sandee's invaluable insights and deep knowledge enriched the book and saved me from many errors.

Thor Ronay and Duncan Sellars at the International Assessment and Strategy Center have offered unstinting support, especially when things looked bleakest. Thank you.

Thanks, too, to Peter Bergen, who, over a bowl of pasta, urged me to write the book and helped set me off on this adventure.

From Stephen Braun:

My family cheered me on from the moment this project was conceived, coaxing me forward, humoring me during my mood swings, and patiently tucking into the manuscript at a moment's notice. They were my first and most careful readers and remained as supportive at the finish as they were at the start.

Much of this book could not have been written without the enterprising and dogged work of a stellar crew of *Los Angeles Times* reporters and editors who teamed up for a run of stories that grew from the terror attacks of September 11, 2001. From the beginning,

Judy Pasternak, my supremely talented collaborator, was as much guide as partner, ferreting out critical leads that always moved the work forward, drawing in important sources, and writing like a dream. John Daniszewski, then a Moscow correspondent and now foreign editor of the Associated Press, was as heroic and indefatigable in chasing leads to Kabul and Sharjah as he was later in enduring the bombing of Baghdad. Without him we would never have cracked the story of the Taliban connection. The fearless and resourceful Sergei Loiko was with John for much of the journey, and came up with defining interviews every time he picked up the phone. Maura Reynolds, a gifted colleague in Washington who then worked in Moscow with John and Sergei, also provided important Russian interviews. When the story moved to Iraq, T. Christian Miller, whose sources are legion in Baghdad and Washington, provided indispensable reporting. Sebastian Rotella pitched in from Paris at a crucial juncture. The late Mark Fineman helped nudge our work forward early on, when we needed it the most. We would all have been lost without the artful spadework of John Beckham, a researcher's researcher. A long parade of *Times* editors brought their sharp eyes to our stories, but three were instrumental in urging us on: former investigative editor Deborah Nelson shepherded all of our major efforts and encouraged us to think big; national editor Scott Kraft provided his commanding writer's eye to early drafts; and former *Times* editor Dean Baquet unleashed us and kept us on the trail.

A special thanks to three writers and friends who provided wise counsel and encouragement over the years and the course of this project: Mark Bowden, Peter H. King, and Mark Arax.

Prologue

Africa was burning. Witney Schneidman read the tide of grim news every morning when he arrived at his office on the sixth floor of the Department of State's headquarters in the Foggy Bottom section of Washington, D.C. Overnight intelligence summaries bearing the latest dismaying developments were usually waiting at his desk. Color-coded by agency, the eyes-only collations were filed from around the world in the predawn hours with terse reports from State's own analysts, cables from embassies abroad, glossy-covered briefings from the Central Intelligence Agency, and electronic intercepts gathered by the National Security Agency (NSA). All through the summer and fall of 1999, the thin summaries piling up on Schneidman's desk detailed the gathering African inferno as it took its toll not on forests, but in thousands of lives.

The fire consuming the continent in 1999 was anarchic slaughter, stoked by tribal enmity, greed, and ambition, raging out of control in too many countries at once. For a decade since the end of the Cold War, Africa had been plagued by internecine conflicts that killed millions by violence and millions more by war-induced starvation. As the rest of the world fixated euphorically on the rapprochement between the United States and the Eastern bloc, Africa's regional wars simmered, capable of erupting into sudden catastrophe at any moment. In 1994, the fast-paced crisis in Rwanda showed what could happen when governments failed to take heed. Rwanda's Hutu-led government launched a campaign to exterminate the Tutsi tribe, and the resulting warfare and spreading famine killed up to a million people. Rwanda's torment had receded by the summer of 1999, but there were new portents of trouble sweeping across the continent.

Sierra Leone, bled by nine years of civil war, was plunged in a lethal free fall. Militias from the Revolutionary United Front (RUF) launched a brutal January offensive against the government's capital in Freetown, lashing out in a spree of murder, mutilation, and arson. The RUF executed two thousand civilians and systematically maimed thousands more, amputating the limbs of their victims and gang-raping women and teenagers by the scores. Exhausted by the carnage, the RUF and the government signed a peace accord in June, but the pact was soon marred by cease-fire violations and more deaths. In Angola, a tranquil lull was shattered by air raids and bombardments, while rebel and government offensives killed thousands and displaced 1.7 million refugees. Two United Nations–chartered planes were shot out of the sky, towns were shelled, and village populations were massacred, leading to war crimes accusations on both sides. Sudan's seventeen-year-old civil war was accelerating as the fundamentalist Muslim government bombed tribal towns and refugee camps, leaving tens of thousands homeless. In the Democratic Republic of the Congo (DRC), rebels tightened control over the eastern half of the country and sparred sporadically with the government forces. Skirmishes in Liberia threatened a tenuous peace while the autocratic government of Charles Taylor consolidated power and intimated opponents amid a wave of torture, killings, and disappearances. And throughout the year, American missions in Africa were on high alert, still jittery in the wake of the August 1998 al Qaeda bombings that had killed 220 people in Nairboi and Dar es Salaam and raised the specter of terrorist penetration across Africa.[1]

Schneidman, the Clinton administration's deputy assistant secretary of state for African affairs, pored worriedly through the reports every morning. A rumpled, cheerfully profane diplomat driven by his fascination with African policy, Schneidman normally dealt with social and economic issues such as the AIDS crisis and the continent's soaring national debts. But the brutal ethnic conflicts and power struggles that flickered alive again in 1999 jeopardized that progress.

Enamored of African history and culture since his college days, Schneidman kept up a grueling pace traveling to South Africa and other emerging democracies. He had studied at the University of Dar es Salaam in Tanzania and written on the decolonization of Angola and Portuguese East Africa before joining the State Department for several years in the late 1980s. Through the 1990s he had worked in South Africa for the World Bank and in other financial roles before rejoining State as a deputy assistant secretary in late 1997.

In his earlier stint at State, Schneidman had served two years as an analyst with State's Intelligence and Research Bureau, so he was familiar with the dry, codified shorthand of the summaries piling up on his desk. Working late hours in a small office decorated with a few tribal masks and totems from his African visits, Schneidman began searching for revelatory nuggets. Over months, he noticed a recurring reference in the SIGINT material—the satellite and electronic intercepts of telephone and Internet communications provided by the NSA. The African summaries kept citing a "Russian national" who appeared to be delivering tons of weapons by plane through Central and West Africa, where much of the latest violence raged. The Russian's last name was unclear—he used too many aliases. The intelligence briefs simply described him as "Viktor B."

"After two or three months of reading this stuff a light went on in my head," Schneidman recalled seven years later. "We needed to go after this guy."

Schneidman quickly learned that a few others inside the government already shared his curiosity. One was a studious, bearded young CIA analyst at the agency's Langley headquarters who had responsibility for "thugs and guns" operating across international borders. For several years he had been quietly building files on the Russian and other arms merchants in Africa, waiting for someone on the policy side to take note. The analyst had already compiled an impressive array of evidence showing that the mystery man's weapons pipelines were fueling the intractable violence in Sierra Leone, Liberia, Angola, the DRC, and other African countries at risk. As the analyst had focused on the movements of massive shipments of relatively new, sophisticated weapons flowing into the warring countries, he caught repeated references to old Russian cargo planes that kept turning up in flights across the region, spotted by over-head U.S. plane-mounted radar in the vicinity of drop zones and airfields where the shipments of Russian and East European–issue weapons and ammunition were off-loaded. The CIA man kept track of the tail numbers of the Antonov and Ilyushin freighters as they reappeared, noting that sometimes the busy planes even armed both sides in the same war.

The sprawling enterprise moved a spectacular tonnage of weaponry thousands of miles by air from Eastern Europe deep into Africa. The range of ordnance was staggering: disassembled attack helicopters, heavy antiaircraft guns, a multitude of crated AK-47s and shoulder-fired rocket launchers, land mines, mortars, artillery rounds, and millions upon millions of ammunition rounds. Month after month, the arms shipments turned up in Kisangani and Mon-rovia and Goma and in dozens of remote bush and hilltop landing strips, dropped off by battered, ancient Russian planes to be wielded by marauding armies of child soldiers and mercenaries. Week after week, the daily summaries provided new references to the man who orchestrated the pipelines. "Russian national transferring arms to subject in Liberia," the dispatches read. "Airplane sponsored by Russian national sighted in Angola."

As the reports mounted, Schneidman and the small circle of intelligence analysts he consulted were fixated on two troubling questions. "Who is this guy?" Schneidman kept asking. "And what can we do about him?"

The enigmatic Russian, the Americans learned, was Viktor Bout, a stout, flint-eyed world traveler most likely born in Tajikistan and barely out of his twenties. He was a gifted linguist with dark hints of a Soviet military intelligence background, a tough, canny business-man whose brief stints as air force officer and Russian government interpreter in Africa had opened up vast possibilities in the arms trade. As both Bout and his business came into sharper focus, the

Americans found themselves confronting a global network with corporate entities and operatives on five continents, including their own. At first they had only a few grainy images of the elusive Bout, passport portraits showing a cipher with a brush mustache. Secure in his anonymity, the phantom Russian had amassed the largest private fleet of vintage Soviet cargo planes in the world. His freighters plied ceaseless circuits across Africa and Asia, flying out of an airport in the obscure dune-swept Persian Gulf emirate of Sharjah and in smaller hubs from Belgium to South Africa. Bout himself turned up regularly in the world's most perilous killing zones, hobnobbing with dictators and warlords before returning to the safety of sumptuous homes in Russia, Belgium, South Africa, and the United Arab Emirates.

The little the Americans had learned about Bout and his organization had come not only from their own electronic intercepts and intelligence sources, but also from European intelligence agencies, UN investigators, and from a small circle of resourceful international activists who worked doggedly to expose Bout's operation and stem his weapons flows across the Third World. The growing trove of data on the arms pipelines provided a sobering window into what became known in the intelligence community as the "shadow infrastructure," the deadly symbiotic web of weapons purchasers and transporters who fueled conflicts around the globe.

Bout had many competitors in the arms trade, but his unique monopoly over the air transport that moved the bulk of the arms streaming into Africa made him a dominant figure who had to be urgently countered, the Americans felt. Their worries mounted as intelligence reports raised suspicions that Bout's planes were also being used to supply the militant Taliban regime in Afghanistan and their patrons bin Laden and his al Qaeda terror network.

"Bout was clearly a guy who needed to be dealt with," Schneidman recalled. "There was evidence he was fueling wars all over Africa. Our job was to promote stability and peace in the region. It fit every definition I knew of in terms of pursuing the national interest."

The American effort to scuttle Bout's operation geared up quickly. Schneidman asked for an informal briefing from the CIA expert. Days later, the analyst showed up with an impressive file on the Russian, filled with the few shreds known about Bout's personal history along with a breakdown of the planes under his command and their extensive flight patterns, and a compilation of the extensive arms deals he had cinched in Africa. Excited that someone on the policy side was finally focusing on the arms pipelines in Africa, the analyst brought along a colleague, a translator from the NSA who spoke the same colloquial Russian that Bout and his colleagues used to veil their long-distance conversations on cell and satellite phones. The NSA official had listened in as Bout and his cronies conducted their deals in Africa and laid plans from their home base in Sharjah, one of the seven United Arab Emirates that include the wealthy kingdoms of Dubai and Abu Dhabi. The NSA official's "drop dead" presentation, recalled one of the impressed government officials who watched, "was absolutely stunning."

The analysts also unveiled a series of black-and-white satellite photographs showing dozens of planes parked in formation on the ground at Sharjah International Airport. They all belonged to Bout's air firms or to allied cargo operations. "These guys were responsible for fueling the war in Angola," Schneidman said later. "I was responsible for that. And this guy was playing both sides in Angola, selling guns to the government and to the rebels. It was outrageous, crazy shit."

The briefing in the early summer of 1999 set off a chain of events that by early 2000 had quietly led to Bout's designation as the highest-ranking international target other than Osama bin Laden and his top tier of terrorist leaders. "People got him right away," Schneidman recalled. "We were dealing with the real possibility of crisis in Africa, and that got people's attention. And Bout was an intriguing, mysterious character, and the sheer size of his operation opened a lot of eyes."

By early 2000, Schneidman was joined by Lee Wolosky, a blunt, aggressive White House National Security Council adviser assigned to devising strategy against transnational threats. An expert on Russian organized crime and political corruption, Wolosky quickly seized on the Bout operation as the quintessential symbol of the unforeseen perils of the new age—stateless rogue organizations that offered material support to any armed camp willing to pay for their services. Wolosky had worked in Moscow at the dawn of Russia's chaotic experiment with capitalism, and had grown alarmed at the emergence of its powerful new class of plutocrats and gangsters. But Bout, Wolosky felt keenly, had risen beyond them, posing a clear and present international danger—more for his ability to carry things than for the things he carried. "Viktor Bout was a bigger problem than just moving weapons," Wolosky said. "He had a logistics network, the best in the world."

Unable to rely on U.S. law because the Bout organization's arms deliveries occurred outside American borders, Wolosky and Schneidman traveled repeatedly to Europe and Africa throughout 2000 and 2001, cajoling and pressuring friendly nations to join in their efforts to build a criminal case against Bout's organization and track him down for arrest. CIA analysts traced his planes. Law enforcement agents scanned phone and banking records. British intelligence officials and other European and Western spy agencies were consulted. At the urging of Richard A. Clarke, the NSC's maverick counterterror czar, Bout's name was even discussed as one of the earliest targets for the controversial practice of "rendition"—the arrest of a foreign national abroad, where the prisoner is handed over to a third country for detention.

But the formidable clout of the U.S. diplomatic and intelligence apparatus had unanticipated limits. America's foreign partners preferred to pursue their own interests. Interagency squabbles took a toll, as did the impotence of international law to keep pace with the arms trade. Bout remained free, and his armada of planes flew on. The Bush administration's attention was diverted, first by the horrors of September 11, 2001, and then by its invasion of Iraq and the postwar fiasco that followed. Despite revelations that his planes had secretly aided Islamic militants in Afghanistan, Bout's organization not only survived, but also flourished—astonishingly, by flying weapons and supplies to the U.S. military and private contractors in Iraq, reaping millions from the nation that once pursued him.

Viktor Bout emerged as a player in the international arms trade in the early 1990s, the unsettled post–Cold War era when most foreign policy experts assumed that the primary threat to U.S. national security was still posed only by nations with nuclear forces and standing armies, fixed borders, and traditional ideological and pragmatic interests. The notion that transnational threats—the Clinton administration's phrasing for terrorists, narcotics cartels, global organized crime, and other dangerous "nonstate actors"—might prove as dangerous as hostile nations was an idea still in its infancy.

But when the Berlin Wall fell, so did that paradigm. Decentralized, far-flung organizations created first by drug cartels and then by ethnic-based crime syndicates that emerged from Russia and China rendered international boundaries and traditional loyalties meaningless. Al Qaeda took center stage in the late 1990s as the most infamous and dangerous transnational threat, but Africa's guerrilla armies and local warlords fit that rubric as well, seizing control of large swaths of territory, terrorizing and killing thousands for private gain, and leaving millions of survivors homeless and destitute.

Bout represented a third breed—Soviet-bloc entrepreneurs who rose from the ashes of the Cold War. These businessmen had easy access to the massive inventories of weapons and ammunition that had been manufactured for decades to sustain a vast military that was suddenly shrinking. They soon realized that there were fortunes to be made from Third World clients who looked to their old former Communist allies to purchase weapons. The system only required a cash influx to become operational again. In the new incarnation, the revived arms pipelines could sell to anyone because there were no longer ideological enemies, only potential clients. The Bout network became the new face of the old system.

With his network's formidable logistical prowess and unfettered access to weapons, Bout became "the poster child of transnational threats," said Gayle Smith, who headed the NSC's Africa office during the last two years of the Clinton administration. "You want to talk about transnational threats? We had [al Qaeda's bombing of U.S. embassies in] East Africa, global warming, and Viktor Bout."

Transnational threats also worried the United Nations, but the Security Council pursued Bout in its own fashion, more concerned with documenting violations of arms embargoes than with shutting down the pipelines. While the work of Wolosky and Schneidman's team proceeded in secret, the United Nations did more than any government to publicly expose the Bout network's activities in Africa. Throughout the 1990s, the Security Council had been imposing arms embargoes on war-ravaged African nations, hoping to dry up the arms flows that fed the violence. But without an international peacekeeping force to enforce the bans, the United Nations could resort only to the public shaming provided by its investigative reports and the limited use of financial and travel sanctions.

To buttress its cases, the Security Council dispatched experts across Africa to report on weapons flows and identify those responsible. UN embargo reports stacked up in the late 1990s, often naming Bout firms as prime culprits. In report after report, the United Nations relied on Belgian investigator Johan Peleman to provide its extensive research. A chain-smoking former philosophy student, Peleman guided a series of reports documenting the movements of Bout's planes and firms, gaining expertise as the foremost independent authority on the Russian and his empire. A globe-trotting detective, Peleman grew adept at exposing Bout's holdings and plane movements by uncovering obscure flight records and "end-user certificates"—international cargo transit papers that were normally used to identify arms clients but that are easily forged. Another UN collaborator was Kathi Austin, a passionate American activist who worked for several nongovernmental agencies. Austin, who joined the UN panel on the DRC, made daring trips into terrorist-run refugee camps and shantytowns to show the lethal impact of small-arms flows in the poorest regions.

Penetrating the veiled, complex corporate structure of the Bout organization was maddeningly difficult for even the most experienced investigators. The Russian deployed a welter of front companies around the globe, including entities in Texas, Delaware, and Florida. Assets moved constantly from one shell to another. Bout network flights were aided by the incoherence of the international aircraft regulation system. Hiding aircraft and companies was almost as easy as flying weapons into war zones, and the Bout network excelled at avoiding international aviation scrutiny by registering planes in compliant nations such as Liberia, where warlord Charles Taylor had turned his country's government into a well-oiled criminal enterprise, and in tiny, remote jurisdictions such as Swaziland and Equatorial Guinea, where oversight was lax. "If you look at all of Bout's various escapades, how easy it was for him to move aircraft and move weapons, get end-user certificates, change aircraft registration, you get an amazing picture of how corrupt many parts of the world are," said Michael Chandler, a retired British army colonel who led the United Nations' panel of experts on the Taliban and al Qaeda.

As his profits soared, Bout cultivated close business and social ties with some of the Third World's most abusive and murderous strongmen. He dealt directly with Charles Taylor in Liberia, Mubuto Sese Seko in Zaire, Paul Kagame in Rwanda, and rebel leaders Jonas Savimbi in Angola, Jean-Pierre Bemba in the DRC, and Sam "Mosquito" Bockarie in Sierra Leone. Bout armed and hunted with Ahmad Shah Massoud, the resistance fighter and Northern Alliance leader who became an Afghan hero but who was also accused of massacring his foes. Bout's organization then nimbly switched sides in Afghanistan, covertly aiding the despotic Taliban regime, secretly providing the Islamic militants with their own fleet of cargo planes and flying in weapons and supplies that aided both the mullahs and their al Qaeda financiers.

Bout's discerning eye for associates complemented his organizational wizardry. He carefully selected his aides, hiring loyal bankers and accountants, pilots and security toughs who got the job done professionally, discreetly, and always loyally. "Viktor Bout was like a jeweler, putting people into place," said a longtime business associate. "He had to select each one, asking who knew the country and the parts of the country, to ensure he did not have any problems there. It took him a long time, and was like making jewelry. Every piece had to be there. That is why he is so successful."[2]

The jeweler still flourishes.

Bout's friends and associates say he has paid a heavy personal price for his success, managing an international operation that continues to draw heavy scrutiny and onerous financial sanctions from the United Nations and the world's superpowers. Richard Chichakli, a longtime American associate and likewise a target of American and UN sanctions for his dealings with the Russian, says that Bout is a decent man who has been misunderstood and deeply wronged by his image as the world's leading arms merchant. The portrayal, he said, is a myth fabricated by hostile officials, intelligence agencies, and journalists.

"He doesn't want to be God," Chichakli said. "He just wanted to retire in Africa, near the rain forest, to raise his daughter. They didn't get the man but they sure killed his dream."[3]

In a world that President George W. Bush divides starkly between those "who are either with us or against us," Bout has become both. Enemy and ally, hunted and hired, he remains useful both to governments and to the violent movements that threaten their security. The endurance of his network remains a thumb in the eye of the new world order, glaring evidence of the impotence of nations to take concerted action against the global arms trade.

"The Viktor Bout story is a story of failure, a failure of the U.S. government," said Lee Wolosky, who lobbied loudly for Bout's arrest after Wolosky left government service, only to be dismayed by the silence of U.S. officials who replaced him. "I am not under any illusion it worked."

The struggle to shutter Bout's empire remains a narrative still unfolding, a chronicle of nations pitted uncertainly against one resourceful man.

CHAPTER 1

The Delivery Man

One evening in April 2001, Jean-Pierre Bemba, a Congolese warlord leading a rebel army of guerrillas and gun-toting teenagers, discovered that he had a problem. Camped with his ragtag troops on a remote mountaintop in the northeastern corner of the Democratic Republic of the Congo (DRC; formerly Zaire) with a magnificent view of Lake Albert, Bemba realized he was low on beer.

The rotund Bemba was hardly cut out for the role of austere revolutionary. Not one to give up the comforts of home to live off the land with his deprived gunmen, the articulate, fastidiously dressed warlord traveled with his own generators, chemical toilets, and hard tents, complete with cots. He was not about to waste a lovely night of revelry in the bush because of a simple oversight of logistics.

Fortunately, Bemba's traveling companion had a solution. Viktor Bout, who was tagging along with the warlord as part of an arms delivery into his remote stronghold, was equipped not only with his usual stores of weapons and ammunition, but also with the means to scour for beer. As part of the full-service package he provided to Bemba's war machine, Bout had rented the rebel leader two aging

Soviet-built Mi-24 helicopters. Bemba and his retinue normally used the gunships to avoid the brutal marches that his troops were forced to make across hills covered with scrub brush and hellish clouds of torturing mosquitoes and small, biting flies. But on this night, Bout's helicopters proved uniquely fortuitous.

Moving swiftly with the authority of a seasoned commando, Bout gathered his crew and, accompanied by a heavily armed escort of twenty of Bemba's men, choppered across Lake Albert into Uganda. There, they occupied a small Ugandan town for about an hour, ordering residents in the town's market square to find all the available beer. When the townspeople had rounded up a few cases—Bout paid a little money for them—he scrambled back into the copter with his occupation force and flew off. Fortified with enough drink to last the night, the revelers sprawled across a secured hilltop as lights twinkled from the fishing boats on the lake below.[1]

Bemba could afford Bout's services because Bemba controlled access to something Bout very much wanted: a rich diamond field that netted the rebel leader $1 million to $3 million a month in sales. These "blood diamonds"—illicit gems that were mined in rebel-held territory and shipped abroad despite international embargoes against their sales—were mostly moved illegally through the neighboring Central African Republic, where both Bemba and Bout had friends and protectors in high places.[2]

When Bout finally bedded down, he slept, as he often did, with some of his crew near one of the helicopters. The aircraft was primed to make an emergency exit in case something went wrong. Bout's willingness to go the extra length for Bemba, despite the risks, made his client happy and kept the good times rolling. But Bout always took care to stay a step ahead, even from his clients.

Bout's ability to supply his customers with whatever they needed under almost any circumstances—while always keeping his options open—has come to define the Russian entrepreneur and his remarkable career. Unlike his rivals in the underground arms trade, Bout has not been content to live from deal to deal. He is a quintessential big-picture man who understands that organizations, not deals, are the underpinnings of meteoric business success. While most of his Russian countrymen struggled with the strange new complexities of international capitalism—the USSR's mortal ideological anathema for nearly three quarters of a century—Bout quickly built a flexible, expanding corporate organization that fused the functional remnants of the archaic Soviet system with the West's fluid, ambition-driven business culture. He built an operation that ranged across continents and hemispheres, carefully scattering planes, handpicked employees, corporate entities, and hidden wealth, creating a formidable empire capable of operating at a moment's notice in dozens of cities across the world.

Not even thirty years old when he first drew the attention of intelligence officials in the mid-1990s, Bout, now forty, remains the preeminent figure atop the world's multibillion-dollar contraband weapons trade, an underground commerce that is outpaced in illicit profits only by global narcotics sales.[3] Bout's corporate earnings have reached easily into the hundreds of millions, and his own personal net worth was conservatively estimated at $5 million in 1998—well before he consolidated his firm's multimillion-dollar take from the Taliban and his organization's post–September 11 supply flights for the United States in Iraq. In Afghanistan alone, U.S. Treasury officials and Western intelligence reports claim, Bout's operation reaped more than $50 million for deals with the extremist mullahs. And hundreds of flights into Iraq for the U.S. military and private contractors may have netted his operations as much as $60 million.[4]

Bout and his associates became masters at outsourcing their arms profits. So careful with his investments that he retained finance experts and even a Swiss bank administrator, Bout stands accused by the Belgian government of illegally laundering more than $32.5 million in arms profits through shell holding companies between 1994 and 1996.[5] Often he took his payments in diamonds and other commodities stripped from the land in areas controlled by his warlord and tyrant clients. Congolese rebels offered coltan, a mineral ore used to make cell phones and computers. Ahmad Shah Massoud, the late Northern Alliance leader and Afghan defense minister, reportedly paid in emeralds. Charles Taylor in Liberia paid in diamonds, and to ensure that the payments were accurate, Bout hired a gemologist who often flew along on weapons flights to assess the stones.

New wars meant more money for Bout and for his competitors in the arms trade. But unlike his rivals, he also had an unfettered ability to deliver his goods. His private air force—which grew to more than sixty Russian cargo planes and a handful of American models by the late 1990s—made him the top private supplier and transporter of killing implements in a world addicted to his products.

Each year over the past decade some three hundred thousand to five hundred thousand people have died in sputtering, little-understood regional wars that have eroded international stability from the Democratic Republic of the Congo to Colombia.[6] Most were killed with light weapons, from semiautomatic rifles to easily carried machine guns. The most popular and durable of them all is the Kalashnikov assault rifle, known as the AK-47, manufactured across the former Soviet bloc, as well as in China, North Korea, and elsewhere.

Invented in 1947 by Mikhail Kalashnikov, the AK-47, with its distinctive banana-shaped ammunition clip, flooded the Third World because of its simplicity of design and ruggedness. It rapidly became the weapon of choice for liberation movements, terrorists, and guerrilla armies. It is simple enough to be taken apart by a child, and often is in Africa's conflicts. It could take a beating and keep on firing long after most other weapons were inoperable. More than a hundred million of the weapons have been manufactured in the past six decades, nearly ten times as many as its nearest rival, the U.S.-made M-16.[7] Ammunition was another vast, lucrative market because most of the armed groups across Africa and Latin America had little training and no fire discipline. Thousands of rounds could be expended in a brief firefight as gunmen fired wildly into the bush until their supplies were exhausted. Similarly, the Russian antitank rocket-propelled grenade known as the RPG or "Ruchnoy Protivotankovy Granatomyot" has flooded the Third World since its invention in 1961. RPGs were skillfully wielded by mujahideen fighters against Soviet forces in Afghanistan in the 1980s and by Somali street fighters against U.S. Special Forces in the Black Hawk Down battle in Mogadishu in 1993. This constant, profligate use of

Russian-designed weapons and ammunition created a constant demand for resupply.[8]

Bout did not take sides in his business. Any and every combatant was a prospective customer. His planes simultaneously armed warring factions in several different conflicts, aiding the Northern Alliance and the Taliban in Afghanistan, rebel and government troops in Angola, and several sides in the prolonged wars that convulsed the Democratic Republic of the Congo.

"He was friends of everyone," said one longtime associate. "They tolerated this because they had no alternative. No one else would deliver the packages. You never shoot the postman. He has no loyalty. His loyalty is to his balls, his sweet ass, and maybe his wallet."[9]

Bout has often insisted he is simply a businessman, and he has long expressed bitterness about being targeted as an international criminal, complaining he is a marked man because of his high profile as a successful Russian. "I exclusively deal with air transportation," he said in 2002 in one of the few interviews he has granted. "And I have never been involved in the arms trade."

Indeed, Bout's aircraft often carry legitimate freight. His planes flew humanitarian supplies to nations ravaged in late 2004 by the devastating Indian Ocean tsunami. And they have hauled UN relief supplies for refugees fleeing the same African conflicts stoked by the guns he sold. Bout-controlled planes have ferried flowers from South Africa to Belgium and shipped beef and chicken around the African continent. Through much of the 1990s, he owned the franchise to sell Antonov aircraft in Africa, and ran one of the few maintenance facilities and aircraft-painting facilities outside of Russia that serviced Soviet-built planes.

Remarkably, even though many of the weapons shipments flown by Bout's planes have had lethal and reprehensible consequences, the deliveries were often made legally. He began just as the world economy was entering an era of fast-paced transformation. The laws governing the sales of weapons, designed to deal with country-to-country sales, simply could not keep pace. The result was a vast "gray market" of gunrunning that might violate UN or regional embargoes, but rarely ran afoul of national arms laws. The Bout network's work with the repressive Taliban did not overtly violate international law—because global arms and trade bans on the militants were enacted too late, and because the world at large remained unaware of his activities until after September 11. Even now, cracks and loopholes in international law often allow the Bout network to continue operating with near-impunity.

Bout was artful in skirting the edge of laws that were clearly unenforceable. Under existing international law, weapons merchants have few obligations—other than moral compunctions—to ensure that their arms supplies go to a legitimate army or state. And though a growing number of countries have enacted toughened statutes covering brokers and even transporters such as Bout, cargo carriers have little legal obligation to view and authenticate what their containers really hold. Customs officials, too, are rarely obliged to check invoices against real cargo. So the shell games continue around the globe, with few brokers held accountable.

"Very few countries have the sort of legal instruments to deal with exactly those middlemen or brokers," said Johan Peleman, a Belgian arms trade expert who investigated Bout's violations of weapons embargoes for several UN panels. "When it comes to making real recommendations and heavy-duty commitments to stop this, most countries don't want this practice of middlemen to end. They don't even want to regulate it."[10]

While often described by casual acquaintances as polite, easygoing, and gifted at picking up languages, Bout did not get by on charm. In business relationships and social situations, he was often fussy in his personal habits, impatient to get to the point, overbearing and aggressive in cultures that prized social niceties and tact. His reputation was built almost entirely on his well-established history of delivering whatever his clients wanted, when they wanted it, and for that, he could be forgiven almost anything else.

He was brash, at times to the point of bullying, and did not brook criticism well. During Bout's hopscotch tour with Bemba of rebel strongholds in the Congolese hills, someone made the mistake of mentioning a verse of the Bible, offering an interpretation that seemed to bother the Russian. In front of a crowd of people, Bout suddenly launched into a loud, extended discourse in fluent French, explaining how the verse should be taken and how foolish the interpreter was. The startled audience of his impromptu exegesis was stunned into silence. No one dared disagree.

"He is really intelligent and could talk about anything," said Dirk Draulans, a Belgian correspondent for *Knack* magazine who tagged along with Bout and Bemba during their rounds in the Congolese bush. "It was sophisticated small talk, anything from the Bible to free trade zones. However, he is not charming and he does not have humor."

Yet at other times Bout waxed lyrical, conjuring up a bleakly haunting vista as he reminisced about his journeys in Afghanistan. "One of the most beautiful landscapes I ever saw was Afghanistan in spring," Bout rhapsodized. "A third of the country is colored blood red by poppies." Bout also showed a sociologist's fascination with tribal patterns in the regions where his guns stoked bloodshed. "He knew all about the historic and current Hutu and Tutsi migrations in the region," Draulans recalled. "He was a very smart guy. He said he was there as a tourist. That was the big joke. He said maybe some bad things had gone on the airplanes, but you know, he cannot inspect the cargo. But we saw weapons being loaded twice onto VB aircraft."

Like a tourist from hell, Bout incessantly videotaped nearly every meeting, every flight, every village and hamlet where he landed. His videotaping habit got him into trouble once on the same African trip, when he wandered away from a political meeting Bemba was holding and began filming a hospital in a nearby town. After Bout was gone about an hour, a local policeman showed up in Bemba's camp to consult with one of the warlord's bodyguards. The policeman confided that he had just arrested a white man, who had written his name on the paper, for illegally filming at the local hospital. This white man was being held in the town's sweltering, fetid prison, angrily demanding immediate freedom. The officer wanted to know what he should do with the prisoner, then showed a scrap of paper bearing the man's name. It was Bout. Informed in no uncertain terms that his prisoner was an important person and had to be sprung immediately, the policeman, suddenly trembling and sweating, rushed back to the jail to let his VIP inmate out. Time and again Bout's carefully cultivated friendships with Big Men would save him from unpleasantness.

"Bout could not have done what he did without the help of princes, kings, and presidents," said Michael Scheuer, a former CIA counterterrorism analyst who headed Alec station, the agency's in-house unit that tracked Osama bin Laden in the late 1990s. "It would have been impossible without help from the very highest levels."

In Sierra Leone, Bout negotiated weapons deals directly with Sam "Mosquito" Bockarie, a wiry hairdresser-turned-battle-commander notorious for savage combat tactics. Bockarie's nickname derived from his boasts that he would suck the life out of his enemies. Bockarie's violent Revolutionary United Front (RUF) forces were sponsored by another Bout client and friend, Charles Taylor, the president of Liberia. Taylor is one of only two sitting heads of government since World War II to be indicted for crimes against humanity and now awaits trial in The Hague on eleven counts, including mass murder and the enslavement of citizens.[11] Taylor's alleged atrocities were legion, but he earned particular condemnation for forming and training Small Boy Units (SBUs), fierce combat units composed of children who were often sent into battle high on amphetamines and cocaine to bear the brunt of the fighting.

Like Taylor, Bemba of the DRC, who was named one of the country's vice presidents as part of a fragile 2005 peace accord, was another Bout client who now faces charges of human rights abuses at the International Court of Justice in The Hague. He was a player in the decade-long spasms of war in which tens of thousands died and hundreds of thousands were forced to flee their homes.[12]

In Angola, Bout's planes shipped weapons to government forces and to the União Nacional para a Independência Total de Angola (UNITA) rebels under Jonas Savimbi. UNITA had degenerated from a once-respected rebel movement seeking to overthrow a Marxist regime to a violent force that preyed on civilians. A 1999 report by the U.S. Institute of Peace said that UNITA "has plunged Angola back into a recurring nightmare of war and human rights depredations."[13]

Despite his easy entry into the inner circles of dictators and warlords, Bout was socially awkward and contemptuous of many of the African leaders he dealt with. Conspicuous among his clients, a white man in a black continent, he would walk in on presidents and ministers without waiting to be announced and demand immediate attention, regardless of what his prominent client might be doing. Several complained behind his back of his apparent racism and lack of respect, but few ever dared to confront him to his face.

Bout's entitled sense of ease was aided by the constant presence of a security detail of Russians who had served with the special forces of the GRU, the former Soviet Union's military intelligence apparatus. Heavily armed and well trained, they made sure no one got too close to the boss if Bout did not want to be bothered. The guards generally kept a low profile, though one redheaded security man was conspicuous for the large hunting knife he carried.

Bout appeared at home roughing it in the bush. When Draulans traveled with him, Bout sometimes chose to pitch a small tent and sleep with his bodyguards next to his aircraft, rather than riding into the villas that Bemba commandeered as his headquarters. Bout dealt with few in the rebel command except Bemba himself, and spent most of his time with his bodyguards and pilots. Most days, Bout would set up his satellite telephone and make a morning round of brief calls, alternating in Russian, English, French, and other languages, usually for about an hour. Mostly he barked orders, juggling several calls in several languages simultaneously if his cellular phone was operational. And he always made sure to hang up after no more than a minute or two—a security precaution to avoid tracing.

If his precautions bordered at times on paranoia, Bout seemed to hew to at least one unvarying personal code: entrusted cargo had to be delivered. Bout almost always came through. Ironically, his widespread network of weapons suppliers and clients, stretching from Afghanistan to South Africa, enabled him to embrace the capitalist ethic of customer service foreign to his Communist upbringing.

No effort was spared, not even in the roughest conditions and terrain. American officials who saw the first spy satellite photographs of Bout's planes in action were astonished by their setting: crude dirt airfields in East Africa. Most of the runways were pocked and rutted to the extent that they posed impassable hazards for most modern air freighters. But Bout's antique Antonovs, Ilyushins, and Yakovkevs—some of them forty-year-old models—

were durable enough to take the punishment. Maintenance facilities were unheard of in the war zones where Bout's planes flew, so his crews had to be adept at jerry-rigging almost anything. Civil radar coverage on the African continent was severely limited and huge swaths of territory went uncovered, making it virtually impossible to track his old planes as they shuttled into the interior—or hunt them down if they crashed. At least five are known to have crashed or been destroyed by ground fire.[14] Several veteran Russian air executives said the actual toll of crashed Bout-owned and Bout-leased planes is even higher, but hidden by his veiled corporate structure and shifting plane registries. There have also been unconfirmed reports of pilot deaths. "They are real kamikaze. There is no better word for it," said one former Bout partner.[15]

The fuselages of Bout's aircraft were often sheathed in lead, which made them heavier but offered crucial protection against sprayed bullets. In May 1997, Bout's friend and client Mobutu Sese Seko, president of Zaire, was refusing to face the fact that his despotic rule spanning three decades in that country was finally over. As rebel forces advanced, he had retreated from the capital of Kinshasa to the lavish Gbadolite Palace, a few hundred miles to the north.

Finally, Mobutu summoned an aircraft to carry him and a cache of plundered loot into exile in friendly Togo, in West Africa. Bout answered the call, sending an aging Antonov to pick up the cancer-ridden dictator and his entourage. But the plane arrived as rebel troops loyal to Laurent Kabila closed in. Mobutu and his aides hurried aboard as the engines were still running. As the old Antonov lumbered down the runway, Mobutu's remaining bodyguards, realizing they had been left behind as targets for the rebels, fired a hail of bullets as the aircraft slowly rose from the end of the rutted landing strip. Bullets peppered the aircraft but did not puncture the armored fuselage. Mobutu lived long enough to die four months later in gilded exile in Rabat, Morocco.[16] "We were lucky it was a Russian plane," Mobutu's son Nzanga later remarked. "If it had been a Boeing it would have exploded."[17]

Once, according to an aviation associate of Bout's, one of his aged Russian planes, scheduled to fly a load of weapons into Angola from South Africa, faced grounding by authorities for safety violations. The plane's tires were so worn that metal bands were showing through. But rather than delay the flight by waiting for a rushed shipment of new tires, Bout suggested that his crew coat the worn tires in black paint to make them appear new, hiding the telltale silver wire.

Taking a look, Bout's agreeable pilot announced that since the Russian plane's tires typically had twenty-one rubber layers and only seven had worn through, "there was no problem," recalled the Bout associate. Only the intervention of Bout's nervous client forced the crew to wait for replacement tires before taking off.

"He did the job, so people came back for more, and he kept delivering, no matter what the circumstances, no matter where he was called on," said an intelligence official who tracked Bout. "People know that and respect that."

Bout may have always delivered, but he never left calling cards. For more than a decade, he shied away from publicity, maintaining a rigid silence with a hermit's fanaticism. Only when he felt threatened did he reluctantly surface to explain himself.

His past is "hopelessly mired in obscurity," said Thomas R. Pickering, who was involved in American efforts to track Bout both during Pickering's mid-1990s tenure as U.S. ambassador to Moscow and later as undersecretary of state for political affairs in the last three years of the Clinton administration. "That is clearly how Bout wants to keep it."

Discretion was of the essence in the arms trade. Too much flamboyance could scuttle a delicate arms deal, or mark a delivery man for capture or death. Customers were happiest when foes were unaware of what lay hidden in their arsenals. The need for caution became even more paramount for Bout when he began playing both sides in some of the conflicts he stoked, arming both the UNITA rebels and government forces in Angola, and later, the Afghan government and their mortal enemies the Taliban. Bout justified his silence by hinting of menacing forces at work behind him. "If I told you everything I'd get the red hole right here," he said to one interviewer, pointing to the middle of his forehead.[18]

To stay safe, routes had to be varied, schedules staggered, landing zones constantly altered. At the same time, deliveries always had to come in on time and weapons loads shipped as advertised. Keeping the customer satisfied kept one's reputation solid. Whatever else his customers felt about Bout, they counted on him to come through.

Bout kept his origins a blur, sparing not a single anecdote from his childhood or recollection of his brief Soviet military career. The first photos passed discreetly to the press were grainy Russian passport snapshots, supposedly taken when Bout was still in his twenties. They showed an unsmiling, prematurely middle-aged man with all traces of youth already extinguished. "It is sort of like Jesus," said one U.S. official. "He suddenly appears on the scene miraculously, as a full-blown character."

The first candid images of Bout emerged in late 2001, taken clandestinely by a Belgian photographer, Wim Van Cappellen, who joined Dirk Draulans on his journeys with Bout in the African bush in 2001. Van Cappellen carefully circumvented Bout's strict photo ban by surreptitiously capturing the Russian in the corner of his picture frames as he snapped with a wide-angle lens. The photos showed Bout in his element, supervising the off-loading of weapons from one of his battered cargo planes, surrounded by blank-faced rebel soldiers. He was dressed, as he almost always was, in a light polo shirt, khaki pants, with a baseball cap and sunglasses. It was the publication of the photographs, rather than Draulans' account of Bout's weapons movements, that prompted a furious call from the Russian to Bemba, bitterly complaining that he had been betrayed. Finally, in 2003, frustrated by mounting press coverage about his work for the Taliban and African warlords, the publicity-averse Bout consented to formal portraits for a *New York Times Magazine* feature. The photographs showed a pensive, aloof figure who could have walked on as a bourgeoisie villain in a Sergei Eisenstein film in the 1920s—preening in a severely tailored suit, staring defiantly at the camera.

By appearance, Bout imposed by girth and stolidity. With his fleshy face, drooping brush mustache, and suspicious, flint-eyed stare, he radiated torpid sullenness. He dressed to the nines when necessary, but formal wear only straitjacketed his barrel chest and ample gut and exposed his massive hands. Bout was more relaxed in the bush, with his freshly laundered, nearly identical sets of polo shirts and khakis, affecting the casual look of Internet-age Western entrepreneurs unconcerned about boardroom haberdashery.

Bout's leaden appearance, intimates said, masked a resourceful intellect; a winning and persuasive demeanor when necessary; and a cunning, radarlike insight that allowed him to quickly size up any client, rival, or pursuer. In person, Bout was opaque, rarely confiding much, even to those who had dealt with him for years. Acquaintances who admired Bout for his deal-making acumen still left business meetings grasping for insights.

"How do you describe Bout? He was a man with a big belly and a big mustache," said one associate. "He was very friendly. He was quiet, he didn't say a lot. He loved to hunt, to be outdoors. He is hard to describe. He was very smart. He had a real gift for languages. He was always everyone's friend."

Bout was often helpful to others in the aviation industry. "If you needed a plane, he would swap routes and things with you," said Gary Busch, an arms transporter who worked around Bout for several years in Africa. "He was competitive, but also very cooperative. I have never heard anyone say anything bad about Viktor on a personal level. He was a nice guy." Sanjivan Ruprah, a Kenyan who worked with Bout in Liberia and the DRC and later tried to broker a multimillion-dollar deal for the U.S. government to use Bout's services in arming anti-Taliban forces in Afghanistan, said that his erstwhile partner "was always on the move and seemed to be very much in demand in the region. . . . He had a jovial, intelligent and shrewd personality."[19]

Bout could be winningly generous, as Vladislav Ketov, a globe-trotting Russian cyclist, discovered when he was stranded in the Persian Gulf emirate of Sharjah during a trip around the world. Bout paid for Ketov's ticket home to Russia, and over the next five years, sent him $50,000 to cover expenses for the cyclist's journeys and altruistic projects. Eager to respond in kind, Ketov offered to paste the logo of Bout's main air cargo company, Air Cess, on his bicycle. The publicity-averse Bout declined the offer, telling Ketov: "My company doesn't need much advertising."[20]

But others described Bout as a hot-tempered control freak who lashed out at his employees. Resentful business rivals and former partners told of a tough, skillful adversary who betrayed at will and discarded old allies without a second thought. "If he had a hobby, it was money," recalled one of Bout's first business partners, Alexander Zakharovich Sidorenko, an aviation executive and decorated former Soviet paratrooper known for daredevil parachute feats. "He was ready to con and stiff even his best friends for a profit. I still don't understand it. It was as if he was walking on the edge of the knife all the time."[21]

After severing relations with Bout in 1994, another former partner, Sergei Mankhayev, said he "watched him grow richer and richer, and it is quite obvious how he did it. I am not sure he has ever done a fair, honest and legal contract in his life. Deception was his strongest point, beginning with the authorities and ending with his partners and even friends. He would cheat on you at the first opportunity."[22]

Bout clearly enjoyed the spoils of his aviation empire, acquiring Mercedeses and Range Rovers and building a far-flung real estate portfolio that included high-priced apartments in Moscow and St. Petersburg and gated estates on the Belgian coast, in Johannesburg, and in a secluded enclave in Sharjah.[23] Even in Monrovia, the hapless Liberian city that had the sad distinction of being the only capital in the world devoid of lights, water, and garbage service, Bout was granted the use of a plush villa near the Hotel Africa with a private generator and water supply.

His pilots alternately praised and despised him. For new hires and freelancers, wages were decent: $5,000 to $10,000 a month. But they hardly made up for planes that one air executive described as "flying coffins." Bout rented apartments in Africa for the crews during their extended stays, or negotiated to make sure they could stay in safe compounds. He kept an entire floor of the Meridien Hotel in Kigali, Rwanda, available year-round for himself and his crews. "He would take good care of his pilots," insisted Vladimir Sharpatov, a star aviator who flew for Bout through the late 1990s. "Once, after we delivered 34 tons of Afghan money [printed by the Russian government] to Kabul, he even invited the whole crew to a Russian restaurant in Sharjah. I remember him as a considerate and kind person and I cannot say anything bad about him."[24]

Bout also had grudging admirers within Sharjah's cutthroat expatriate community of Russian air entrepreneurs, pilots, crewmen, and mechanics. "Viktor was very professional and he had a very professional staff, too," said former partner Igor Abdayev, general manager of Jet Line, Inc., which operated in concert with Bout's network. "But he sometimes tended to get carried away in his business operations. He got involved in those bad contracts in Africa and that in the end ruined his business reputation."[25]

Though willing to banter when necessary with his clients, Bout often seemed to be uncomfortable in large social settings. He had a dark, fatalistic sense of humor, veined with an ominous strain of menace. Draulans recalled how Bout "told the story of how a Belgian guy named Olivier Piret, one of his financial people, had come to visit him in South Africa. He came with his fiancée. On their way to Bout's house they were robbed. The thief threatened to cut off the girl's finger to get off the diamond ring. Viktor thought that was funny as hell. He laughed and laughed." Bout, Draulans sensed, was "vulgar, low-class and always overwhelming in conversation."

In the few interviews he has given over the years, Bout carefully sidestepped penetrating questions about his own activities. He complained perpetually of being targeted by enemies because he is Russian. When asked about his career in the arms trade, Bout usually responded with the well-rehearsed evasion that he was only in the air transport business and had no obligation to know what his cargo was.

"When a client orders a certain kind of transport and pays the lease per hour, what is transported and how it is transported is regulated not by the owner of the transport but by that organization or person who undertakes to organize the transportation," Bout said in a 2002 interview after he was named by the international police organization Interpol in a "red notice" warrant requesting his immediate arrest. "You see, it looks as if an airplane can take off by itself and fly somewhere. But what about somebody's decision to load it? A plane isn't parked in an open field. There are authorities, there are customs, security controls."[26]

Viktor's older brother, Sergei Bout, who has long worked at Bout's side as a detail man, sounding board, and the one person he trusts without hesitation, put it more succinctly during a terse exchange the same year: "Imagine a taxi driver who is supposed to give a lift to a customer who asks him to take him to a certain location. But suddenly this taxi driver asks the customer what is in your suitcase. It is not my bloody business what my customer has in his trunk. I am a taxi driver, I am a carrier. I don't know what I carry. Maybe I carry a nuclear bomb. No one is informing me about it."[27]

CHAPTER 2

Planes, Guns, and Money

What little is known about Viktor Bout's early years has emerged from his own clenched narrative and from the scavenged leavings of a hidden life. Intelligence agencies have tracked him with spy satellites and electronic intercepts, scoured his bank records, and charted his network's hierarchy for more than a decade. Shreds of personal history have been lifted from passports, from Soviet school and military documents, and from the few Russian colleagues willing to talk.

According to official Soviet and Russian records acquired by Western intelligence, Viktor Anatolijevitch Bout was born on January 13, 1967. The most official of the array of Russian passports Bout has used on his travels pinpoints his birthplace in the faded Soviet outpost of Dushanbe, Tajikistan, a Central Asian capital hemmed in by mountains and sunken in rural poverty. Bout claimed an alternate birthplace during a 2002 radio interview in Moscow, saying he was born near the Caspian Sea in Ashgabat, Turkmenistan, a provincial capital near the Iranian border racked by heat and dust storms. He said his father was an auto mechanic and his mother a bookkeeper.[1] A South African intelligence report from 2001 lists him as Ukrainian, and his mother is said to have German ancestry. His Interpol arrest warrant says he may have been born in Smolensk.[2]

Bout has acknowledged graduating from Moscow's Military Institute of Foreign Languages in the late 1980s and then earning a degree in economics from the Russian military college. According to intelligence documents, he attended school 47 in Dushanbe between 1974 and 1984, and took a sociology degree in intercultural communications before attending the foreign languages institute from 1987 through 1991.[3] He served in a military aviation regiment, including a two-year stint in Mozambique, most likely his introduction to Africa.

For years, journalists and Western officials speculated openly that Bout had a KGB background, whispers he strenuously denied. Some reports suggested that one or both of his parents were senior Soviet intelligence agents. His mother wept, Bout complained, after she read the KGB allegations in a newspaper. Other reports raised the possibility that Bout's wife, Alla, who reportedly ran fashion studios in Johannesburg and Sharjah, and also may have run one of Bout's travel agencies, was the daughter of a senior KGB official who met an untimely and suspicious death. Bout angrily denied all the talk, saying he "never served in the KGB or any other organization linked to the KGB."[4]

In fact, the Moscow foreign languages institute where Bout first emerged in the dying Soviet star system was well known among Western intelligence experts as a feeder academy for the Soviet espionage services, and Bout was a prize student. He speaks almost perfect English, as well as nearly flawless French and fluent Spanish. During his time in Africa he claimed to have learned several more, including Xhosa and Zulu in South Africa. Other reports suggested he had a familiarity with German, Portuguese, Farsi, and Urdu.[5] Bout's "big advantage" in starting out in the air transport industry, said Sidorenko, his former partner, "was that he spoke several foreign languages: Portuguese, English, German. It seemed to me like a great asset at the time. It was very important in our business."[6]

The language school, said Western defense analysts, was in fact most closely allied with the GRU, the vast, secretive Soviet military intelligence network that for decades oversaw the flow of Russian arms to revolutionary movements and Communist client states in the Third World. "Language training was usually a pretty good tip-off to a GRU officer," said Graham H. Turbiville Jr., former chief of the U.S. Defense Intelligence Agency's Soviet/Warsaw Pact Strategic Operations Branch. "These GRU guys had privileges that weren't available to the normal Russian military. And they had the know-how and the flexibility and the assignments to reach beyond their borders." British intelligence concluded early on during their investigations of Bout's background that he emerged from the GRU. "They never had any doubt that Bout was GRU material," said an analyst who has worked with British intelligence.[7]

Bout has acknowledged his stint in the Soviet military, saying only that he retired "with an officer's rank."[8] Other reports have identified him as a former major. Dirk Draulans, the Belgian journalist who traveled with Bout in Africa, reported that the Russian began his military career as a navigator at a Russian air base near Vitebsk in Belarus, and later trained air force commandos there for the GRU.[9] Early British and South African intelligence reports said that Bout was stationed in Rome by the KGB from 1985 to 1989, but U.S. officials now say that was unlikely. A more reliable account by UN officials placed him as a translator for Russian peacekeepers in Angola in the late 1980s. Sidorenko affirmed his Angola posting. "Bout was a trade representative in Luanda," Sidorenko said. "His friend was chief of the Russian submarine base in Angola. They had lots of business connections in this country and when the Soviet Union broke up they chose not to return to their homeland, but stay and do business in Africa."[10]

Russian intelligence services, particularly GRU agents, maintained a strong presence in Angola for years, using their embassy and outposts there to keep up contacts with rebel movements and to serve as a bridgehead for moving arms throughout the region, said the British intelligence analyst. "Bout was stepping into existing relationships," the analyst said. "He didn't simply show up and say, 'I'm some Russian you never heard of, let's do some business.' He was the new face of the old pipeline."[11]

Former CIA analyst Michael Scheuer said Bout's contacts and

protection by the former Soviet military "were a given" in the CIA's analysis of Bout's activities. There was no other way he could have an organization mushrooming over several continents and maintain the far-flung empire, Scheuer said.

When Bout struck out on his own in 1991, the year of the final death throes of the Soviet state, he was able to take swift advantage of the convergence of several fortuitous economic and political factors that came to the fore as the USSR disintegrated. The most critical factor for his future as an air transport magnate was that the bloated Soviet aviation fleet was suddenly on life support, and its massive assets—its planes—were up for grabs. Thousands of pilots and crewmen were suddenly unemployed. Funding for maintenance and fuel had evaporated. Hundreds of lumbering old Antonov and Ilyushin cargo planes sat abandoned at airports and military bases from St. Petersburg to Vladivostok, their tires frayed and their worn frames patched with sheet metal and duct tape.

"The entire Soviet civil air system collapsed," recalled Thomas Pickering, who served as U.S. ambassador to Moscow from 1993 to 1997. Pickering saw the detritus of the Soviet commercial fleet at close range whenever he flew into the Russian interior. From the door of his aircraft, the ambassador viewed aged cargo planes sitting stranded and idle—the perfect transports for hustlers eager to move contraband. "Everywhere you'd fly, you'd see these parked airplanes, always with flat tires, just sitting there, useless," he said.

Ownership of the squat, old Antonovs, Ilyushins, Tupelovs, and Yakovlevs that clustered on civil airfields across the Soviet interior had always been in the hands of the government. The planes carried dual civilian and armed forces identifications, each attesting to the separate missions long forecast by Soviet planners—carrying commercial cargo in peacetime and matériel and troops in the event of war. "The [Soviets] built an aircraft for every route," Pickering said. "It was a state-subsidized thing and their reserve air force. So they just built aircraft."

Most of the planes were the property of the old Soviet commercial fleet, Aeroflot. But with the disappearance of Communist overseers, Aeroflot was left paralyzed, "too big to know what it had and where," said Mark Galleoti, a British historian who specializes in the modern Russian military and organized crime. "In some cases, local administrations or military authorities took them. There were spats between the local airports and central authorities over some of the planes. And at some airports, they sat, completely abandoned. In that state, planes just disappeared."

Despite their age and often dilapidated condition, the heavy-duty freighters were perfect vessels for the lift and range requirements that Bout needed for long-distance transport of weapons and ammunition. The older Tupelovs and Yakovlevs and the newer-generation Antonovs and Ilyushins were particularly well suited for handling the blasted terrain of Third World landing strips and making fast exits under fire. They were ear-splittingly noisy, with dirty, inefficient engines. But their sturdy undercarriages could take rough landings and were equipped with extra wheels and reinforced pneumatic systems. Designed simply, the engines, hulls, and instruments were not hard to maintain, and their parts were easily replaced. The durable hulks turned up at remote landing strips across Africa and Central Asia, whining loudly, bullet-pocked, wingtips gouged, hulls laced with gaffer tape. "The planes were literally built to last until they frayed away," Galleoti said. Experienced Antonov and Ilyushin pilots were often trained, Galleoti added, to operate on short runways and without the benefit of air traffic controllers—both critical advantages for arms flights into remote, rugged territory and quick getaways.

Moving speedily to establish himself as a player in the nation's struggling new capitalist society, Bout acquired several cargo planes destined for the scrap heap. By his own account, Bout, then twenty-five, bought his first trio of old Antonovs for $120,000, hiring crews to fly cargo on a maiden flight to Denmark, then on longer-distance routes to the Third World. But he told intimates a markedly different version. "The GRU gave him three airplanes to start the business," one associate said. "The planes, countless numbers of them, were sitting there doing nothing. They decided, let's make this commercial. They gave Viktor the aircraft and in exchange collected a part of the charter money. It was a setup from the beginning."

Bout began renting his tiny fleet to customers either in "wet leasing" arrangements—aviation parlance for providing plane and crew—or "dry"—just the plane. Years later, Bout insisted he was the sole investor and that he had no difficulty raising the initial cash.[12]

In reality, according to Bout associates and Western intelligence officials, Bout's senior GRU contacts were critical for his start-up, and his initial flights were sanctioned weapons runs to approved Third World clients. Most likely Bout paid little or no money down on the planes, but had an extended lease agreement that provided some seed money in return for administering the initial arms shipments. Through the years, Bout's GRU benefactors remained as his "rabbis," said one associate, and presumably still benefited from his burgeoning operation.[13]

"What he was doing, he was doing with a wink and a nod from the GRU," said Pickering. "He was an international entrepreneur. He really did not care who he was mixed up with or how."

In the Russian underworld they called it *krisha*, a roof, a favored tie to an official or powerful criminal benefactor who offered protection and hidden advantages. Over time, said longtime Bout watchers, he cultivated ties with the critical people he needed to find new planes and keep the arms shipments flowing: military and intelligence officials, most importantly, but also friendly faces in the Russian foreign and interior ministries, plane and weapons plant managers, civil aviation and airport officials, and banking and finance officers.[14] Sergei Mankhayev, a former partner who became general manager of Republic Air in Sharjah, concluded early on that Bout had "very powerful backing and protection back in Moscow. At first, he just implemented the orders of bigger men in Moscow, telling him where to go and what to take. Later, he started his own business, but I believe the strings attached to Bout in those years have never really been cut."[15]

Bout grew adept at acquiring the old cargo planes for his own operation by whatever means necessary. "His eyes sparkle when he sees an aircraft," said Chichakli.[16] Valery Spurnov, a Soviet civil aviation official in Chelyabinsk who later became general director of the SpAir aviation firm in Yekaterinburg, openly suspected that Bout played a central role in the disappearance of several civil aircraft from the southern Urals region in the early 1990s. Spurnov said his private investigation discovered that "a company in Russia which owned planes wrote some of them off, then sold them to another Russian company, which in fact was a front company, for Bout's operations. At that time Bout was very actively doing business in Angola."

Spurnov and other Russian air industry hands said aviation and airport officials often wrote off old planes as scrap—then sold the aircraft to Bout's network for pittances. Bout's avionics crews would retrofit the junkers with enough spare parts to make them airworthy. In one deft 1992 operation, Spurnov said, "Bout acquired four old and written-off [Antonov] An-8s, which were nothing more than a pile of scrap metal. According to my information, Bout paid $20,000 to $30,000 for each of them." The purchase of the decrepit planes quickly paid off. "In Angola at the time, every An-8 [cargo flight] brought him about $30,000 a week."[17]

Buying written-off aircraft provided another benefit. Once the planes were recorded as unworthy to fly and taken off the international aircraft registries, it was much harder to track them or determine their origins. The aircraft would often just appear on a Bout company's fleet as if they had flown in from the ether.

A veteran Russian air executive who competed against Bout's air firms said at least three hulking Ilyushin Il-76s were spirited out, along with eighteen Il-76 engines. "The engines were written off as having exhausted their service-time limits," he recalled. "But Bout had these engines put on those planes and the planes, which had no right to fly, worked for years for Bout." His hard-boiled philosophy, the executive said, was "to profit at every stage of business."[18] An official at the Kyrgyzstan Air Star Company (KAS), a Gilbraltar-registered firm that did frequent business with Bout's companies, recalled that the Bout firms he dealt with in the late 1990s stored "all sorts of papers, permissions, licenses, and certificates, fake or real, that made it possible for him to deliver anything, at any time and without necessary noise and publicity."[19]

Bout's most audacious acquisition was his appropriation of a jumbo Il-76 freighter that had been consigned to stand as a monument in front of the Smolensk Rocket and Artillery School. The old aircraft was never delivered to its pedestal. Instead the plane was written off as scrap with the aid of compliant officials and smuggled out of the country into Bout's fleet. "Anything for money, anything for risk," said the Russian air executive. "The more risk the better."[20]

The same political and economic chaos that left scores of cargo planes available for the taking in Russia in the early 1990s also swung open the gates at arms factories and massive storehouses of weaponry.

Across Russia's interior and in its far-flung satellite states, arms factories that had churned out AK-47 assault rifles, millions of rounds of ammunition, land mines, surface-to-air missiles, tanks, sniper rifles, and night-vision equipment were suddenly idled, assembly lines shuttered because of a lack of money for matériel and salaries. Security at the sites also was fraying: plant managers and base commanders suddenly found themselves in charge of vast storerooms of matériel as the local Communist Party hierarchy withered. Military conscripts who worked as guards faced layoffs and uncertain pay schedules, and some responded by cutting deals that allowed outsiders to pilfer weapons stocks.

The newly privatized Russian arms factories and the military's stockrooms were filled to capacity with massive inventories of older rifles, ammunition, and matériel that would not sell easily to Russia's blue-chip clients. Often these less-desired weapons were written off as destroyed, then shipped off to unwitting Third World clients disguised as top-grade arms. According to Western intelligence reports, nearly a third of the vast stock of Kalashnikovs disappeared in this fashion from the factories at Tula, the main source of the ubiquitous Russian-built rifle.[21]

The most loyal customers were former Third World clients of the Soviet Union—rebel movements, anti-American warlords, dictators spurned by the West. They needed reliable sources of arms to replenish the massive stockpiles that fueled the regional outbursts and civil wars that had replaced the Cold War feints of the past. In the new world order, there were few impediments to cranking up the levers of Russia's old war machinery. "It was like a Pavlovian reaction by people after the wall fell," said one Bout associate. "They had been trained with Soviet weapons, the Soviet Union had always given them weapons, and so they wanted to keep going with Soviet weapons. They didn't want to have American weapons. So they kept coming."[22]

As the old Soviet arms pipelines began to flow again, the West paid little attention. In the euphoria of the Eastern bloc's liberation, the stealth movement of excess weapons to African and Central Asian backwaters did not register as an ominous trend to U.S. and European officials preoccupied with smoothing Russia's path toward democracy and free market principles. With the Cold War buried, U.S. intelligence agents were recalled from remote African capitals just as the new arms routes began to hum. In a world seemingly devoid of enemies, what possible harm could come from making a tidy profit from a glut of guns and ammunition? In the early 1990s, this was the atmosphere of obliviousness that allowed Bout to painstakingly lay the groundwork for the expansion of his budding empire of planes, guns, and money. An admiring U.S. defense official would later compare Bout's appearance at the birth of the world's transformed arms trade to the emergence of two seminal American business figures. "Viktor Bout is like the Donald Trump or Bill Gates of arms trafficking," the official said. "He's the biggest kid on the block."[23]

The surge in available weaponry had its greatest immediate impact in Africa, where automatic weapons had previously been expensive and hard to obtain. The influx of the new, high-powered weapons soon wreaked havoc, dramatically beefing up the killing power of the continent's guerrilla movements. But few cared, at least in the beginning.

"A few planeloads of arms going to an African country just didn't make the cut, in terms of an issue governments would want to pay attention to," said Tom Ofcansky, a State Department African affairs analyst. "But the impact of a few planeloads of arms, as we've seen repeatedly in Africa, had a devastating impact on fragile African societies."[24]

It did not take long for Russia's new generation of oligarchs to see the potential for profit. Military and intelligence service leaders quickly cashed in on the privatization of the Russian economy, well aware that the nation's arms stockpiles had "tremendous value to warring countries in Africa and anywhere you need guns," said Jonathan Winer, a former deputy assistant secretary of state for international law enforcement in the Clinton administration. "It's capitalism, comrade."[25]

Base commanders could be persuaded to part with crates of weapons straight from their warehouses for a fraction of market value, allowing for high profits when the matériel was resold. Bribes worked wonders. Even before the end came, Soviet military officials saw the signs of rampant sell-offs from weapons stocks at their military bases. In 1989, official Soviet statistics indicated that weapons thefts had spiked 50 percent over the previous year. One arms merchant who dealt with Bout described the ease with which even the most dangerous weapons were accessed. He said he has an old photograph of himself, happily drunk, driving a tractor pulling a fully operational Russian nuclear warhead. "They let me ride it for the hell of it," he said. "They all laughed and said they hoped it didn't go boom."

In a 1995 report for the U.S. Army's Foreign Military Studies Office, the former DIA official Turbiville found "poorly paid, badly housed, and demoralized Russian military forces at home and abroad are deeply immersed in criminal activities conducted for personal and group profit. Smuggling crimes of all types (particularly drug and arms trafficking), the massive diversion of equipment and materials, illegal business ventures, and coercion and criminal violence, all fall under the umbrella of military organized crime."[26] There was an underground trade in heavy matériel, from armored vehicles to MiG aircraft. Mark Galleoti noticed on a research trip through Russia in 1991 that even low-ranking former soldiers were hustling for their piece of the action. "You'd see them in hotel lobbies, tough guys out of uniform, now all wearing track suits. There was money to be made."

As graft and organized crime enterprises grew rampant, Bout could hardly have been expected to steer clear of their influence. Western intelligence documents reported that at least two men who rose to prominent roles inside the Bout network had solid ties to Russian organized crime groups. One was a director of a Russian weapons manufacturing firm; the other was a top pilot who later left Bout's employ and became an aviation executive.[27] Bout also worked with a far-flung network of weapons providers. In Moscow, according to Western intelligence officials, his main arms contact was Alexander Islamov, an associate who was named in a 2001 UN report examining arms embargo violations in Liberia and who was charged in that same year by Slovakia with illegal arms sales. In Bulgaria, according to U.S. officials, Bout dealt with Petar Mirchev, an arms broker who operated out of Burgas, a free trade zone where several arms factories were based for easy air access.[28]

Experienced former Soviet pilots and flight crews, grounded by the lack of aircraft flying, were available for work at rock-bottom wages. The Soviet Air Force had fourteen thousand pilots and five thousand aircraft when the Berlin Wall fell, and thousands faced unemployment as the service shrank.[29] A base salary of $900 per month and the chance to avoid Russia's harsh winters lured many former Russian aviators to fly in dangerous and remote regions. The task of moving weapons was made even easier because many of the far-flung weapons factories and arsenals had landing strips built on the premises, designed to make loading the cargo fast, efficient, and cheap. All the ingredients were available for a master chef to work wonders. Bout, with his African connections, language ability, and entrepreneurial daring, quickly took possession of the kitchen.

"On the surface, it might seem easy to get those weapons out [of Europe], but in fact it was not an easy thing to do," said a U.S. intelligence official who monitored Bout. "There were only a few individuals capable of moving large amounts of weapons to African countries. This was the expertise Bout developed. If you had an Antonov and wanted to get into the arms business, you needed strong contacts and excellent language skills. He had all of these."

From early on, Bout and his associates grew practiced in the manipulation of shell companies, plane registries, and offshore jurisdictions. Financial barriers were breaking down as the world transformed in the post–Cold War era. Soviet intelligence agencies also were experienced in setting up front operations and disguising money movements. Indeed, as the Soviet bureaucracy imploded in the last years of the USSR, the KGB, the GRU, and other state intelligence agencies moved vast amounts of cash into foreign banking accounts and facade firms to prepare for the post-Communist era. "They salted money into Swiss bank accounts and front companies in the Soviet Union and elsewhere in the world," said the British intelligence analyst. "There was a well-designed program for setting up foreign bank accounts and companies."[30]

Bout's firms were often set up in jurisdictions where lax corporate reporting laws veiled ownership. Bout-linked firms sprouted in Belgium, the UAE, Switzerland, in several African nations, and even in Delaware and Texas. Similarly, his aircraft could take advantage of spotty international aviation regulations, often registered in countries far from where they were actually based—moves that made it difficult for the host countries to take any action against them. "His structure is a lot what we see in drug cartels," said a U.S. Treasury official. "He uses lots of interlocking corporate structures, capital-intensive assets, shifting names and associates. Everything with Viktor is one big ball of wax that can be molded any way he wants. It's really just one big company, really, and he uses different names and structures when it suits him."[31]

Bout's own identity was just as elastic. When he traveled, he had at least five varying Russian passports he could show prying border officials. Adopting the modus operandi of spies and criminals, he sometimes altered his name on documents and in personal encounters, allowing him to adopt and shed aliases at will. In South Africa he used Vitali Sergitov. Elsewhere he was Victor Buyte, or Butte, Byte, Bont, or Boutov. In the UAE he signed as Victor Butt, the name that bemused U.S. government pursuers wryly preferred to use in the late 1990s as they tried to scuttle his operation. Elsewhere, Bout was "often referred to in law enforcement circles as Viktor B because he uses at least five aliases and different versions of his last name," a UN panel of experts related in a 2000 report on arms embargo violations in Sierra Leone.

In 1996 Bout moved his aircraft registrations to Liberia. A UN panel investigating his activities later discovered why: just as Liberia had long been a haven for the maritime industry's most hazardous and unregulated ships, the African nation also had become a flag of convenience for the fringe air cargo industry. A company incorporated in Liberia could locate its executive offices in another country and conduct business activities anywhere in the world. Names of corporate officers or shareholders did not need to be transparent, there was no minimum capital requirement, and incorporation could be accomplished in one day. Businessmen in several countries competed with each other to attract customers for these offshore registrations. The system led to a total disregard for aviation safety and a lack of oversight of Liberian-registered planes operating on a global scale.[32]

From 1996 through 1998, Bout associates Michael Harridine and Ronald De Smet conducted business in the United Kingdom on behalf of the Liberian Aircraft Register. This presented no logistical problems, since the aircraft did not need to be physically present to receive certificates of airworthiness that allowed them to make international flights.[33] Other countries offered similar systems of registration without accountability, and when UN officials and others began focusing on Liberia, Bout was already shifting his plane registries elsewhere—Swaziland, the Central African Republic, and Equatorial Guinea among the most notable.

As his aviation operation grew, Bout heeded the first rule of the air transport industry: never fly empty. Like Milo Minderbinder, the cheerily infernal war profiteer in Joseph Heller's World War II novel *Catch-22*, who filled returning bomber planes with shipments of fresh eggs and Egyptian cotton, Bout often scheduled lucrative cargo pickups wherever his planes dropped off weapons shipments. The practice ensured that his Russian freighters always carried a moneymaking load when they were airborne. If an Ilyushin Il-76 was bringing helicopter gunship parts into Goma, it might leave with a consignment of coltan, mining equipment, or blood diamonds. On a run of Kalashnikovs and MiG fighter jet tires into Kandahar, a load of lumber or carpets might be waiting for a flight out. RPGs or gladiolas, diamonds or frozen chickens, it made little difference as long as there was a profit to be made from one destination to the next.

In that manner, Bout's air fleet flew the world in endless circuits. In the mid-1990s his Antonovs and Ilyushins would often fly out with empty cargo holds from Ostend Airport in Belgium. They would head for Burgas, a free-trade zone in Bulgaria conveniently near several arms factories, or any number of other East European airports where weapons consignments were loaded aboard. From there, Bout's options were almost limitless. His planes might fly on to Sharjah, where the weapons shipments could be stored for later flights, transferred to other planes, or flown on, after refueling, toward night landing zones in Afghanistan. Alternately, the planes could fly south into Africa, taxiing down with crates of weaponry at Kigali Airport in Rwanda, at Kisangane, in Zaire, or on scores of landing strips hidden in African forests and hills. From there, the planes would rumble back toward Sharjah or other friendly airports. Sometimes their cargo holds brimmed with ordinary shipments of refrigerators and appliances bound for Afghan merchants. But more often the cargoes were spoils that warlords and dictators preferred to turn over to Bout's crews as payments for their weapons deliveries—blood diamonds, coltan, gold, any natural resource that Bout's network would then convert to cash. Eventually the planes would return to Sharjah or Ostend, poised for their next circuit.

Bout has said that his business took off exponentially in 1993 when he began flying his aircraft out of the UAE, overrun at the time by nouveau riche Russian vacationers and business hustlers. The bustling emirate of Dubai offered duty-free shopping and a wealth of Western products still unseen in Russia itself—the latest models of satellite telephones, televisions, stereos, refrigerators, and a heady array of American and Japanese cars. Bout saw the opportunity to increase his wealth by servicing his countrymen in their gallop toward once-decadent conspicuous consumption. He was welcomed in Dubai's poorer neighbor, the emirate Sharjah, where airport officials eagerly sought to attract new cargo firms to increase business.

Bout's Russian customers "bought everything from pencils to cars to electronics to IKEA furniture," the Russian recalled. "I saw a gap in the transportation market and flew it all back for a premium." When Bout discovered he could buy gladiolas in South Africa for $2 apiece and sell them for $100 apiece in Dubai, his business really took off. "Twenty tons per flight," said Chichakli, who met Bout in Dubai while Chichakli headed Sharjah's growing free-trade zone near the airport. "It was better than printing money." Bout said his idea was to "create a network of companies in Central Africa, Southern Africa and the Emirates. I wanted to make a cargo and passenger airline like Virgin Atlantic."[34]

By the late 1990s, at the height of his fortunes, Bout's network was mixing arms flights and standard cargo deliveries at will. In South Africa, where his planes found a new base in 1997, Bout built an expensive refrigeration unit at Pietersburg Airport to chill the massive quantities of frozen chicken and meat he shipped across the continent. Chickens cost about $1 in South Africa, but they sold for $10 in Nigeria.[35]

The Bout organization made a tidy fortune off the legitimate business deals. And the steep profits reaped on the return flights allowed the expansion of its weapons operation. Figuring out how to load up empty aircraft with profitable goods "is where Bout showed his entrepreneurial spirit," said Gary Busch, an arms transporter who worked around Bout for several years in Africa, often supplying weapons to the armies who were fighting rebel groups armed by Bout. "He grew as demand grew."[36]

He also expanded by playing hardball with rivals in the air cargo business, and sometimes with his own partners. Alexander Sidorenko, the general director of the Russian aviation firm Exparc Air, took Bout on as a partner in 1991 and quickly found himself being deftly outmaneuvered by the novice businessman. Bout repeatedly struck deals with other firms for services while leaving Sidorenko with the bills. In one incident, Sidorenko laid plans with Bout to export Russian army airborne parachutes and platforms— only to discover that Bout had cut a deal on his own on the side, selling the equipment on his own for a much greater profit. "When he made these deals in my presence he chose to speak a foreign tongue and I couldn't follow it," Sidorenko recalled. "So he took these paratroops platforms for $200 (apiece) from me and sold them for $2,000 each—and he sold about 1,000 of them. I learned the real facts too late."

The last straw, Sidorenko said, came when one of Bout's henchmen entered his office and demanded the use of one of his jumbo Ilyushin Il-76 freighters for two months for flights into Afghanistan, Yemen, and Africa. "You can take a vacation in the emirates. Here is your down payment," Bout's associate told him, pointing to a briefcase filled with cash. "I didn't open the case," Sidorenko recalled. "I told him to get out. That was the end of my cooperation with Bout." But it was not over. For months afterward, an enraged Sidorenko discovered, Bout's planes made "about 200 flights using my company's name, stamp and even [aviation] call signs."

Finally, in 1998, Sidorenko confronted Bout face to face in a shopping mall in Dubai. "He looked me in the eye and said that he hadn't done anything wrong," Sidorenko recalled. "I wanted to say a lot of things to Bout there and then, but a mall in Dubai is not a place you make a public scene."[37]

CHAPTER 3

A Dangerous Business

V iktor Bout's entry into the air transport business brought early success in the unlikeliest of places—in Afghanistan, the war-torn nation abandoned at the close of the Cold War by demoralized Soviet forces retreating from a punishing decade of occupation and war.

In 1992, Bout's small fleet of Antonovs began flying east toward Central Asia carrying military-green crates packed with Kalashnikovs, machine-gun rounds, and rockets. The munitions were destined for a fragile Afghan coalition government that had just seized power after the collapse of the Communist puppet regime left defenseless by the Soviet withdrawal.[1] Bout's aggressive push into Afghanistan filled a weapons procurement vacuum left by the vanished Soviet overlords, and he built on his rapid success by expanding elsewhere in the Islamic world. Bout's associates were soon covertly supplying Bosnian Muslim fighters in the Balkans. And he began stationing his cargo planes in the obscure Persian Gulf emirate of Sharjah, a centrally located air hub where his fleet could easily ply its circuitous routes among Africa, Europe, and Asia—and where a wave of hustling émigré Russian merchants had discovered tidy profits in the offing.

The arrival of Bout's planes restored a modest Russian presence inside Afghanistan just as the country took its first shaky steps toward a coalition government. Following months of skirmishes that threatened civil war, a new administration had coalesced around Burhanuddin Rabbani, a white-bearded Islamic academic and mujahideen leader who had formed the ruling Afghan Islamic Council. Ahmad Shah Massoud, the battle-tested warlord and poet known as the "Lion of the Panjshir," joined Rabbani as defense minister. Massoud would later oppose the Taliban as commander of the Northern Alliance resistance forces before his assassination by al Qaeda henchmen in September 2001.

During his stint as defense minister, Massoud promoted Bout as a miracle man who could replenish the regime's depleted weapons stocks. Bout, in return, openly admired his new clients. "Rabbani and Massoud were the only hope" for Afghanistan, Bout said later. "I had a major pact with the Rabbani government. We sustained them."[2] Massoud may well have bankrolled some of Bout's initial plane purchases, a Bout associate said, "paying in emeralds and other things." At first Bout "was delivering packages. Some were weapons. He was like DHL. You pay up front, you give the destination, and he would deliver."[3]

Massoud and Bout shared a love of hunting and weaponry, and met often in Afghanistan. Bout admired Massoud as a host, both for his fine table and his magnanimous entertainment of guests—especially visitors who kept him well supplied in weapons. The Bout associate, who occasionally joined the Russian and Massoud on hunting trips in the high, rugged Pamir Mountains that straddle Central Asia, said that the Afghan's favorite entertainment was flying in his guests by aging Soviet helicopters to hunt Marco Polo sheep, a big-game trophy prized for their exquisite horns.

"Sometimes people would shoot at the helicopter, and it was okay to shoot back at them," Bout's associate said with a laugh. "No one cared. Massoud was very nice, a great host. Because of that I gave him my favorite hunting rifle, one with a special electronic scope. He kept looking at it when we were at dinner. He had a great kitchen, too, let me tell you. The food was fantastic. He gave us permission to hunt in his side of the Pamir. He gave us guides and everything."

The Northern Alliance leader delegated the logistics of his arms resupply needs to his weapons procurer, Abdul Latif, who was ordered to find a new weapons connection days after Northern Alliance troops swept into Kabul in April 1992. Soon Latif was flying to the UAE and to Eastern European capitals to cinch the details of the arms deals with Bout and his assistants. Latif, a wily political operator whom Massoud later cashiered amid allegations of corruption, boasted that "I was the person contacted between our government and Mr. Bout." Latif traveled with suitcases stuffed with cash. He would hand over the money to Bout in Dubai, and in return the Russian would "provide transport of these [arms] shipments," Latif recalled.[4] Bout's planes brought rifles, shells, and tank ammunition from Prague and from the Bulgarian arms depot near the free-trade zone at Burgas, said Ahmet Muslem Hayat, a longtime Massoud aide known as "Commander Muslem." But despite his private warmth toward Bout, Massoud chafed at the high prices the Russian demanded for his services. Massoud scorned his provider as "Russian Mafia," a term Hayat echoed years later. "Bout charged a lot," Hayat grumbled. "One tank shell was $60. From Russia, officially, it was $10."[5]

The Russian government was not selling weapons to Afghanistan in the early 1990s—at least not officially. Under its new president, Boris Yeltsin, the Russian Foreign Ministry preferred distance to engagement. Relations between the two nations remained cool, strained at times by outbreaks of ethnic unrest along the borders between Afghanistan and the Central Asian buffer states of Tajikistan, Uzbekistan, and Turkmenistan. In 1993 the Russians sent twenty-five thousand troops into Tajikistan to stabilize the country after a brief, violent civil war. Moscow suspected the Afghan government of aiding Tajik insurgents, and the two nations traded threats after rebels destroyed a Russian military outpost. In such a tense atmosphere, Bout's planes had to operate clandestinely. Afghanistan had been Russia's Vietnam, and bitter memories back home about the loss of fourteen thousand Soviet soldiers ensured that Bout's crews took care not to draw attention to their covert arms flights.[6]

Vladimir Sharpatov, a decorated former Soviet Air Force pilot, flew many arms sorties for Bout into Afghanistan during the mid-1990s. Sharpatov, a crusty veteran airman who had worked off and on for Bout for years, first met Bout "at a hotel in Sharjah where we used to stay. He impressed me as a calm, reserved and soft-spoken man, who at the same time knew what he was talking about." During the years he worked for Bout, Sharpatov said, "we never had any conflicts." Sharpatov took his orders from both Bout and his brother Sergei. He found Viktor "a bit tougher than Sergei; he has got more grit."[7]

When Sharpatov joined Bout's Transavia air firm, the Russian's fleet in the UAE consisted mostly of smallish Antonov An-8s known as "Camps." The twin-engine, propeller-driven aircraft, built in the 1960s, were useful only for medium-range transport and limited to carrying an eighteen-ton payload, adequate for ferrying smaller munitions. But by 1995, Transavia had begun to field a leviathan Ilyushin Il-76 capable of long-range flights and hauling a forty-four-ton payload. The plane was not Bout's. It had been leased from Aerostan, a Russian-owned firm in Tatarstan. The bulbous-nose, swept-wing "Candid" could easily lift tanks, heavy artillery, and dis-assembled helicopter parts as well as monstrous loads of guns and munitions.[8] Sharpatov's skill quickly won him a slot as the Candid's pilot. He and his crew "worked on the best plane in the entire company," he bragged.

In 1994 and 1995 Sharpatov piloted the Candid on a series of arms runs between Kabul and Tirana, Albania. The Il-76 would pick up its crated payloads in Tirana, usually a vast tonnage of "subma-chine gun and assault rifle rounds." As a military veteran, he was familiar with the oblong, military-green crates. "I had carried muni-tions and matériel before and when the soldiers in Tirana loaded those green boxes on board our plane, I knew exactly what was in those boxes." When he returned to Sharjah, Sharpatov also knew not to ask Bout prying questions. "I knew that it was not something illegal," he said. "Nor was I nervous—I had done such things before."[9]

The flights were usually uneventful except for a brief stretch when the Ilyushin neared the city of Kandahar, controlled by the fanatic Taliban. The Talibs patrolled the airspace around Kandahar with a single MiG-21 jet interceptor. But as long as Sharpatov kept the Candid at a safe distance, he had no problem reaching Kabul and dropping off his arms payload. When he returned to Transavia's headquarters in the dune-swept emirate, Sharpatov could relax at the airport hotel where Bout's crewmen and fellow Russian émigrés often met and drank.

Afghanistan was not the only place where Bout developed close ties to Islamic groups that only a few years earlier would have been considered enemies of the Soviet state. In 1992, soon after he went into business, NATO intelligence officials uncovered Bout's involvement in the intractable conflicts spawned by the breakup of the former Soviet bloc.

The first of these new wars centered in Bosnia and Herzegovina, one of six Balkan republics that emerged from the disintegration of the former Communist nation of Yugoslavia. Serbs living in the new Bosnian state feared minority status and opposed its independence, preferring that the region remain attached to Serbia. Bosnia's Muslims, backed by Croatia in a sporadic alliance of convenience, strongly supported independence. As the European Community announced recognition of the Republic of Bosnia and Herzegovina in April 1992, one of the most brutal European conflicts since World War II erupted, with the Belgrade-aided Bosnian Serbs on one side and Bosnian Muslims and Croats on the other.[10]

In an effort to keep the bloodshed from escalating, the United Nations imposed its first post–Cold War arms embargo on all sides. Bout, setting the template that he would follow in coming years, cut his teeth in his new capitalist incarnation by violating the sanctions.

The embargo gave a de facto advantage to the Serbs, who were better positioned to smuggle in the weapons necessary to attack the new state. Muslims in Bosnia had no standing army or stores of munitions to fight back. A brutal Serb campaign of "ethnic cleansing" sparked a wave of international sympathy for the beleaguered Muslim population. The United States and most of Europe paid lip service to the arms embargo, but were more than willing to turn a blind eye to weapons funneling into Bosnia.

As the international community debated how to respond to the carnage, the Muslim world raced to aid the Bosnian Muslims. Hundreds of battle-hardened mujahideen who had fought with Osama bin Laden in Afghanistan descended on Bosnia. Giddy at having defeated the former Soviet Union and anxious to prove that Allah would perform another miracle, the militant fighters viewed the Bosnian conflict as an opportunity to establish an Islamic state near the heart of Europe.[11]

The fundamentalist Islamic regime of Sudan, a country where Bout was already developing close ties with senior leaders, was at the forefront of the efforts to supply Bosnia. The vast desert nation had just installed a regime that would soon embrace Osama bin Laden and other terrorists from around the Islamic world. The Sudanese effort was aided and abetted by the fundamentalist Islamist regimes of Saudi Arabia and Iran. Despite religious differences between the Sunni Muslims of Saudi Arabia and Sudan on one side and Shi'ite Iran on the other, the donors were able to put aside their sectarian disagreements to work for a common Islamic good.

The primary weapons broker for the Muslim side was an obscure organization called the Third World Relief Agency (TWRA).[12] TWRA was no-run-of-the mill charity. From 1992 to 1995, when it was shut down by Austrian officials, some $400 million flowed through the organization's coffers, including donations from a who's who of Muslim radicals and al Qaeda supporters. Among the prominent TWRA supporters was bin Laden, who was moving his newly minted al Qaeda operation from Afghanistan to Khartoum, Sudan.[13]

The infusion of cash beginning in early 1992 allowed for the Bosnian miracle the mujahideen prayed for. In July 1992 TWRA received more than $20 million for a single account in the First Austrian bank. Three months later a Saudi government official walked into the same bank with two suitcases stuffed with cash and deposited another $5 million.[14] Flush with money, TWRA embarked on a weapons-buying spree. By September 1992 an Il-76 was making weekly flights from Khartoum to Maribor, an airport in Slovenia, next to Bosnia.[15]

The plane had been hired from Bout's fleet. "The TWRA agency had their first big operation in September 1992," said a multiagency European intelligence assessment of the Maribor operation. "They hired a Russian transport plane, from well-known sanctions buster and arms trafficker Victor Bout, out of Khartoum, the Sudanese capital, to transport equipment over to the Maribor Airport marked as humanitarian aid. However, instead of humanitarian assistance, the plane carried over 120 tons of Soviet manufactured rifles, RPG's, mines and ammunition."[16]

It is not clear how TWRA found Bout or how he found them.[17] But because of the lack of American understanding in the early 1990s about both the Bosnian conflict and the radical nature of the Islamic forces arming Bosnian Muslims, the Clinton administration allowed the weapons shipments by Bout to proceed.

A senior Western diplomat in the region said the Clinton administration knew about TWRA and its activities beginning in 1993 but took no action to stop its fund-raising or arms purchases, in large part because of the administration's sympathy for the Muslim government and American ambivalence about maintaining the arms embargo. "We were told [by Washington] to watch them but not interfere," the diplomat said. "Bosnia was trying to get weapons from anybody, and we weren't helping much. The least we could do is back off. So we backed off."[18]

Militant Islam was not yet perceived to be a national security threat in 1992. None of the fund-raising and other terror-related activities that would recur in al Qaeda's future campaigns were yet illegal, and the pervasive roles of nonstate actors, from terror-based charities to weapons merchants such as Bout, were not even dimly perceived as threats in U.S. policy and intelligence circles.

Austrian officials, in a refrain that would become familiar in the hunt for Bout, also failed to move against TWRA. They had documented the organization's weapons-trafficking activities but were unable to take action because none of the shipments actually passed through Austria. "They did a lot of talking here but as long as they did not move weapons through our territory, we could not arrest them," one Austrian investigator said.[19]

Viktor Bout set up shop in Sharjah, in the United Arab Emirates, in the spring of 1993. He needed a secure hub for his growing operation. As Bout grew from footloose trafficker to international businessman, he need a more organized, stable operation. Sharjah was perfectly located for flight routes to Afghanistan, Bosnia, Africa, and other places where his business was expanding. The first known record of a Bout firm is a trade license issued by the United Arab Emirates' Ministry of Justice on March 11, 1993, to the Transavia Travel Agency. The firm's business activities were listed as "travel, cargo, tourist." The license was registered to "Victor Butt" and an Emirati businessman who served as Bout's local sponsor in Sharjah.[20] "Transavia was just a travel agency," scoffed longtime Bout associate Richard Chichakli, who worked in Sharjah during the mid-1990s and later ran a Bout-network firm called Trans Aviation Global Group, Inc.[21] But U.S. officials said Bout repeatedly used several permutations of the Transavia name for his air operations.[22]

Alexander Sidorenko, the veteran paratroopers and air industry figure who worked early on with Bout, said he brought Bout and his brother Sergei to the emirates, touting the UAE's prospects as a strategic business location. "I introduced them to the sheikhs, to representatives of big air companies," Sidorenko said.[23] Bout has said only that his business took off exponentially in 1993 after his planes started flying out of the UAE. Russians began flocking to the emirates soon after the Soviet Union collapsed, first as vacationers, then as consumers and merchants.

The emirate of Dubai, where many visiting Russians disembarked, offered cut-rate and duty-free shopping and a wealth of Western products that the amazed visitors could not obtain even in the most exclusive stores in Moscow. Eager to profit on a wave of conspicuous consumption once condemned as decadent and bourgeois, expatriate Russians settled into Dubai by the thousands, hawking everything from jewelry and electronics to prostitutes. "Dubai became one big mall full of Russians," recalled an American diplomat stationed in the region. "They'd come off the planes with empty shopping bags. The nouveau riche would buy up TVs, VCRs, every electronic item they could get their hands on. Pretty soon you had the Russian Mafia in place and hundreds of hookers in the streets and hotel rooms."[24]

Bout shrewdly realized that he could make a windfall by bringing the UAE's products directly to Russian buyers. His planes were soon flying appliances and other coveted goods out from Dubai and Sharjah and back to the motherland. His profits soared as he sold everything from flowers to IKEA furniture to pencils.

The UAE seemed a perfect match for Bout's profit lust. The federation of seven sheikhdoms welcomed foreign-owned companies with economic incentives, low taxes, and weak, laissez-faire oversight. There were no requirements for banks to practice basic "know your customer" policies, and there were virtually no financial regulations on the books. Money laundering was not criminalized until 2002, and then only under strong international pressure.

Unified as an independent nation in December 1971 after decades as a British protectorate, the emirates had plunged into three decades of feverish growth. The UAE was governed by Sheikh Zayed bin Sultan al Nayhan, an autocratic Bedouin whose extended royal family steered the new nation's commercial expansion. The sheikh centered the UAE's national government in his home base of Abu Dhabi, the largest and richest of the sheikhdoms, where the royal family kept lucrative interests in the vast oil reserves beneath the dunes.

Dubai, a bustling gulfside emirate to the north, made up for a lack of natural resources by exploiting its role as a vital sea and air center connecting the Arabian peninsula to Pakistan, India, and the Middle East. It also became the center of the world's gold trade, a vital commodity in the Pakistani, Indian, and Arab cultures.

Arab traders, pirates, and smugglers had operated out of Dubai's souk, or marketplace, for hundreds of years, and even into the 1990s, they still plied the waters off Dubai in their dhows, curved wooden sailboats that carried every conceivable cargo, legal and black market. Under the commercially savvy Makhtoum family, Dubai pulsed with economic growth. The special gold souk takes up several city blocks of the downtown areas, jammed with stores that sell only gold and gold jewelry. It is so safe that the businessmen walk the narrow corridors with suitcases full of gold or cash, with no security. No matter what time of year, the gold souk is lit up with so many lights at night that it makes New Year's Eve on Times Square in New York look dim in comparison.

Glass- and aluminum-faced office towers sprang up over the waterfront, and lavish new hotels tended to the whims of wealthy sheikhs and tycoons. The most spectacular was the Burj al Arab, fashioned in the shape of an angular dhow sail, where diners were taken by submarine to an underwater restaurant and prime suites cost $15,000 a night, each equipped with a butler.

The young crown prince of Dubai, Sheikh Mohammed bin Rashid al Makhtoum, was the architect of Dubai's fever-pitch growth and a major investor in the emirate's massive development projects. A horse fancier who owned stables in Kentucky, the prince backed the Dubai World Cup, the world's most lucrative racing stakes. He was also a self-proclaimed poet and inventor, funding the cross-breeding of a llama and a camel that he called "Rama the Cama." And as the UAE's defense minister, he openly admired the Taliban in the late 1990s, playing a key role in the emirates' decision to recognize the militant Islamic regime.

Under the prince's watch, Dubai's seaport became a free-trade zone that lured foreign investors by eliminating taxes and duties. Dubai International Airport rapidly grew into the busiest air hub in the Middle East, a sprawling glass-and-steel complex constantly chilled to below seventy degrees despite the unrelenting desert heat that surrounds it. The structure hosts more than a hundred airlines and has miles of motorized walkways and a sprawling, duty-free bazaar crammed with cheap electronics, jewelry, perfume, and liquor stores. To keep wealthy passengers amused, Dubai officials staged a monthly raffle at the airport, charging visitors $100 and up to buy tickets for giveaways of Porsches, Mercedes, and Rolls-Royces. "In one sense, they were mimicking the American business culture, but it was the most freewheeling commercial atmosphere I've ever seen," said the American diplomat. "Their desire to stimulate business growth was so great that they lost control over everything, good businesses and bad." [25]

Sharjah, an emirate southwest of Dubai, also coveted business growth, but was late to the race. The emirate's city center was a drab cluster of brown office buildings and mosques where residents practiced a strict form of Islam similar to the puritanical tenets of Saudi Arabia's Wahabism. Liquor sales were forbidden, and officials had once banned the wearing of short pants. The ruler, Sheikh Sultan bin Mohammed al Qassimi, had tried to distinguish the emirate as a center of Muslim learning by building Islamic universities. But by the 1990s, impatient Sharjah officials turned to their sleepy airport as an economic engine.

A one-runway field that opened in 1977, Sharjah International Airport could not hope to catch up to rival Dubai as a hub for passenger airlines. But officials began wangling financial incentives to lure foreign-owned air freight firms in the hope of turning the airport into a major cargo center. By the time Bout arrived in Sharjah in 1993, airport officials were touting plans to open a major free-trade zone similar to Dubai's seaport, eliminating taxes and import and export duties for companies that relocated there. As work crews broke ground in 1995 at an abandoned military base near the airfield, Sharjah officials hired a Syrian-born former U.S. Army sergeant as the free-trade zone's new commercial manager. He was Richard Chichakli, who would soon become Bout's close friend, confidant, and business associate. "Sharjah always felt it was living in the shadow of Dubai," Chichakli said later, explaining the emirate's desperate push for expansion.[26]

Richard Ammar Chichakli emerged from a large, influential Syrian family that he later described as decimated by a wave of politically motivated murders and jailings. Chichakli escaped by studying in the early 1980s at Riyadh University in Saudi Arabia, where he claimed to have met and befriended Osama bin Laden and many of his siblings. The two students often sat over sandwiches, singing. Bin Laden was "a lot of fun" in those days, Chichakli recalled. Chichakli moved to Texas in 1986, obtained American citizenship, and joined the U.S. Army, serving in the first Gulf War and earning several decorations. He remained a soldier until 1993, specializing in aviation, interrogation, and intelligence.[27] Then he returned to the Middle East, relocating to Sharjah to tout the emirate's free-trade zone to skeptical businessmen and diplomats. "The U.S. attaché there laughed at us," Chichakli recalled. "He didn't think it would work."[28]

Chichakli's efforts paid off handsomely. The free-trade zone opened in June 1995 with 55 foreign firms, a number that quickly doubled in 1996 and grew to more than 2,300 companies by 2003. Sharjah's airport was soon crowded with more than 160 air cargo firms and freight forwarders. A trim, blunt-spoken man known among friends as "Stone Face" for his somber countenance, Chichakli moved easily among Russian airmen and emirati princes, sheikhs, and moneymen, constantly talking up the virtues of his free-trade zone.

One of his earliest converts was Viktor Bout, who moved his air offices into the zone and also invested in the facility. The two men had met at an air show in 1993. "We used to sit ass to ass on the runway and smell the kerosene," Chichakli recalled.[29] They remained friendly as Bout's operation grew at Sharjah, adding dozens of planes, hangars, and a cavernous avionics shop that would eventually employ scores of mechanics and crewmen. Bout's primary operation in Sharjah was San Air General Trading FZE, a holding company that controlled several other companies that operated in Sharjah. A similarly named firm later opened a branch in Richardson, Texas.[30]

When Chichakli left his free-trade-zone job in 1996, he began doing consulting work for Bout. Returning to the Dallas suburb of Richardson, he earned an accounting degree at the University of Texas, Dallas, and began working as a CPA. According to a 2000 résumé cited by U.S. Treasury officials, Chichakli identified himself as the controller and chief financial officer for Air Cess, Air Pass, and Centrafican Airlines—all key Bout-linked firms. (Chichakli later denied those roles, insisting the résumé was a fake.)

Chichakli blithely downplayed his work for Bout, saying he only "provided some accounting advice here and there. I'm a gun for hire. I helped him advance his cargo business."[31]

As Bout's businesses boomed, he generated millions of dollars that moved through the accounts of various front companies and partners. The UAE's lax banking standards were already an ongoing concern among some of the Gulf nation's largest banks, whose senior officers worried that the unbridled freedom of emirates' financial structure was leaving them open to fraud and damaged reputations. A 1999 internal audit by the Sharjah branch of HSBC Holdings PLC, a major bank, found that hundreds of Russians had opened 1,186 bank accounts in that branch office—and that the rapid turnover in the accounts indicated "money laundering on a massive scale."[32]

Among the Russian accounts—later shut down by auditors—were several belonging to the "Semenchenko Group," named for Andrei Semenchenko, who was listed on paper as the sole proprietor of San Air General Trading, a Bout-network firm later targeted by the U.S. Treasury Department. The "group" included San Air

General Trading and several individuals who ran the company accounts. The report found that "a number of unusual transactions (including large cash transactions and transfers to a local money exchange) have taken place over the [San Air] account over the past year."[33]

In one case the auditors found that an individual in the Semenchenko Group named Maridiboy Kakharov, an Uzbek national "believed to be closely connected to San Air," had a declared income of $817 a month. Yet he had a turnover of $1.53 million through his account from December 1998 to February 1999, prompting the bank to note that such transactions are "clearly not commensurate with this level of salary." The report noted that Kakharov's account had received a transfer of $648,017 from the "Uzbekistan Ministry of Defense" during the period in question. An internal HSBC June 11, 2000, memorandum said that an internal bank compliance officer "has acknowledged that the bank is guilty of money laundering in the case of the Semenchenko Group at Sharjah branch." But the compliance officer concluded that in the absence of any UAE law making money laundering illegal in the emirates, "the bank is under no legal compulsion to inform the central bank of the UAE."[34]

By 1995, Bout's Sharjah airport operation had become the nerve center of an expanding Third World operation and his financial situation was improving dramatically. Already regularly flying weapons shipments into Afghanistan, Bout's Sharjah-based Transavia flagship was also active in Africa.

With many of his planes already settled in Sharjah, Bout moved in March 1995 to add a European hub at Ostend, a seaport on the Belgian coast. He set up an office in Ostend for another tentacle of his Transavia operation, using the name of the NV Trans Aviation Network Group, also known as the TAN Group.

The tiny Ostend airport, less than a mile from the North Sea, was ideal. It was one of the few airfields in Western Europe that still allowed the large Antonovs and Ilyushins to land on its runways. The deafening engine noise from the Russian-made aircraft had already led many other European airport officials to ban them from their fields.

Ostend's management had also adopted a relaxed stance toward the air cargo firms that operated there, welcoming any company that promised steady freight operations. Bout's competitors included an American firm linked by a Belgian parliamentary commission to clandestine arms flights to Iran and UNITA rebels in Angola in the early and mid-1980s; and another U.S. cargo operation that was tied in the early 1990s to rebel movements in Rwanda and the DRC. Both firms went out of business, as did a number of other Ostend-based cargo operations that were also suspected of using the airfield as a launch point for arms shipments.[35]

Most importantly, Ostend provided easy flight lines to Burgas, the Bulgarian free-trade zone, and to other East European transshipment points where Bout's planes could load up with arms shipments and other cargoes before flying south to Africa or east toward Afghanistan. "We think he came here for cover for his flights to Burgas," said Ronny Lauwereins, Ostend airport's security director.

Bout showed up on occasion to personally take the reins of the operation, although he also had two partners—at least on paper. One was Michael Victor Thomas, a Frenchman whose name never cropped up on paper in any other Bout enterprises. The other was a Belgian shareholder, Ronald De Smet, a pilot who had reportedly flown for the Saudi royal family and who would later work with Bout in Liberia and South Africa.

The Russian set up his new offices on the first floor of a lowslung white brick building known as the Jet Center. He hired a secretary and installed a telex machine and a few pieces of leased furniture. Although Bout spent much of the time during that period in Sharjah and in African locations, Lauwereins would see him at odd hours, scheduling arrivals and departures of his earsplitting Ilyushin Il-76. Bout left hints that he planned to settle in Ostend. He got in the good graces of the Jet Center's owner by buying the man's gated estate for $500,000. Soon expensive cars were prowling in and out of the mansion. And Bout even raised his public profile, staking out a helpful role in the high-profile disappearance of three Belgian girls by consulting with a Russian clairvoyant.[36]

"He paid his bills on time and took care of everything," Lauwereins recalled. "He had a lot of flights going in and out all the time.

He must have been a good businessman because he was making a lot of money in those days."[37]

In the summer of 1995, Bout and his crewmen were given a harsh lesson in the perils of working in the arms trade.

Afghanistan's government desperately needed guns and ammunition. Bout's hulking rented Ilyushin Il-76 was pressed into service. For three years, the Rabbani regime had survived a grueling series of clashes with rival warlords. Soldiers and civilians had died by the thousands. Kabul had been raked by rockets and artillery fire, but the government held—only to face its stiffest challenge from the sudden rise of the young fundamentalist students known as the Taliban. Under the command of the one-eyed Islamic zealot, Mullah Omar, an army of bearded, fundamentalist Pashtun students and battle-tested mujahideen had seized control of Kandahar in November 1994. The following spring, armed by Pakistan with heavy weapons and swift, gun-mounted four-wheel-drive pickup trucks, the mullahs launched a blistering offensive, attacking government troops from Kabul to Herat. Taliban forces reached Kabul's suburbs before they were driven back, but by the summer of 1995 the Talibs controlled nine of the country's thirty-one provinces and had dug in, rearming for an expected attack in the fall.[38] Rabbani and Massoud were anxious to replenish their exhausted munitions supplies, and they turned to Bout for a quick fix.

On August 3, 1995, Transavia's Il-76 set course for Kabul. Sharpatov was in the cockpit, leading a crew of six. The plane's vaultlike cargo bay was crammed with AK-47 ammunition clips. The plane had stopped in Tirana, where Albanian soldiers spent hours loading green crates containing more than 3.4 million Kalashnikov rounds. Massoud had struck a deal with Albanian sources for five munitions flights, using Bout as the transporter. The Ilyushin's tail carried a Russian federation decal, but its nose was emblazoned with a green, white, and red Tatarstan band—representing the Central Asian air firm that had leased the plane to Bout. The ammunition crates were labeled as "spare parts."

"Albanian authorities signed a contract with the government of Afghanistan to ship ammunition to government troops," Sharpatov recalled. "And since we were not involved in delivering ammunition or weapons to guerrilla forces, we were sure there was nothing wrong with what we were doing. Since it was a delivery sanctioned by the government, there was nothing criminal about it."[39]

The crew had already made two runs between Tirana and Kabul, and they "went flawlessly," Sharpatov recalled. But on the third flight, the Ilyushin veered too close to the perilous air corridor over Kandahar. "Our radio operator was stupid enough to establish radio contact with the [Taliban] control tower in Kandahar. There was a person there whom the radio operator knew and he got on the air just to say hi. The person asked where we were headed and when they found out we were flying to Kabul, they decided to [force] land the plane."[40]

Within minutes, an ancient MiG-21 jet flying for the Taliban's ill-equipped air force intercepted the Ilyushin and escorted it to the airport at Kandahar. An informant in Kandhar for the United States who was on the scene hours later told American diplomats in Islamabad that he saw "three crewmembers, one of whom had blonde hair, resting on cots beneath the aircraft wings."[41] The Talibs transferred the hostages to a converted storeroom near the governor's mansion at Kandahar. With their prisoners safely stowed, Taliban troops swarmed over the Ilyushin, seizing the massive payload of munitions for their own Kalashnikovs. But as they cracked open crate after crate, they found—to their growing ire—that many of the rounds were corroded and useless.[42]

Bearded mujahideen fighters stood guard outside the storeroom all day and night. Sharpatov and his men were given cots to sleep on, but the frames were rusted and creaky. Instead, they stretched out on thin rugs laid over the concrete floor. They were fed under-cooked rice that often sat for hours outside their door, accumulating pebbles and rat droppings. Several men cracked their teeth on the roughage. The Talibs bolstered their meals with occasional servings of fried potatoes and meager rations of meat and fruit, but the "primitive" diet took its toll. "Every one of us would have terrible diarrhea after eating," Sharpatov said.

For the first several days, the crewmen wondered if Bout was trying free them. "We just sat around waiting for something to happen," Sharpatov recalled. Back in Sharjah, Bout tried to negotiate by phone with the mullahs, and daringly even flew to Kandahar, only to be turned away. But the mullahs insisted on the involvement of Russian negotiators, convinced that the Ilyushin had been on an official government mission. On August 10 the Russian Foreign Ministry ordered Zamir Kabulov, a veteran of Afghan and Central Asian diplomacy, to fly to Sharjah and join Bout on his next flight to Kandahar.

Yeltsin's diplomats were furious about being dragged into the affair. "This incident only caused irritation with the Russian government, since what had been done had been done without our knowledge," Kabulov recalled later. "We did not know what was going on while he, naturally, was making money."[43] Kabulov arrived in Sharjah the same day, then joined Bout in one of the Russian's Antonov An-32s, and by nightfall they were in Kandahar. Bout and Kabulov were ushered to the governor's house, not far from where Sharpatov and his crew were held under guard. They were met by Mullah Muhammed Rabbani (no relation to the Afghan leader), who was in direct contact with Mullah Omar, who led the Taliban's side of the negotiations.

"It was a very slow, sticky and unfriendly talk with the Talibs," Kabulov recalled. The mullah stuck to a hostile tack—the crew, he intoned, had been "supplying arms," and only a Taliban Islamic Sharia court could decide their fate. "They totally rejected our reasoning," Kabulov said. "I tried to explain to them the entire chain of events, that the company did not have anything to do with Russia." But the mullah "thought that it was just a cover for an operation by the Russian state secret services." The Talib "would leave the room to confer with Mullah Omar, come back and repeat the same stance." The mullah further complicated the talks by insisting that Russia had to compensate "the material damage to Afghanistan over the years of the civil war." Hours later, the only progress was a Taliban agreement to allow the Russians to deliver food packages that Bout had packed on the Antonov.[44]

As the weeks dragged on, Sharpatov and his crew grew desperate with boredom and pessimism. They spent much of their time sleeping—or trying to sleep. They occupied the long hours devising new ways to kill the armies of ants that swarmed through their makeshift jail. They were given brief exercise periods in a courtyard and began collecting scrap metal for dumbbells. They had to tread carefully to evade scuttling scorpions and tarantulas.

In December, despite the hardened stances of both sides, the Talibs gave Sergei Bout permission to bring shipments of canned food to the imprisoned crewmen. When he entered the storeroom, the Bout brother motioned Sharpatov over to a corner. "Be ready to leave," he whispered. "Do not take off your clothes when you go to bed at night. Do not take anything but your documents with you. There will be someone who will come for you at night and will take you to a safe place."[45]

The crew lay awake for the next two nights, but there was no rescue. Sergei Bout returned several weeks later with more canned food and new orders. He told Sharpatov that he and his brother were working on a ransom deal. "He told us to sit tight and not do anything stupid," Sharpatov said. Again, nothing happened. There were no further visits from the Bouts. The crew sank into despair. "We realized that no one was interested in saving us anymore," Sharpatov recalled.

Despite the stasis, Bout's Transavia planes continued to fly into Kandahar. A Bout lieutenant brought more food deliveries, and Kabulov kept up his dismal negotiations, also flying into and out of Kandahar on Bout's planes. The diplomat found it odd that despite the strained relations between Bout and the Talibs, the mullahs allowed Bout's planes to make regular visits. The planes would stop in Kandahar, dropping Kabulov off, then fly on to Jalalabad, where they would unload cargo shipments. "I was somewhat surprised," Kabulov said, adding, "but not very much." Veteran Russian aviation executive Sergei Mankhayev, a former Bout partner, later claimed that Bout used the Kandahar flights to deliver clandestine shipments to the Talibs. Bout "used this opportunity to fly there [to Kandahar] very often, sometimes to make 5 to 6 flights a day with a cargo of TVs, clothes and consumer goods made in China or Taiwan," Mankhayev claimed. "In Kandahar, the Talibs would unload the stuff into trucks and take it across the open and uncontrolled border to Pakistan."[46]

Kabulov tried to break the logjam by seeking out Russia's Central Asian allies, conferring with Tatar officials and Afghan warlords. He approached the Pakistani government, trying to find leverage with the ISI, the secret service that had armed the Talibs and directed their military operations. The Taliban delegation changed faces regularly, but their responses did not vary. There was no progress for a year.[47]

In mid-July 1996, Sharpatov recalled, the mujahideen guards suddenly gave his crew permission to climb into the Ilyushin for the first time to fire up its engines. Over the next few weeks, the engine tests became routine. Kabulov learned later that the mullahs had been considering selling the seized plane and had dropped hints to Sharpatov and his crew. According to Sharpatov, the hostages shrewdly seized on the opening, telling their guards that the plane had to be in top condition for resale and required regular engine tests.

An escape plan began to form, Sharpatov recounted. On August 16, he and his crew took advantage of a momentary lull when most of their guards drifted off briefly for Friday prayers. The crew overpowered two remaining soldiers, and Sharpatov fired up the engines, taxiing down the runway. Several Taliban guards tried to block the moving plane with a fire truck, Sharpatov said, but by then the massive plane was picking up speed. Airborne seconds later, Sharpatov and his crew flew to Sharjah, ignored by the Taliban's lone MiG, and returned to Moscow as heroes. The Bouts treated them to lavish dinners, and Russian president Boris Yeltsin honored them with medals.[48]

But in the years since, Western intelligence officials and Russian aviation veterans have raised doubts about the scenario, describing it as a convenient cover story for a staged escape and a secret deal between Bout and the Talibs. Several Russian aviation executives who were based in Sharjah in the mid-1990s insist that Bout crafted an arrangement with the mullahs that set his crew free in return for his agreement to supply the Taliban's military with weapons. One veteran director of a Russian air firm described it this way: "When the Talibs captured the plane, they wanted to shoot the crew and keep the plane and the bullets. But Bout conducted very long talks with them and the Talibs told Bout to run several free rides with arms for them in exchange for the crew and the plane. Then the Talibs arranged for the so-called escape of the crew at Bout's request. After that, Bout began supplying weapons to the Talibs as well." [49]

Even Bout has intimated that the escape tale was a flimsy cover.

But he hesitated to divulge more, hinting that the real story remains too sensitive because of the collusion of an unnamed government. "Do you really think you can jump in a plane that's been sitting unmaintained on the tarmac for over a year, start up the engines and just take off?" he asked interviewer Peter Landesman in 2003 in Moscow. After a pause, Bout added: "They didn't escape. They were extracted." When Landesman pressed for an explanation, asking if the Russian government was involved, Bout clammed up. "There are huge forces," he began, then lapsed into silence.[50]

Kabulov, who went on to become Russian ambassador to Afghanistan and then director for Asian affairs at the Russian Foreign Ministry, said he had no inkling of any covert dealings between Bout and the Russian government in the crew's liberation—and added that he was unaware of Bout's alleged secret arms arrangements with the mullahs. But ever the diplomat, Kabulov allowed that nothing could be ruled out.

"In Afghanistan," he said, "anything is possible."

CHAPTER 4

Continental Collapse

I n March 1997, an American with a short, grizzled-gray beard stood watch on a crumbling tarmac in Zaire, squinting into the tropical sun past the broken-down hangars that passed for an airport on the outskirts of Kisangani. He was eyeing Russian cargo planes as they rumbled down the airfield's rutted runways, laden with supplies for a nation in crisis.

He had arrived days earlier in the provincial capital, a sweltering, strategic jungle outpost on the Congo River that Joseph Conrad used as the backdrop for *Heart of Darkness*, his fictional descent into the moral netherworld of nineteenth-century colonial Africa.[1] Unlike Conrad's doomed European imperialists, the American had come to Kisangani on a mission of mercy, trying to help figure out how to avert a humanitarian disaster.

A veteran Africa hand who worked for the U.S. government, the American had spent long years ranging across the continent on countless thankless official assignments. But as he waited at the airstrip outside Kisangani, it seemed as if he had been suddenly dropped into his own modern version of Conrad's hell. His immediate mission had been to see if the airfield, Kisangani's sole airport and last remaining link to the outside world, was still serviceable.

In the days before the U.S. official arrived at the airport, thousands of Congolese refugees had been streaming toward Kisangani over ruined jungle roads, driven by war and starvation in a country on the brink of disintegration. Behind the desperate throngs were rampaging rebel forces led by Laurent Kabila and backed by the armies of Uganda and Rwanda. While Kabila and his rebel army fought to wrest control of Zaire from its aged, weakening dictator for life, Mobutu Sese Seko, the Rwandans and the Ugandans were bent on revenge, aiming to eliminate Hutu tribesmen hiding among the crowds of fleeing refugees. Accused of the genocidal slaughter of hundreds of thousands of Tutsi tribesmen in Rwanda in 1994, the Hutu killers had fled to United Nations–run refugee camps inside Zaire. Now Kabila's advance had driven them toward Kisangani, along with thousands of other displaced Congolese.[2]

Kisangani was a prize for whoever controlled it. The city was the regional hub of the lucrative diamond trade, run by clans of Lebanese merchants who had controlled the flow of stones since the early part of the twentieth century. In earlier days ivory also was smuggled through the city, 750 miles northeast of the capital, making Kisangani a hub of black market trade and violence. Called Stanleyville during colonial times because of its proximity to Stanley Falls, Kisangani was already home to five hundred thousand people. But by 1997, after years of war and neglect, it was a city in name only.

The American had already seen the first arrivals of the approaching human flood. The dispossessed were selling anything they could get their hands on. Refugees and locals hawked everything from jugs of water to auto mirrors ripped from the doors of passing cars. The hustlers milled among crowds of women and children, hoping for a single sale that might allow them to feed their starving families a small portion of rice. The U.S. official's job was to help sort out the real refugees and help them get emergency shipments of food and aid that were about to be flown in by the United Nations' World Food Program.

The American had no idea how to pick out deserving refugees from Hutu mass murderers. His resources were limited. He had no defined policy guidelines from Washington. All he had been asked to do was to help streamline the movement of food supplies and other humanitarian aid and to monitor the overall flow of events. He was to report back to Washington on any prospects that might help U.S. decision makers fashion a coherent response to the crisis—even though it lay at the bottom of the list of American foreign policy priorities.

The American cared, but his mission was daunting, and there were few others helping him do it. He was among the remnants of a shrinking pool of U.S. intelligence officials and humanitarian aid providers still based in Africa. Their ranks had steadily diminished since the end of the Cold War, numbers thinned by attrition and budget cuts. Africa had seen more than two thirds of its CIA stations closed since the collapse of the Soviet Union. Embassy staffs were slashed, development aid offices shuttered, and knowledgeable field workers sent Stateside without replacements.

By the mid-1990s, most stations in the countries at risk did not have regular CIA stations. Sierra Leone was covered from Conakry, Guinea. Liberia and Burkina Faso were covered from Abidjan in the Ivory Coast.

The station chiefs, once among the most influential U.S. officials abroad, were reduced to what the CIA and diplomats disparagingly called "circuit-riders," moving from one country to the next and relying almost entirely on liaison relationships with often corrupt and brutal local intelligence services. Almost all capability to run human intelligence operations had been irretrievably lost.

Arriving at the airport, the American recognized quickly that despite its cratered runway and broken hangars, the facility, carved out years before as a lifeline for white administrators who worked for the Belgian government, was still usable. Old Russian cargo planes circled in and took off at a desultory pace. But the rest of Kisangani was in no shape to receive a flood of refugees. The jungle was encroaching, leaving Kisangani's Belgian-built cement administrative buildings overgrown with moss and decaying in the relentless humidity. The city's tin-roofed shantytowns stank, stagnant and fetid. Functioning hospitals, running water, and garbage service were distant memories, and electricity was provided only by private generators. Once-paved streets were in such disrepair that it was easier to walk or ride a bicycle than navigate over the enormous craters in a vehicle. Even transportation by boat on the dark, slug-gish Congo River was slow and dangerous, a throwback to Conrad's day. The railroad link to Kinshasa was now a rusted set of tracks to nowhere, unused for decades and retaken by the jungle.

The airstrip would have to do. By the time the U.S. official had showed up to look the facility over, the situation in Kisangani had taken a turn for the worse. Just days before the American arrived, Kabila's rebel troops had seized the city. Tons of food would have to be moved by air, and Kabila had abysmal relations with the UN relief organizations. And the United Nations, which had precious little airlift capacity of its own, would have to scurry to charter as many aircraft as it could find.

The arrival of Kabila's troops was an ominous development for more than just the American's hopes for an aid airlift into Kisan-gani. Even for a superpower that was not paying attention, the dire situation around Kisangani had the tragic timbre of a disaster in the making. Kabila's forces had swept through the already ravaged countryside, looting like freed criminals and devouring like fam-ished locusts. Many of the volatile gunmen were teenagers, some adolescents and children. Many had been kidnapped and impressed into military service. They had little to eat and were often doped up on gin and amphetamines. Lugging heavy bandoliers of ammuni-tion, they could barely lock and load their AK-47s, and some held guns almost as long as they were tall.

Kabila, a rotund despot with a fondness for safari suits, had received personal tutoring from the legendary Argentine-Cuban guerrilla Ernesto "Che" Guevara in the 1960s. The Congo was rich in natural resources, and Kabila had bought support from Rwanda, Uganda, and other foreign allies by promising rights to the coun-try's bountiful diamond, uranium, timber, coltan, and iron conces-sions once he took power. He placated his troops by giving them license to loot and rape at will. As his forces swept in to Kisangani, Kabila was poised to ride the wave of good fortune all the way to the presidential palace in the capital of Kinshasa.

Once assured that the airport still functioned, the American official moved quickly to jump-start the relief pipeline. The airfield was swarming with Rwandan, Ugandan, and Congolese soldiers. In their drab uniforms, T-shirts, flip-flops, and cheap wrap-around plastic sunglasses, the troops were impossible to separate from the refugees. They were thugs more than soldiers, using their AK-47s and RPGs to loot from the exhausted refugees who drifted nearby on foot and bicycle, in search of food and a place to camp. The American finally found Kabila's officers, and once he had negotiated guarantees that the relief supplies would not be looted, the airfield was ready to receive aid.

Russian Ilyushin Il-76 and Antonov An-24 cargo planes began arriving with pallets piled with food, medical supplies, and plastic sheeting. The planes were easily identified by the UN World Food Program (WFP) logos on their tails. Piloted by veteran Ukrainian crews, the Russian planes flew in day after day, ferrying tons of emergency staples for tens of thousands of refugees.

As he stood at the tarmac, the American found himself watching one of the mammoth Il-76s creak downward for a rocky landing. Grinding to a halt, the freighter lowered its rear door and began its off-loading of food parcels. Oddly, the crew members brought out a ladder, set it against the tail, climbed up, and removed a UN logo that gave the plane its official protection. The startled American continued watching as the crewmen then began loading the Ilyushin with crates of weapons.

"I didn't know those tail markings were magnetic, but I guess they were," recalled the official, who still works for the U.S. government. "Then guys in uniforms were moving quickly, taking good old-fashioned crates of AK-47s and ammunition onto it. When it was loaded up, it just took off. We don't know where it went." The entire turnaround time was less than an hour.[3]

Reporting the strange events at the airfield back to his superiors, the American soon learned that the plane—and its cargo of weapons—belonged to Viktor Bout. The Ilyushin had flown the food supplies into Kisangani under official UN auspices and left with a load of weapons destined for parts unknown, most likely delivered to Rwandan troops on another battlefront. The departing flight was just one of the hundreds, if not thousands, of arms runs that made Bout infamous during the 1990s as the preeminent weapons provider to Africa's dictators, warlords, rebel leaders, and terrorists. And the inbound flight of food supplies for the WFP was an example of Bout's deft ability to keep his planes airborne with

moneymaking cargoes and to ingratiate his operation with governments and global organizations.

The American had heard about Bout's operation. Sparse intelligence reports had linked the Russian's aircraft to the arming of the
Hutu killers only a few years earlier, although hard evidence of
those flights remained sketchy. There were newer reports that Bout's
crews were flying for Rwandan troops, helping them project a military presence far from their home base in their tiny country. But in
1997, the Bout network was not a U.S. priority, only "of interest,"
the American recalled later. He could look into the movements of
the Bout planes in Kisangani. But he could not touch.

In a model he would repeat in other killing fields, Bout was
profiting from several sides in the Congolese conflict. His planes
were feeding refugees, shuttling in the weapons for Kabila's rebel
forces while Mobutu, Zaire's fading president, remained a close
client and personal friend.

Mobutu had been well worth cultivating. Famously fond of
leopard skin hats and capes, Mobutu had skillfully portrayed himself as a foe of international communism to loosen the spigots of
American financial aid. For years he had effectively blunted calls for
reform in Zaire—his chosen name for the Congo—by repeatedly
threatening to switch sides in the Cold War. But by 1997, the United
States and other old foreign friends were no longer willing to rush
to his aid. Mobutu, who had memorably spent tens of millions of
dollars to lure Muhammad Ali and George Foreman to Kinshasa in
1974 to fight the "Rumble in the Jungle" heavyweight championship
fight, had almost nothing left but his well-stocked Swiss bank
accounts. He was dying of cancer, and his empire was slipping
through his aging fingers.

Three months after the American officials saw the Bout plane
loading weapons at Kisangani, the Russian sent another aircraft, on
a dangerous mission to extract Mobutu and his entourage from
their last stronghold. Mobutu escaped into exile. Renaming Zaire
the Democratic Republic of the Congo (DRC), Kabila ascended to
his place.

Bout's flagrant arms shipments to both combatants stunned
even the most jaded observers. Belgian researcher Johan Peleman,
who mastered the flight routes and corporate structure of Bout's

network as he investigated UN arms embargo violations in Africa, came away unnerved "in the way that ideology or politics are not at all involved. And it shocks me in that, if I can find out who's supplying these rebels or this government, they themselves can find out as well. So they very often knowingly do business with the very person who's supplying their enemies." [4]

Toward the end of 1997 the U.S. official returned from the DRC to attend a classified year-end review session with senior American intelligence officials who headed African divisions from several government agencies. One of the primary topics was the DRC and the Rwandan-backed incursion that had propelled Kabila into power. The intelligence community had entirely failed to foresee the developments.

"We did not realize that Rwanda could project power halfway across the continent," the official recalled. "They had to have Il-76s flying to do that. Specifically, the Rwanda experience brought home to us that you can't just look at the order of battle for a state, but you have to look at the gray market, nonstate actors that can be brought to bear."

Viktor Bout had begun to alter the landscape of modern war.

Bout's Africa operations left bloody footprints across the continent. Chaos gave rise to instability. Instability bred more chaos. The results, writ large, were staggeringly bleak. The massive continent has fifty-three countries and is the size of China, the United States, Europe, India, Argentina, and New Zealand combined.[5] Yet a 2003 World Bank study found that only nine nations merited even a barely acceptable fair-governance rating. The rest, comprising more than 80 percent of the continent, were judged as failing or failed states.[6]

The private global arms trade had surged, reaping as much as $10 billion a year—an industry that researchers believe had its most rapid growth in the decade following the end of the Cold War.[7] The effects were immediate and pronounced on African countries that were suddenly awash in guns. African tribal factions had long fought territorial wars using a patchwork of simple and outdated weaponry—rustic hunting rifles, shotguns, spears, and machetes. Even the more modernized streams of arms that had been covertly shipped to African rebel groups by the Soviet Union during the

Cold War were carefully meted out and controlled. But everything changed as the African market was flooded with a tide of assault rifles, rocket-propelled grenades, antitank cannons, and endless supplies of ammunition.

In northeastern Uganda, the Karimojong tribe had used traditional weapons for centuries to settle territorial disputes. Deaths were rare, and feuds usually were settled by clan elders. But by the late 1990s, according to a 2001 State Department fact sheet on African weapons flows, the tribe and its neighbors had been armed with an estimated forty thousand AK-47s. "Not surprisingly," State Department officials said, "cattle rustling and clan warfare became more lethal." Kalashnikovs became a common wedding dowry. Efforts by the government to disarm the tribe led to violent clashes, and a once-peaceful area had "become part of the arc of conflict that stretches from the Horn of Africa to east, central and southern Africa."[8]

The Eastern bloc was not alone in culpability for rising weapons flows in Africa. Between 1991 and 1998, U.S. weapons and training deliveries to Africa totaled more than $227 million—and American military aid to the seven African nations involved in the DRC wars totaled $125 million over the same period. But the ubiquitous AK-47 and other Eastern bloc weapons far outstripped American varieties in popularity. In the post–Cold War era thirty-five million to fifty million AK-47s were churned out by Russian and East European factories. By contrast, about eight million American M-16 varieties were manufactured.[9] The flow of Russian assault rifles was so vast that in Kenya, the barter rate for a single AK-47 dropped from ten cows in 1986 to two cows in 2001, the nongovernment organization Oxfam reported.[10] Easy access to weaponry gave the rudimentary armies of drugged children and untrained militias the firepower to level entire societies.

One group whose ascendancy can be traced, at least in part, to Bout's weapons provisions is the Revolutionary United Front (RUF) in Sierra Leone. The RUF's battlefield advances coincided neatly with Bout's weapons deliveries. The luckiest victims in Sierra Leone were those who escaped the RUF's onslaughts of amputations, rape, and torture and eked out a hardscrabble existence as slaves in the conflict's diamond fields.

There, the men and boys, watched by armed guards cradling Kalashnikovs and wearing their ubiquitous wraparound plastic sunglasses, were forced to dig diamonds all day, six days a week. The heaviest activity was during the rainy season, when the alluvial diamonds were easier to wash from the rivers and streams. Stripped to their underwear, the slave laborers would haul gravel from pits dug by shovel deep into the muddy riverbeds. Cave-ins were endemic, often bringing death by suffocation.

Others would haul the gravel to the river, to be washed in rudimentary gravel sifters called "shake-shakes," where the diamonds were picked from the stones and turned over to mine bosses. At times the digging grew so frenzied that the workers dug under pylons holding up bridges and the foundations of houses, causing their collapse.

The men were forced at gunpoint each night to strip and wash each body cavity under the watchful eyes of the guards, to ensure that they were not smuggling out any stones, a crime that brought an automatic death sentence.

As Bout-supplied weapons flowed to the RUF in 1998 and 1999, both in direct flights and through weapons transshipped by Charles Taylor in Liberia, the rebels were able to carry out campaigns that were as chilling and destructive as their names: "Operation No Living Thing" and "Operation Pay Yourself." The commanders directing the mayhem dubbed themselves with equally mordant nicknames: Kill Me Quick, Superman, Poison, Mosquito, and Mosquito Killer.

The child soldiers bore the brunt of these operations. Often they were given mixtures of cocaine and amphetamines the night before setting off on "mayhem days," the endless hours when they would rampage through the countryside, killing, mutilating, raping, and pillaging until they collapsed from fatigue and hunger.

To ensure that the children could not abandon the rebel forces, the commanders would often take razor blades and carve the initials "RUF" into the young soldiers' chests. The brand was tantamount to a death sentence. An escapee caught on the road by the RUF could easily be identified as a deserter. And if the enemy caught him, it was equally fatal because he would be unable to deny his affiliation to the rebel movement.

Large swaths of eastern and northern Sierra Leone were reduced to abandoned, barren wastelands that resembled hellish scenes out of Goya paintings. Burned and bombed-out villages populated by those too weak and ill to flee were slowly retaken by jungle growth. Dilapidated, unused clinics, schools, and businesses that had been razed to the ground were stripped of anything of value, from the aluminum roofing to plumbing hardware. The rubber plantations and palm trees that produce palm oil were slowly chocked by overgrowth after years of neglect.

In the overcrowded refugee camps in the eastern regions of the country, where most of the war was fought, relief workers found that close to 70 percent of the women were victims of sexual assault, and the percentage was almost as high among the men. The crisis was so overwhelming that doctors and nurses would not even test for HIV/AIDS because they had no way to treat the infection if it were found. Instead they limited themselves to testing for traditional sexually transmitted diseases that could be treated with antibiotics.

The scorched-earth campaigns left thousands of maimed victims. The rebels often mocked their victims before amputating their limbs, asking them if they wanted to be "short-sleeved"—with the limb chopped off above the elbow or knee—or "long-sleeved," with just the hands or feet amputated. Many of the maimed still live in tattered, crowded homes built out of plastic sheets and aluminum roofing.

The fragile domiciles are clustered in the Amputee and War Wounded Camp, a den of human anguish by the side of the main road in Freetown, Sierra Leone. Disfigured men, women, and children eke out a numbing existence there, squatting in abject poverty and living off international food donations. They are largely ignored by their own government and now almost forgotten by the world outside. Dust, flies, and mosquitoes hover over the camp. Visitors are no longer welcome. Too many foreigners have arrived, promising relief. Few have delivered.

Sitting beside an open sewer canal a few years ago at the camp, a man with both arms hacked off cursed his young son as the boy tried to light a cigarette. The boy was missing a leg, and teetering on crutches, he was unable to light a match to help his father out.

When he saw an American visitor watching, the old man demanded that the stranger avert his eyes.

"We are reduced to living like animals!" he yelled, overcome by shame and rage. "Go. You have seen how we live. You will do nothing about it. Now go."

As his planes flew tons of guns into the chaos of sub-Saharan Africa, Bout's network also aided two northern African states that were directly opposed to U.S. interests and often widely considered to be international pariahs—Libya and Sudan. Libya was, at the time, the world's foremost sponsor of terror. Its enigmatic and megalomaniacal leader, Muammar Gaddafi, was also the chief sponsor of the rebel armies that were being serviced by Bout and ravaging the subcontinent in the name of pan-African unity and liberation. Selected cadres from different nations were hosted at special Libyan training camps at the World Revolutionary Headquarters in the desert. Libyan special forces and secret services trained thousands of potential revolutionaries from Africa, Latin America, and Asia.

By the 1980s Gaddafi's headquarters had become "the Harvard and Yale of a whole generation of African revolutionaries." [11] Many of Gaddafi's star graduates would become loyal Bout customers, and Bout opened several air charter companies there, including one called Cen Sad/Sin Sad, which operated out of Tripoli but was registered in the Bahamas. Western intelligence officials also learned that Bout air crews had begun regularly servicing not only Sin Sad planes but also Gaddafi's personal fleet. That relationship continued, officials said, at least through early 2000, and perhaps beyond. [12]

Sudan, too, was in the grips of a radical Islamic revolution led by the National Islamic Front (NIF). The NIF leadership that took over Sudan in a bloody 1989 coup d'état came from the Muslim Brotherhood, a loosely knit organization that has spawned many of the radical Islamic groups that espouse terrorism, including the Islamic Resistance Movement (Hamas) and al Qaeda. The NIF offered refuge to Osama bin Laden and several hundred of his Islamic combatants in 1991 when they were forced from Afghanistan. In Sudan, bin Laden opened training camps, farms, and businesses, and helped found a bank to stash the money that would later help him carry out a series of terrorist attacks.[13]

As early as 1992, Bout used Khartoum as a base to fly weapons to Bosnian Muslim forces in Sarajevo, something he could not have done without connections at the highest level of the regime.[14] He continued to use Khartoum as an operational hub for many years, including flying relief flights for humanitarian groups during the Darfur crisis in 2005.

The regime was not as hospitable to its own people as it was to Bout and bin Laden. Throughout the 1990s, the NIF waged a series of wars against different groups in Sudan in what became a "systematic policy of scorched-earth clearances. Many hundreds of thousands were killed or displaced."[15] Yet Bout was able to open up air transport companies there, transit through the totalitarian state, and move weapons, all indicating a high level of access in one of the world's most shuttered regimes.

Bout's first known commercial excursion to Africa was in 1992, when he flew UN peacekeepers to Somalia. Like much of Bout's history, the accounts of the origins of his African adventures are vague and contradictory. What is clear is that Bout figured out a lucrative niche in breaking the flimsy UN weapons embargoes that existed almost exclusively on paper. New information that has emerged about Bout's activities in Africa suggests that his operation was busy at work there in the early 1990s, much earlier than the official timeline constructed by U.S. intelligence agencies—which places Bout's emergence in Africa at about 1995.

In his initial African ventures, Bout seemed to concentrate largely on legitimate operations, and much of his early business came from the United Nations and other official groups. In addition to the 1992 flights to Somalia, he flew French troops, WFP food deliveries, and aid workers across the continent. South African records show that he visited South Africa on a work permit in 1992, and twice more on similar visas in 1993, a sign of how strong his interest in that region was from the beginning of his business ventures.[16] But he was also almost immediately looking beyond government and official business.

Bout was in contact with Liberia's Charles Taylor in the early

1990s, when Taylor was still fighting in the bush, according to eye-witnesses. When Taylor became Liberia's president, Bout earned millions of dollars in his business with the former warlord. In November 1992 the United Nations placed an arms embargo on Liberia, seeking to stanch the flow of weapons that inflamed violence there. A year later, a similar ban was imposed on arms deliveries to Jonas Savimbi's UNITA forces in Angola. Despite the United Nations' growing international use of arms embargoes to keep the peace in Africa, Bout's expanding client list soon included a host of African nations and rebel groups that had been targeted by the sanctions.

In theory, the embargoes were designed to prevent each UN member state from selling arms to the country under the sanction. The measures were the United Nations' first real attempt at curbing the flow of weapons in the post–Cold War era. But the embargo measures contained several fatal flaws. There were no enforcement mechanisms built into international law, and no police or military forces were issued orders to enforce the embargoes. In effect, the only penalty for breaking the international weapons embargoes was public censure.

"You've had UN members, on the one hand, applauding the imposition of arms embargoes, while on the other hand selling arms to the countries under arms embargoes," lamented Tom Ofcansky, a State Department Bureau of Intelligence and Research analyst who helped track Bout.[17] To date only one person in the world has been charged and convicted of violating a UN weapons embargo.[18]

Even if the governments of the region had wanted to enforce the embargoes it would have been almost impossible. Much of Africa, especially the central and western regions, had no radar coverage. Semiliterate civil aviation officials often made their livings by collecting landing fees and bribes while keeping virtually no records. Frustrated by arms traffic into Sierra Leone, UN investigators warned in 2000 that aviation "authorities are frequently informed of violations of their airspace by pilots who come across illegal traffic. They are also aware that aircraft operators can operate with impunity in their sphere of sovereignty, without their knowledge." And African military authorities "do not have the means to intercept such traffic."[19]

There was another inherent weakness in the new world order. Recognizing the need for toughened arms controls after the Cold War, the United States and thirty-two European and former Soviet bloc nations met near The Hague in 1996 and signed the Waasenaar Arrangement, a pact that created a global system for monitoring the flow of arms. But the arrangement depended on the political will of the participants and the severity of their arms laws and tracking systems.

Under the agreement, nations buying weapons are required to obtain meticulous documents, including transshipment papers known as "end-user certificates" (EUCs), from sellers. The EUCs are designed to ensure that the weapons were legally purchased, delivered for the sole use of a purchasing government, and will not be resold to a third party. All of the signing nations are obligated to report twice a year on all their arms transfers and make their documents available for inspection. But they are easy to forge. There are no standardized forms for the certificates. Some governments type their EUCs on letterhead stationery of the Ministry of Defense. Others are even less formal. Companies or governments selling the weapons have no legal requirement to ensure that a government allegedly purchasing the weapons is, in fact, the actual destination of the cargo—even when the purchases fly in the face of credibility.

For example, from July 1997 to October 1998, planes flying for Bout's Air Cess company made thirty-seven flights with weapons from Burgas, the center of Bulgarian weapons production, to the West African nation of Togo, a country smaller than West Virginia and with a population of about 5.6 million. Bout had spent parts of the previous two years visiting different weapons factories in Bulgaria and setting up a network for future shipments. Then he or his clients forged a series of Togolese EUCs and provided the forgeries to a company called KAS Engineering, based in Gibraltar, an offshore haven. The company names where the weapons would be purchased were real, and the certificates could pass as genuine.

KAS Engineering, using the forged EUCs and an apparently false affidavit empowering the company's Sophia, Bulgaria, office to represent the government of Togo, then contracted for the weapons in Bulgaria. Bout's aircraft would deliver the shipments. "Some of the end-user certificates had been provided to the representative of

KAS Engineers (Gibraltar) through the captain of a flight coming from Togo and some by express mail from Dubai, United Arab Emirates," the UN investigation found. "Further investigations disclosed that the mail was sent by a Mr. Victor Bout."[20]

The routes of the weapons were fairly standard. The planes flew out empty from Ostend, Belgium. They headed for Burgas to load the weapons. Most of the flights then transited through Nairobi, Kenya, and Khartoum, Sudan, listing their final destination as small airstrips in either the DRC or Kenya.[21]

On paper the transactions appeared legal, among thousands that are carried out each year. No questions were raised. No one selling the weapons in Bulgaria was required to explain why a peaceful, small African nation, with a tiny military that had relied for forty years on French weapons, suddenly needed to spend $14 million for Soviet bloc weapons, including fifteen million rounds of ammunition; twenty thousand 82-millimeter bombs; or six-three hundred antitank rockets.[22]

In reality, the matériel was shipped to UNITA rebels in neighboring Angola and did not stay in Togo except for the bribes, in weapons or in kind, that Togolese officials extracted for their transshipment services. The EUCs had been crudely forged, copied off a document that UNITA had acquired. And the person whose name appeared on the document as authorizing the purchases on behalf of the government of Togo was not in the government when the flights were made. A single telephone call or a quick Internet search would have revealed potential problems with the deal.

Landing heavy cargo planes with illicit cargoes in wartime conditions required more than individual effort. It took an internationally organized network of individuals, well funded, well connected, and well versed in brokering and logistics. In Africa, the only organization that fit that description was Viktor Bout's network.[23]

In the case of the "Togolese" shipments, no one was ultimately held responsible for the arms trafficking. The company in Burgas fulfilled its legal responsibility by having a certificate on hand, even a forged one. Togolese officials could correctly claim the document was forged. Under those rules, accountability was not possible.

"When it comes to making real recommendations and heavy-duty commitments to stop this or that, most countries don't want this practice of middlemen to end," said Johan Peleman. "They don't even want to regulate it. They don't even want to start processing legislation that would enable them to go after this go-between who uses their territory to organize his deals abroad but is nevertheless the brains of the operation, who cannot be caught under current legislation." [24]

The UN arms embargoes were ineffective, but the Security Council's efforts to track the violators were not. A core group of UN investigators, along with nongovernmental organizations interested in tracking the flow of weapons, set out to slowly and methodically map the weapons trafficking networks. Under the terms of the international embargoes, the United Nations could send panels of experts to different countries to monitor the effectiveness and name violators. The "name and shame" campaign led to the first detailed, public reports on Bout, his aircraft, front companies, partners, and protectors. They received virtually no attention, however, from the Security Council's superpowers or in the mainstream press. And the lack of an ability to actually punish the alleged offenders soon left a small dose of public embarrassment as the only price one had to pay.

The UN investigators had few illusions. Peleman recounted how he was mocked by one of Bout's chief operators during a confrontation. The Bout associate, Pavel Popov, taunted Peleman for being unable to put Bout out of business and even dared him to ground a Bout plane. "They basically laugh about it," Peleman reflected ruefully after the encounter. "As long as the United Nations takes action, puts experts in the field, and issues reports, and the countries where these individuals are doing their business do not act, then, indeed, few things can be done. Of course, the United Nations is only as powerful as UN member states allow it to be. And the United Nations, as such, cannot arrest people, has no subpoena rights or whatever. It's up to the individual member states to act." [25]

By 1993, Bout had turned to South Africa as a base of operations on the continent. Although many of his aircraft were already operating out of Sharjah in the UAE, Bout began using Pietersburg Airport,

180 miles northeast of Johannesburg, as a hub from which he could ply his assorted trades. Bout was already flying gladiolas and other flower species out of Africa to the UAE, at a considerable profit. He began flying beef and poultry from South Africa to other African nations. On a continent with little transportation infrastructure, air freight was the only way to move perishable goods any distance, and Bout's companies soon grew from the original three to several dozen. Aircraft that Bout could acquire for $30,000 would pay for themselves after just two or three flights. If they fell from the sky, cheap replacements were easy to find. If crews became disgruntled, there were always more pilots waiting to be hired. It was a growth industry for the foreseeable future.

Bout built up enough air capacity to fly twenty-five hundred French troops to Rwanda in 1994 in a futile effort to halt the genocide there. There are persistent but sketchy intelligence reports that Bout also had flown weapons to the Hutu *genocidaires* to facilitate the killings that the French were later ordered to prevent. But the French were not the only government forces using Bout planes.

At about the same time, Bout was also supplying the Força Aérea Popular de Angola (FAPA), the Angolan air force. Included among the services Bout was offering, according to one intelligence report, were two parachute teams of forty men each. The teams could have been mercenaries or trainers or both.[26] The Angolan government, a longtime Soviet client, was a natural fit for Bout, and a lucrative one. It had the largest Soviet-built air fleet in Africa, one that Bout could provide maintenance facilities for. Given the likelihood of Bout having spent time in Angola in the late 1980s, just a few years before, setting up the new business there did not present any serious difficulties. To handle the business he set up a company called the Air Charter Center (ACC) in Belgium.

According to Bout's Interpol arrest warrant, from 1994 to 1999, some $325 million in funds were deposited into the ACC's Belgian bank accounts. The money came from "the Liberian company Simportex, the Angolan air force and the Angolan armed forces." The money was then systematically transferred to the Belgian bank accounts of shell companies named Vial and Yuralex Corporation, both registered in Delaware. Bout had the power of attorney over the Vial account. "Various foreign payments were made from these accounts, which were clearly transit accounts," the warrant says. "There are indications these funds could come from apparently illegal activities (weapons trafficking)." [27]

When the Angolan government discovered in 1998 that Bout had been dealing with the UNITA rebels at the same time, they cut him off, becoming one of the few customers to ever sever ties over his double dealings. Bout had discovered that he could more than double his earnings if he supplied UNITA. The movement's leader, Jonas Savimbi, had flourished as the charismatic anti-Communist leader during the Reagan administration's efforts to contest the dominance of Marxist revolutionary movements worldwide. Reagan even invited him to the White House, and hailed him as a hero. In June 1985 Savimbi hosted a secret meeting of the world's "freedom fighters" at his jungle base in Jamba, including representatives of the Nicaraguan contras and the mujahideen of Afghanistan. The meeting was organized by a then little-known Republican operative named Jack Abramoff, whose code name during the meeting was "Pacman." Twenty years later, Abramoff, after becoming one of Washington's most influential lobbyists, was convicted of political influence peddling and corruption.[28]

Affectionately known as the "Black Cockerel" by his supporters, Savimbi had the unique distinction of being the only guerrilla leader during the Cold War to be simultaneously supported by the CIA and the People's Republic of China as he battled against Angola's Soviet-backed regime. But when the Cold War ended, Savimbi scuttled several peace accords and drove the exhausted nation back to civil war by refusing to accept the results of the 1992 elections that he lost. Even as he lost his international legitimacy, Savimbi retained a wide range of supporters. He had been staunchly supported by South Africa's apartheid government, and elements of the white-dominated security forces continued to route weapons to Savimbi after they formally lost power in 1994.[29]

Mobutu of Zaire, one of Bout's early clients, was another longtime supporter of Savimbi and UNITA in Angola, and it is likely that Bout made his first UNITA contacts through Mobutu or his henchmen. UNITA maintained offices and a quasi-diplomatic presence in Kinshasa, part of the legacy of the Cold War when both UNITA and Mobutu were staunch U.S. allies and urged to help each other. Mobutu provided EUCs for Savimbi, as well as warehouses to store his weapons. However, by the early 1990s Savimbi was already aware of the increasingly precarious position of his longtime ally and began to take precautions. In 1993 Savimbi sent a special envoy to Togo, hoping to open another avenue for weapons. Savimbi was particularly anxious to obtain another source of the precious EUCs.

Savimbi's envoy, Colonel Alcides Lucas Kangunga (known as "Kallias"), had little difficulty cutting a deal with President Gnassingbe Eyadema on the matter. A hulking man with a badly pocked face and weak eyes usually covered with wraparound sunglasses, Eyadema was one of Africa's classic "Big Men." He seized power in 1967, while Lyndon Johnson was still president and the Vietnam War was raging. Through corruption, intimidation, and brutality, Eyadema had survived long past most of his peers, and did not relinquish power until he died in February 2005. Kallias was instructed to tell Eyadema that Zaire was a country of many problems and that UNITA needed to prepare itself militarily. Kallias was to emphasize to Eyadema that UNITA needed weapons and credible EUCs.

A UN investigation summarized the results of the meeting: Savimbi's proposal that Togo play a more active role in support of UNITA (a proposal that also included Togo hosting some of Savimbi's children) was accepted by President Eyadema in late 1993. As a token of appreciation, Kallias gave to Eyadema a "passport-sized" packet of diamonds on Savimbi's behalf. According to Kallias, the working arrangement between Togo and UNITA provided for Togo to keep a share of the arms and military equipment that was imported for UNITA, normally 20 percent. In each case Eyadema could decide whether Togo would take its share in kind or in cash.[30]

Savimbi placed his bets well. Mobutu was less and less able to work the network that Savimbi relied on, and Eyadema proved to be a capable, if somewhat expensive, alternative. By 1996, Bout was regularly using the certificates provided by Eyadema and his cronies to ferry weapons and mining equipment to Savimbi.[31]

Burkina Faso and the region's economic and weapons hub, Ivory Coast, were also supporters of Savimbi. Within a few years Bout had gained entrée into the upper echelons of these countries as well. While not at war, they, like Togo, could be useful, and all formed vital links in a chain of civil wars that required a constant supply of weapons. Bout procured EUCs and landing rights in these countries, building a network that would allow his weapons deliveries to go forward seamlessly.[32]

Ivory Coast's aging dictator Félix Houphouët-Boigny was not only a longtime Savimbi supporter but also was the key regional backer of Charles Taylor when Taylor launched his 1989 Christmas Eve insurrection against the government in neighboring Liberia. Through this web of connections, Bout met with Taylor in the early 1990s but did not begin doing serious business with him until Taylor assumed the Liberian presidency in 1997. The meeting served to open a valuable channel of communications that would later prove to be mutually beneficial.

CHAPTER 5

At a Crossroads

B y 1996, Bout's air cargo operation was busy across Africa. With air operations expanding in South Africa, Bout laid plans to move his entire family, including his mother-in-law, from Sharjah to Johannesburg, where he had been spending an increasing amount of time.[1] While Sharjah was more centrally located and convenient for his ongoing business in Afghanistan, Bout told friends that Africa was where he wanted to live. Bout loved spending time and hunting in the sparsely populated bush. He talked often about the chance to acquaint his young daughter with African life and allow her to grow up close to the jungle.

He also sought new horizons. Bout was reportedly interested in broadening his transportation empire into the telecommunications business.[2] His air operations in Africa were consolidating and growing rapidly, with steady business from Mobutu, UNITA, and Rwanda. He was branching out to Europe, and he still maintained his schedule of flights to Afghanistan as Taliban forces advanced on Kabul, on the verge of triumph. In Africa his air fleet thrived, rarely troubled by ground control or inspections. Gary Busch, who was Bout's rival in arming the other sides in some of the same African conflicts, said he once found that three of Bout's airplanes were operating with the same tail number and using the same air operations papers. "That's just the way it was," Busch said. "No one cared."

"He was always on the move then," said an African who spent a great deal of time with Bout in the mid-1990s. "He was visiting Taylor, Mobutu, Savimbi, and flying back to Sharjah. He was trying to get planes and moving them around. It seemed like he didn't really have time to sleep."

South Africa was attractive for several reasons. He could remain relatively close to the Great Lakes region, where he was working, and to his operations in Angola. Despite the 1994 election of Nelson Mandela, the white-dominated security forces continued to send weapons to UNITA. And South Africa offered the best opportunities for legitimate business, something Bout correctly sensed could be a lucrative, if not dominant, part of his growing empire. No other African capital could match Johannesburg's urban charm and sophistication. Bout's daughter had been born in Kinshasa in 1994, but the town was a nightmare. Bout began looking for a partner in his budding South African air business, someone who would give him legitimacy and allow him to operate unmolested by the sometimes inquisitive South African authorities.

By early 1997, Bout's plan was unfolding. He and his family moved to Johannesburg, staying first at the luxurious Sandton Sun International Hotel and later the Intercontinental Hotel. His wife, Alla, opened a clothing business called AB Fashions. Making good on his talk about altruistic ventures, Bout persuaded the manager of AB Fashions, Leslie Whalley, to set up a training school for disadvantaged children.

He established his new South African branch at Gateway Airport in Pietersburg, near the border with Zimbabwe. Pietersburg was in a part of the country where wildlife abounds and the climate is temperate. It was also an airport where Bout would be under far less scrutiny than in a commercial hub. He found a South African partner named Dierdre Ward, who could obtain the necessary business permits and who owned a company that already had valid air operating certificates. Norse Air, Ward's firm, was looking to increase its charter capacity. She had the routes Bout needed, and Bout, through his ability to acquire aircraft, had the capacity. It seemed like a perfect match.[3]

On February 19, 1997, Bout's Liberian company, Air Cess, and Norse Air registered a new company in South Africa called Pietersburg Aviation Services and Systems Pty. The new company, like many Bout entities, actually did business under another name, Air Pass. Bout owned 90 percent of the new company (spelling his name Butt on the ownership papers), and Ward the remainder. In exchange for her 10 percent ownership stake, Ward let Bout use Norse Air's charter operator's license, which allowed the new company to operate in South Africa. Air Cess, Bout's original company, used Norse Air, Ward's company, to apply for its own foreign operator's license in South Africa.[4] According to Richard Chichakli, Bout paid for his stake with $2 million in cash.[5] Bout's South African air fleet soon numbered about thirty, capable of handling as much as 150 tons of cargo, and he hired several dozen employees. Within six months, Air Pass flight operations extended to Angola, the DRC, Malawi, Zambia, Mozambique, Kenya, Somalia, and Liberia.[6] Bout also imported millions of dollars' worth of spare parts for a maintenance facility for Russian aircraft that he planned to open in Pietersburg.[7] In addition to the air freight business, Bout invested in a cold storage unit, at one point carrying $4 million of stock in a hangar at the airport.

Bout mulled bigger plans. One was to open a South African version of Sharjah's free-trade zone with the help of Chichakli. Bout also wanted to start a garment business and a clothing factory. To help with his finances, he brought down another financial handler, Olivier Piret, a banker friend of his from Switzerland. To lure him down, Bout promised to help Piret, who was under investigation by Swiss authorities, acquire South African citizenship.[8]

Bout's move to South Africa offered the opportunity to ease up on his grinding lifestyle. Entranced by the breathtaking landscapes of unsullied forests, tangled jungle, sweeping deserts, and barren cliffs that he saw on almost every flight into Africa, Bout had intimated to associates that he was mulling over another career besides selling weapons and moving dangerous freight. Much later, when he was traveling with Bemba, Bout told Draulans that he had wanted to build modern agricultural projects and satellite-based telecommunications systems in the DRC, a country riven by war and devoid of electronic infrastructure. He talked of preserving the environment and helping local indigenous groups organize themselves to fight poachers. He wanted to protect elephants and create hunting preserves for businessmen willing to invest in the region. He jotted his ideas down on paper and told Draulans that he had even flown in technicians from Dubai to study the feasibility of his schemes. But it was never clear if his ruminations were a real change of heart, deeply cherished fantasies, or artful conversation pieces devised to present an altruistic facade to outsiders.

"He talked about this all the time, but no one thought any of it was very realistic," Draulans concluded.

Chichakli claimed that Bout invested in some projects in the DRC, including two bakeries and a water treatment plant in Goma, one of the rebel strongholds. But no one else familiar with the region recalled any of Bout's humanitarian gestures coming to fruition.

By August 1997 Bout was set to make South Africa his primary residence. He paid about $3 million for a mansion in the plush residential Sandhurst district of Johannesburg, and then considerably more to renovate the facility to look like a castle—reportedly a request from his wife. The result was imposing, if not quite aesthetically pleasing. The house and property had fifteen-foot walls topped by electric and barbed-wire fences. It was patrolled around the clock by heavily armed security guards and watchdogs—at a cost of $12,000 a day, more than most South Africans earned in a year. The team of twenty-six guards and five dogs was led by a senior South African intelligence officer.[9] Chichakli, who stayed with Bout there, described the house as having the look of a "detention facility from hell."[10]

Inside the walled compound Bout built a luxurious retreat. There were two swimming pools; a large, well-appointed guesthouse; cascading waterfalls; and lush tropical plants. In January 1998 Bout cleared $20,000 worth of furniture through South African customs. The next month he and his wife, daughter, and mother-in-law moved into their new home.[11] It was an opulent prize for a thirty-year-old Russian pilot with no family wealth to draw on.

Just three months after Bout moved his family into the mansion, disaster struck on several fronts. The sudden crises showed how difficult it would be for Bout to ever go legitimate, even if he wanted to.

One warm March afternoon, Bout's mother-in-law was cutting up fruit in the kitchen while Bout and his wife played tennis across the street. Suddenly a series of grenade blasts forced open the main door and several armed intruders stormed inside. The highly paid guards put up little resistance.

The elderly Russian woman grabbed a watermelon and smashed it on the head of one of the gunmen. She was knocked unconscious by a rifle butt. When Bout arrived on the scene, he also was roughed up. The intruders stole $6 million in cash, leaving expensive painting and jewelry untouched.

The well-executed attack was a message. Intelligence services believed it could have been a warning by rival Russian organized criminal gangs who felt Bout was growing too big—or else from someone to whom Bout owed money or merchandise. South African police opened an investigation, "Operation Jacuzzi," but turned up little information. This was not a surprise, given that the guards, who apparently had ties to the government security forces, appeared acquiescent in the assault. Other incidents followed. A gunman reportedly fired shots at Bout's car, though appearing to intentionally miss. The accountant Piret was mugged, and his fiancée lost a diamond ring to thieves who also threatened to lop off her ring finger. "The message was you're vulnerable, so get out," said Chichakli.[12]

Message received, Bout put the house up for sale and moved everyone back to Sharjah. His South African business hub soon unraveled. Questionable accounting practices in his aviation and commodities businesses had led to growing strife with Ward and other partners. Losing the $6 million invested in his house left Bout in a financial crunch. South African government organizations opened up investigations into his business practices and eventually found 146 violations of civil aviation law. Before the South African authorities could act, Bout shifted most of his operation to neighboring Swaziland. South Africa's Department of Home Affairs declared Bout an "undesirable alien" and refused to grant him a visa to return from Sharjah.

Ward claimed that Bout had left behind large debts and was

responsible for her crumbling business prospects. On March 20, 1998, she sent a memo to Bout in Sharjah, urgently requesting money. When none was forthcoming, she sent follow-up memos, then turned on him, alerting South African officials of a possible Bout attempt to sneak into the country. "We believe that VB is traveling under a false passport under the name of George Trodannov," she wrote to the prosecutor handling his case. "We are told he has grown a beard . . . he will be leaving South Africa by road into Swaziland between now and Tuesday."[13] But Bout was not arrested.

Bout has never talked about who might have made the threats. But Chichakli openly accused Ward of saddling Bout with high debt—$1 million for an air firm, Metavia, that went bankrupt. Chichakli also railed that Ward was the source of arms flights attributed to Bout. But Ward, like Bout, was never charged in South Africa for any weapons sale offenses.

"He doesn't come off as a crook," Ward said several years after her falling out with Bout. "He could charm you in seven or eight languages."[14]

In May 1998, aviation officials in neighboring Swaziland, under pressure from South African authorities, grounded forty-three aircraft from five Bout companies, accusing the firms of a lack of adequate documentation and illegal gun running from Mozambique to Angola. Among the cargo found on one of the grounded aircraft were two disassembled Russian military helicopters packed in crates labeled "machine parts." Investigators suspected that the gunships were destined for Rwanda.[15] Swazi officials stripped the Bout planes of their civil registrations. But though supposedly grounded, the aircraft were soon spotted flying elsewhere in Africa.

For Bout, it was a return to business as usual. His chance for a different life in South Africa—if he had ever truly considered it— was gone now. His organization was barely slowed by the government actions. His planes were simply reregistered and flown out across porous, poorly patrolled borders. In several cases the tail numbers were not even repainted. No one noticed.

Bout's successor airline was Centrafricain Airlines, registered in the Central African Republic and based at the offices of his Transavia Travel Agency in Sharjah. Several of Centrafricain's planes had been Bout aircraft that were deregistered in either Swaziland or Liberia. Soon Centrafricain planes were sighted delivering weapons to UNITA, freshly painted with the "TL" call letters of the Central African Republic.[16] Bout registered another company, Cessavia, in Equatorial Guinea in 1998. The operation was painless. Bout's associate Michael Harridine ran Equatorial Guinea's aviation registry. Cessavia was relisted as Air Cess, operating out of Sharjah. Neatly, even though the two companies registered in the Central African Republic and Equatorial Guinea had different addresses, they shared the same phone and fax numbers in Sharjah.[17]

Bout's cash bind appeared to ease. He and his family were settled in Sharjah, but his business was brisk enough to allow him to rent a floor of the Meridien Hotel in Kigali, Rwanda, for himself and his pilots. Bout received a lucrative contract to train the Ugandan air force, a contract described in one intelligence report as making him "basically responsible for the creation of the new Ugandan air force."[18]

Business activity in West Africa was also growing, and Bout found another home away from home in Monrovia, the broken-down capital of Liberia. Monrovia had the distinction of being the only capital city with no lights, water service, or garbage pickup. Already friends with Charles Taylor, Liberia's new president, Bout was soon a regular visitor and was assigned a special bodyguard to make sure he got what he needed and had direct access to Taylor at any time.

"His big advantage is that he was portable," said former State Department veteran Thomas Pickering. "He could move his support system around. He had a hub, but he could do what he did anywhere."

Bout soon began using the Liberian base for audacious new plans. He became an intimate in Taylor's circle, granted access that few others had. In acknowledgment of his influence, Taylor's underlings began referring to him simply as "Mr. Vic."

CHAPTER 6

The Chase Begins

The Western world caught on slowly to the expanding dimensions of Viktor Bout's arms network.

In Afghanistan, evidence of his weapons deliveries had surfaced briefly during the Taliban's 1995 capture of his Ilyushin freighter and crew and their sudden escape after a year of imprisonment. But the episode barely registered in the United States other than a few brief news wire items and perfunctory diplomatic cables to Washington. In strife-torn Africa, where Bout's weapons delivery routes had penetrated deep into remote war zones, he remained a phantom, mostly unknown except to the Big Men and rebel leaders he catered to and the fixers, mercenaries, and rival weapons dealers who plied the same circles.

His massive shipments of rifles and ammunition were evident only in the carnage they left behind in bullet-pocked villages and cratered battlegrounds across the African interior. His weather-beaten cargo planes were common sights at African airfields, but few veteran aviation hands realized that the Russian aircraft shuttling in and out regularly were part of Bout's global fleet. Even in the regional capitals where his planes landed, his name was unfamiliar to most of the continent's foreign diplomats and rarely recognized by intelligence agents posted there.

During a three-year stint as U.S. ambassador to Sierra Leone from 1995 to 1998, John Hirsch never heard the Russian's name. He never read it, either, in any of the confidential intelligence cables that came across his desk. From his embassy office in the capital in Freetown, Hirsch was well aware that the corrosive five-year-old civil war between the government and RUF rebels still flared in Sierra Leone's rural eastern sector. While the rebels methodically ravaged the region's hills for contraband diamonds, uncounted thousands died each year amid atrocities committed by both sides.

UN investigators who later looked into massive violations of the arms embargo imposed by the Security Council on Sierra Leone in 1992 concluded that arms deliveries were repeatedly carried to the RUF both on Russian-made Mi-18 helicopters and by airplane— and that Bout and his accomplices were "key to such illicit practices, in close collaboration with the highest authorities in Liberia."[1] But at the time, Hirsch had almost no intelligence backup and few reliable African sources to provide firsthand reports from the distant front lines. There was hardly any interest from Washington to learn more. Hirsch surmised from his own readings that Liberian strongman Charles Taylor was behind the reported weapons deliveries to the RUF factions. And the ambassador also suspected the involvement of Libyan dictator Muammar Gaddafi. But Hirsch had no hard evidence showing where the weapons were coming from and who was behind the logistics of supplying them. Even if he had, it was clear that his superiors in Washington were preoccupied with other diplomatic spheres. "It was very difficult to get anybody to pay attention about the RUF in Washington," Hirsch recalled. "It was considered a very secondary, tertiary matter."

All of Africa, Hirsch felt with a rising sense of gloom in the mid-1990s, seemed a tertiary matter in the eyes of the U.S. government. The October 1993 Black Hawk Down debacle in Somalia that left eighteen American soldiers dead after running gun battles on narrow Mogadishu streets had curbed the Clinton administration's tentative impulse toward African peacekeeping. The harrowing spasms of genocide and famine in Rwanda in 1994 sealed the matter. By the mid-1990s, the State Department was preoccupied with brighter prospects for peace in the Middle East and the spread of democracy in the former Soviet bloc. Africa was low on Washington's radar, perceived both as a diplomatic backwater and an intelligence wasteland. Already sensing their distance from Washington, Hirsch and his counterparts across the continent keenly felt the loss of up-to-date, detailed intelligence assessments.

The inability to cull accurate information came at the worst possible time, just as Sierra Leone, Rwanda, Angola, and Zaire reeled from a new spate of internecine violence. "The Africa operation was stripped after the Cold War," recalled former CIA analyst Michael Scheuer, who headed the bin Laden unit at the agency's counterterrorism center. "It came back to haunt us." One station chief in West Africa described himself as a "one-armed guy trying to hang wallpaper by himself. I read the newspapers, meet some officials, and have no assets in the field. My secretary knows as much as I do."[2]

With only the CIA's circuit-riders sporadically helpful, Hirsch resorted to trading stale bits of information with his diplomatic counterparts from Britain and the other nations still based there. "Everybody just lived on the rumor mill and passed the same rumors around," Hirsch recalled. "By 1997, the rumor was that the RUF was on its last legs. That turned out to be totally inaccurate." When Hirsch heard from his superiors in Washington, he was told to stay upbeat and concentrate on efforts to solidify peace talks between the government and the RUF in Abidjan. "The focus then was on building up the government and strengthening its capacity," Hirsch recalled. "I think it was a naive view that the process was sorting itself out. We assumed the guarantors on both sides would keep the agreement. But it wasn't solid at all. The troublemakers weren't party to these negotiations. Looking back now, the troublemakers were Taylor and Gaddafi."

Both dictators, intelligence officials would learn, had hired Bout. But at the time, Hirsch saw no effort by either the U.S. or the British government—perceived as the stewards of their former colony's independence—to learn more about how the peace process was being disrupted. "Neither the United States nor the United Kingdom devoted any intelligence assets to tracking the trail of money, arms and diamonds in the West African region," Hirsch later wrote in an unsparing account of his tenure in Sierra Leone.[3]

The situation was little improved for Hirsch's successor Joseph Melrose, who served as ambassador from 1998 through 2001. Melrose was forced to evacuate the embassy staff in Freetown when the RUF attacked in December 1998. When he returned several months later, the permanent embassy staff was reduced to two Americans: Melrose and a security officer. A few Sierra Leoneans manned the phone on the off-chance that the country's shoddy communications system might patch through a call, and others performed secretarial services. Melrose's intelligence coverage from the CIA circuit-rider in Conakry was "extremely spotty. They hardly ever came." The Defense Intelligence Agency, which also had personnel in Conakry, provided more regular coverage of the RUF and the war's overlap into Guinea, but almost nothing about the weapons networks feeding the conflicts.

The coverage was so haphazard, in fact, that even when Bout's arms pipelines were at their busiest, during Melrose's tenure, the CIA never mentioned the Russian or his weapons activities to the ambassador. Even if Melrose had been tasked to look into Bout's movements, Melrose later noted, he had no one to do the job. Melrose finally learned about Bout's operation during a 2000 visit to Sierra Leone by the United Nations panel of experts, who, over dinner, laid out what they had learned.

But despite the embassy's lack of intelligence, the first nascent signs of U.S. intelligence-gathering against Bout's operation had quietly begun. As early as 1995, both American and British intelligence had separately started culling the first strains of information about the Bout organization. They would be joined later in the decade by Belgian, French, and Dutch intelligence operatives, and also by South African agents.

The American effort was more automatic than deliberate at first, the result of the NSA's broadly targeted sweeps of foreign telephone chatter. U.S. electronic surveillance aircraft flying out of Angola began picking up cryptic references to Bout amid intercepted conversations about arms shipments supplied to African rebel groups. Spy satellites equipped with long-distance cameras occasionally captured the fleeting presence of Bout planes at landing strips and airfields near battle zones. "Nineteen ninety-five is the period where we first picked him up," said a U.S. official involved in the early effort. "We were following conflicts and insurgencies and the African rebel movements and these planes and registries kept showing up. But we were focused mostly on the conflicts, not the sources of arms, at that point."[4]

Part of the problem was that the intelligence community was prevented from talking among its sister agencies and to the State Department by bureaucratic and legal walls that had dated back to the Cold War. These internal dead ends, known as "stovepipes" in the jargon of the intelligence community, made certain that the information gathered remained tightly compartmentalized.

The repeated references to Bout also failed to filter out from CIA headquarters at Langley because there was no direction from senior policymakers at State or elsewhere in the Clinton administration to target African weapons flows. "Why wasn't Bout picked up earlier? It's not the job of intel people to do policy," one former U.S. official said somewhat ruefully. "Their job is to gather intelligence and bring it to the policymaker."[5] On the diplomatic end, Hirsch said, "the interest from Washington was more in the political dynamics of these groups" and not in the arms trails that kept them going. Besides, he added, "Sierra Leone was perceived to be a British responsibility. The U.S. worried about Liberia, the Brits worried about Sierra Leone, [the] French worried about Guinea. No one saw West Africa as a regional matter."

Within the U.S. government, analysts and intelligence officers usually focused on single countries—a Cold War tendency that grew from monitoring habits directed at stationary targets such as missile silos and weapons factories. It would take years before the shift in the new world order would begin to be recognized, and there would be some impetus to shift the focus to regions and transnational analysis. Fittingly, the sharp-eyed CIA analyst who first noticed Bout's growing empire was assigned to cross-border transnational trends.

Unknown to Hirsch, the British had also begun to glean intelligence on Bout's operation. Unlike the technologically dependent American operation, the British picked up their information on the Russian's arms flows from case agents stationed at government embassies and from informants on the ground in Sierra Leone and elsewhere in West Africa. The British had not allowed their network to atrophy as the Americans had, but even so, their access to the RUF and its allies was severely limited. The effort to learn more about Bout was directed by MI-6, Britain's foreign-aimed Secret Intelligence Service, and also involved the Defence Intelligence Staff, the secretive arm of the United Kingdom's Ministry of Defence.

"They became aware as Bout grew into an entrepreneurial presence in their backyard," said the analyst with ties to British intelligence. "It was the extent to which he facilitated the arms trade and made it easier for rebel leaders to operate in Sierra Leone and elsewhere." A few British activists concerned about the deteriorating situation in Sierra Leone had begun calling for the United Kingdom to send in a peacekeeping force. That did not occur until May 2000, when Britain launched Operation Palliser, flying a parachute regiment into Freetown to evacuate Commonwealth and European citizens threatened by the advance of RUF troops.

But the broadening flows of weapons from Bout's network and other arms suppliers in the mid-1990s stimulated backstage discussions among intelligence experts about the possibility of inserting peacekeeping forces. The prevailing concerns were "proliferation and force protection," said the British analyst. "They began to look at him long before peacekeepers were deployed. They wanted to know what they would have to contend with."[6]

Like their American counterparts, the British did not widely disseminate the results of the early intelligence gathered on the Bout network. The information remained closely held at the Africa desks at MI-6 and in the Ministry of Defence until Bout's activities in Sierra Leone reached a crescendo in 1999 and 2000. "Until someone decided Bout was a policy issue," the analyst said, "no one did much more than keep watch."

With the sharp reduction of Western intelligence-gathering and diplomatic personnel in the remote regions of Africa, global nongovernmental organizations (NGOs) filled the vacuum, fanning across the continent to tackle the growing need for humanitarian aid in nations broken by violence. In the process, NGO activists saw firsthand the devastating effects of the arms pipelines and began to advocate for solutions.

The NGOs often based their people for extended stays in conflict zones where diplomats and intelligence operatives rarely traveled. Unencumbered by stifling bureaucracy and the confining trade-offs of international diplomacy, the activist groups used their newfound knowledge about the logistics of Africa's violence to advocate for change. In Rwanda, where NGOs rushed to the aid of masses of victims of the Rwandan genocide of 1994, field workers got their first glimmerings of clandestine arms flights and began to raise alarms, pressing Western political leaders and diplomats to act.

"NGOs were the only entities putting out information to the world about [Bout's] importance," said Jonathan Winer, who was a senior official in the State Department at the time. "This was especially true because U.S. intelligence in this period was focused on Europe, transition in the former Soviet Union, Middle East, South Asia and the Pacific Rim, almost everywhere *except* Africa, which was generally viewed as being of lesser importance."[7]

One of the first crusaders against unrestricted arms flows was Africa specialist Kathi Austin. For eight months in 1994 and 1995, Austin, a dark-haired idealist based out of San Francisco, worked to unravel the arms routes into the Great Lakes region in East Africa. Dispatched on a fact-finding trip to Central Africa for the Institute of Policy Studies, Austin daringly slipped into refugee camps on the border with Zaire and found former Rwandan Hutu soldiers rearming with new stocks of weapons. (CIA investigators later confirmed that Bout's planes had armed the Rwandans after they sought refuge in neighboring Zaire.)

A short, dynamic woman who drove herself and others hard, Austin recognized early on that aircraft were the key components of the illicit arms networks she was tracking. At first she and other activists were uncertain whether Bout was as big a player as other veteran arms traders who also made their mark in Africa. "We didn't feel he was a kingpin in the early days," Austin said. "But he really grew into a monster. By 1997 or 1998 he had taken over."

Austin and other NGO workers honed their knowledge of the arms pipelines by getting to know the players on the ground, often at their own personal risk. They developed relationships with pilots and couriers, learning how aircraft registrations worked. They watched as the same aircraft and pilots moved among different weapons-trafficking organizations, and could see how Bout-run companies gained dominance over smaller operations. By the end of her Rwanda tour, Austin was convinced that the Bout network was a serious player in the weapons game, and began to write internal reports citing his operation.

At the same time, at the London office of Human Rights Watch, British arms analyst Alex Vines had also picked up traces of Bout's operation. Vines began talking to African sources about Bout in 1995 as he took part in an examination of the United Nations' sanctions-enforcement process. Some of the group's African information had also come from Austin, who moved over to Human Rights Watch to continue her work in Angola and elsewhere in Africa. A Dutch colleague, E. J. Hogendoorn, also assembled an early unpublished report for Human Rights Watch on Bout's flights out of Ostend Airport in Belgium. "E. J. was ahead of the curve," Vines said, "but his report was under review for 4 or 5 years and by then, everyone had picked up on Bout."[8]

By the spring of 1997, the frequent arrivals and departures of the oversized Ilyushins at Ostend had triggered an investigation by Belgian federal police. "There were rumors about what he was doing with these planes," said Devos Bart, a federal police officer based at Ostend. Bart and other investigators began a series of spot checks on the cargo holds of TAN network planes. The bays were empty, leading investigators to assume that Ostend was being used as a jumping-off point to the arms loading zones at Burgas and other transshipment points in East Europe. "His planes would always leave without cargo. This was suspicious, eh?" Bart said. In December 1996, Bout's TAN operation at Ostend suddenly folded, replaced by a new flagship, Air Cess. But the constant presence of police and Bout's growing notoriety among local activists in Ostend took its toll.

Ronny Lauwereins, Ostend's security director, arrived one morning in late July 1997 to find Bout's Air Cess office abandoned. "He just stopped paying his rent and went away," Lauwereins said. "He took all his files with him."[9]

Bout's Ostend flights also piqued the curiosity of Johan Peleman, a Belgian peace researcher based in a converted Franciscan monastery in Antwerp. Working for the International Peace Information

Service (IPIS), an Antwerp-based group that studied the roots of international conflict, Peleman was trying to trace the clandestine channels that had delivered weapons to the Rwandan Hutus. Operating from a cramped office that once served as a monk's nook, he began looking into the curious TAN network flights out of nearby Ostend.

He learned more from Ostend activists who helped force Bout's exit from the airport by printing leaflets exposing his activities. Peleman suspected that some of the outbound flights of Bout's Ilyushins were ferrying weapons to the Hutus. The planes were registered in Liberia—an immediate tip-off of clandestine activity. Soon Peleman had learned what Belgian police already knew— Bout's planes "took off at Ostend without any cargo aboard, but later were loaded with weapons in Bulgaria or Romania, and flew on to Rwanda. Because under Belgian law, foreign firms whose airplanes ply between other states may not be prosecuted, it was impossible to charge Bout." [10]

Peleman, like Austin, had no formal investigative training. He was a philosophy student who spent his college years burrowing into the writings of French psychoanalyst and thinker Jacques Lacan. A conscientious objector against Belgian military service, Peleman had started out with no knowledge of weapons. But with a scholar's obsession, he became a self-taught expert in deciphering arms trade EUCs, port-of-shipment records, and flight plans, using the obscure documents to uncover the mechanics of what he called "war economics." A wiry, somber man with hooded blue eyes, Peleman chain-smoked unfiltered cigarettes and repeatedly downed espressos through his long days of research.

By 1996 he was filling the IPIS's heavy metal file cabinets with records that began to sketch out the enormity of Viktor Bout's operation. As crumpled blue Gaulois packs littered a research room fogged by clouds of cigarette smoke, Peleman slowly sketched out a profile of how Bout's network operated. He turned up flight documents that showed the route of Bout's planes as they made their way from Ostend to Burgas and then on to African airfields. He learned the names of Bout's Russian aides and top Ukrainian pilots. He picked up intelligence about Bout's bank accounts in Sharjah and New York and learned that the Rwandan government owed him $21 million for unpaid arms deliveries. He even found suspect weapons shipment lists on the Internet.

"Bout is not like any of his competitors," Peleman explained several years later, surrounded by mounds of bulging folders and strewn documents. "With Bout it's different. He runs a fully integrated operation. He sources the arms, he organizes the transport, and he sources the financing. I even have evidence of direct Bout payments to arms factories."

Peleman could rattle off details about Bout's operation like a management consultant dissecting a *Fortune* 500 company. There was a bit of awe and mordant amusement in Peleman's obsession, but he never lost sight of the ultimate victims of the Russian's handiwork. "This person was a major supplier of arms to African rebels whose military operations took a toll of thousands of lives," he said. As he learned more about Bout's operation, Peleman grew openly disillusioned by what he saw as a lack of interest from countries with the biggest stake in a secure Africa—the United States and Britain. At times he felt as if he were working alone on Bout, ignored by intelligence services and diplomats with unlimited resources. "Africa is not high on the agenda. There are no classrooms of analysts and secret agents looking into the situation in Sierra Leone and Liberia. These countries are just not important enough on the national agendas of those states, I'm afraid." He called them "black holes."[11]

Austin was finding much the same thing. Armed with her own files on the Bout organization and other arms supply lines, she organized a round of closed-door briefings for congressional staffers in Washington. A bipartisan group of aides voiced curiosity, but little changed. Austin tried the State Department's Bureau of Intelligence and Research (INR) and Bureau for International Narcotics and Law Enforcement Affairs (INL). At the INR, intelligence analyst Tom Ofcansky showed interest in tracking the movement of weapons. At the INL, Austin found another willing listener in Winer, who did pioneering work on mapping criminal networks that operated beyond state control.[12]

But before American policymakers could act decisively against Viktor Bout's arms pipelines, they first had to have a clear understanding of what his vast business represented. And they needed a clear signal from the White House that the Third World arms trade was a foreign policy priority.

"Transnational threats" was the new national security catchphrase in the Clinton administration. But how those threats were defined and how they needed to be blunted were issues very much in flux throughout the 1990s.

Bill Clinton had entered the White House in January 1993 with a fresh take on the international landscape evolving after the fall of communism. Priding himself on his ability to cast an eye to the future, Clinton viewed a new world awash in global opportunity, freed of the Cold War yoke of competing ideologies. The Soviet threat had eased, and while China and smaller obdurate players such as North Korea, Iran, and Iraq remained nettlesome, Clinton was already concerned about new perils rising from terrorist and criminal groups that were independent of state sponsors and able to diffuse their violent activities across continents. "Today as an old order passes, the new world is more free but less stable," Clinton said in his January 20 inaugural speech. "Communism's collapse has called forth old animosities and new dangers." [13]

The Colombian drug cartels that had operated unchecked through the 1980s, ravaging U.S. cities with cocaine, seemed the most obvious examples. The *narco-traficantes* were soon joined by other perceived global perils. Russian mobsters operating in Odessa, Moscow, and other Eastern bloc cities now had cells in American enclaves such as Brighton Beach in New York and West Hollywood and San Fernando Valley in Southern California. And just a month after Clinton took office, the February 1993 bombing of the World Trade Center in New York—a portent of the September 11 terror attacks—quickly riveted the attention of his new administration to the threat posed by violent Islamic militants on American soil.

Within weeks of entering the White House, Clinton's senior cabinet officials started to transform the upper levels of the bureaucracy to accommodate new offices capable of responding to transnational threats. Clinton's new secretary of state, Warren Christopher, pushed for the creation of a new deputy secretary position for international law enforcement. "Clinton realized, and Christopher was sensitive to it as well, that drugs, crime, and terrorism all needed to be dealt with simultaneously out of the same framework," said Jonathan Winer, who would later occupy a scaled-down version of the post. A hard-charging former staffer for Senator John Kerry, Democrat of Massachusetts, Winer had cut his teeth as an investigator in the late 1980s and early 1990s pursuing the scandal that rocked the Bank of Credit and Commerce International (BCCI), an Islamic-run financial institution with major holdings in the UAE that suffered the biggest banking collapse in history at that time. Winer also oversaw the hard-hitting Senate report on the ties between United States–backed contras in Nicaragua and drug traffickers.

Les Aspin, the new defense secretary, also drew up plans for a deputy secretary to oversee the newly created Office of Peacekeeping and Humanitarian Assistance. "The Pentagon was still very focused on conventional wars and had been very reluctant to get into counternarcotics and counterterror efforts," said Brian Sheridan, who would later oversee the Office of Special Operations and Low-Intensity Conflict of the Department of Defense (DOD). "So Les Aspin whipped up this new architecture to handle counternarcotics and other do-gooder stuff."

But both efforts ran aground, spurned by congressional Republicans skeptical of the transnational threat concept. Unable to win budget approval, Clinton officials were forced to scatter the duties of their new transnational-themed offices through the government's upper echelons, with terror, narcotics, and organized crime functions still kept separate. When Winer took over the new State post as deputy assistant secretary for international law enforcement, his portfolio included drug cartels and organized crime but not terrorism. At the Pentagon, Sheridan's office dealt with counterterror issues but not narcotics.

"Clinton realized, astutely, that international drugs, crime, and terrorism all needed to be dealt with out of the same framework," Winer said. "They each required cross-border law enforcement, evidence-gathering, international access to bank records, sharing of intelligence and police resources—the whole infrastructure had to be coordinated from a central point. But he ran right into a brick wall in Congress."

Not everyone in the Clinton administration saw the wisdom of focusing on transnational threats, especially in the early days. "I was not convinced at first," said Rand Beers, who served in senior positions in the National Security Council (NSC) and State for several decades, under both Republican and Democratic administrations. "Jonathan [Winer] convinced me. I certainly came to see money laundering and other elements as important. Russian organized crime was growing. Nigerian criminal groups were operating. We were seeing drug trafficking spin-offs in other areas. All these were factors that helped change my mind. Also, my greater appreciation for how corruption is undermining development in many parts of the world." Beers would later quit as the Bush administration's counterterrorism director at the NSC, blaming the failure of Bush, Cheney, and other senior officials to understand and counter transnational threats, most importantly, al Qaeda.

Still pressing for his transnational focus, Clinton responded by gradually shifting oversight for counterterror policy and counternarcotics efforts to the NSC. The NSC's close advisory role in the White House and its streamlined ability to respond rapidly in realms of foreign policy and law enforcement gave Clinton more flexibility to tackle transnational threat issues on a broad basis—and on his own terms.

The man who began knitting together the disparate "transnational threat" threads at the NSC was Richard A. Clarke, a career civil servant whose canny policy analysis and skillful bureaucratic maneuvering had enabled him to flourish in three presidential administrations, dating to the Reagan era. Clarke had done stints at the Pentagon and State, and by the tail end of the Bush administration in 1992, he was ensconced at the NSC, where he had been assigned to oversee "drugs and thugs," a loose amalgam of crime, narcotics, and terrorism. A national security Jeremiah who openly warned that the United States needed to gird against terrorist perils, Clarke assumed a primary counterterror advisory role after the 1993 World Trade Center bombing. A massive car bomb set off by Islamic militants in an underground garage beneath one of the Twin Towers killed six people, injured more than a thousand, and panicked thousands into fleeing down smoke-filled stairwells. As investigators centered on a group of Muslim extremists inspired by Omar Abdel Rahman, a blind Egyptian cleric who exhorted violence against U.S. civilian targets from his New Jersey mosque, Clinton ordered the NSC to ramp up the nation's defenses.

Ruddy-faced, blunt, and decisive, a mandarin who cultivated fierce loyalists inside the government and influential contacts in foreign capitals, Clarke was given the reins of a new interagency panel, the Counterterrorism Security Group (CSG). The CSG began coordinating terrorism strategy, drawing experts from the NSC, CIA, and senior levels at State, Defense, and Justice. Meeting once a week, Clarke's committee sifted through the latest classified reports on terrorist activity. Their reports reached the highest tiers of Clinton's administration.[14]

Clarke quickly expanded his portfolio into other transnational issues. He pressed NSC officials to consider using a presidential emergency designation to target Russian organized crime syndicates. He also played a behind-the-scenes role in the covert American effort to apprehend Colombian cocaine kingpin Pablo Escobar.[15] As his influence grew, so did its trappings. He won a third-floor office with a vaulted ceiling in the Old Executive Office Building—a suite once occupied by Colonel Oliver North, the secretive White House aide at the center of the Reagan administration's Iran-contra scandal. Clarke's aggressive approach and relentless focus on the perils posed by terrorism in general, and al Qaeda in particular, impressed like-minded Clinton staffers. They admired his hard-edged outlook and his ability to cut through the chatter of formal meetings and harness the government's complex budgeting process. "Dick's a lightning rod. He gets in twenty to thirty minutes what other people take months to synthesize," said Witney Schneidman, the State Department official who started the hunt for Bout. "That attracted a core of people who had no patience for the usual bureaucratic BS."

Clarke's position was strengthened by a series of presidential directives that firmed up the Clinton administration's intent to act against transnational threats. They flowed directly from a new spate of spectacular terrorist crimes. In March 1995, the bizarre attempt by Aum Shinrikyo cult members to release nerve gas in a Tokyo subway added biological and chemical attacks as a perceived threat in the terror arsenal—along with growing worries about loosely controlled nuclear materials. A month later, the Oklahoma City bombing by right-wing extremist Timothy McVeigh raised new fears of attacks on government buildings.

Clinton responded with a classified June 1995 directive that identified terrorism as the most urgent national security issue, putting all agencies on notice to "deter, defeat, and respond vigorously to all terrorist attacks on our territory." In October, Clinton codified his concerns about transnational threats. Signing Presidential Directive PDD-42 to combat "International Organized Crime," he ordered federal agencies—including the NSC, Justice, State, and Treasury—to integrate their efforts against terrorism, international criminal syndicates, drug traffic, and money laundering. The next day, Clinton elaborated during a speech in New York to UN delegates celebrating the fiftieth anniversary of the global organization. Linking the World Trade Center and Oklahoma City bombings to narcotics-linked abductions and executions in Latin America and harassment by criminal gangs in Central Europe, Clinton called on the United Nations and allied governments to take on "the increasingly interconnected groups that traffic in terror, organized crime, drug smuggling, and the spread of weapons of mass destruction." As he listed his priorities to the General Assembly, Clinton added another that had received scant attention during his first term: he urged the delegates to "intensify our efforts to combat the global illegal arms network that fuels terrorism, equips drug cartels, and prolongs deadly conflicts." It was the opening that would eventually allow U.S. intelligence and national security officials to target Viktor Bout's arms network.[16]

But beyond bold speeches, American officials were ill equipped in 1995 to even recognize the head of a worldwide arms transport network, let alone pursue one. In the past, arms traffickers had been targeted on a piecemeal basis, and prosecutions were limited to illegal transactions made on U.S. soil or clearly involving American weapons procurers. Rogue international arms merchants such as Edwin P. Wilson, the former CIA officer accused of illegally selling weapons to Libya in the 1970s, were pursued only through rare Justice and intelligence agency cooperation. U.S. arms trade laws remained narrow, focused only on direct sales.

In 1996 the Clinton administration finally added teeth to the statutes, nudging Congress into regulating arms brokers under the

Arms Export Control Act. Recognizing that weapons merchants provided their lethal wares not only by direct sales but also by acting as brokers and transporters, the United States now outlawed any arranging of arms deals not licensed by the State Department. The new law defined brokering as "financing, transportation, freight forwarding, or the taking of any other action that facilitates the manufacture, export, or import of a defense article or defense service."[17]

That definition neatly described the activities of Bout's organization—except for the glaring problem that he had no known American presence and was not known to have shipped any United States–made weaponry. Sheltered behind layers of shell companies and airplanes that constantly shed old identities, Bout appeared safe from U.S. law. With its far-flung business interests and scattered aircraft fleet on several continents, Bout's network was a post–Cold War phenomenon, operating with clandestine ties to numerous governments but beholden to none. Its hidden structure was comparable to Latin America's drug cartels, with their offshore bank accounts, small fleets of drug-carrying planes, and highly mobile legions of smugglers stationed from Medellín to Miami.

But where cocaine-ferrying organizations were flagrant criminal enterprises, the international legal status of Bout's arms deliveries remained murkier—and there was no certainty that any other nation possessed the political will to shut down his organization. The United States' tough new antibrokering law had broken new ground, but in Europe, regulations covering arms middlemen were much weaker, and in most of Africa, nonexistent. For the moment, all that American intelligence officials could do was learn more about his operation and watch him work.

Even hobbled by shrunken resources and minimal legal authority, the U.S. intelligence operation that had stumbled on Bout's arms routes began to make headway. Now grown to a small circle of Africa analysts, the operation developed a small trove of material on the Russian's transport empire. Many of the initial leads and information came from the NGO community.

U.S. intelligence officials assembled an early list of Bout's aircraft, traced some of his African routes, and with the aid of British intelligence, started to learn more about his background. "Looking at his planes, we could see there was a large capacity," said a U.S.

official involved in the effort. "We began going through the process of scrubbing and verifying his holdings. We started seeing his fleet in all parts of Africa."

But they were still only gathering string. There were no calls from State or the NSC to learn more about Bout.[18] Other European arms dealers operated freely in Africa, and some even had a few planes at their command, leading some officials to question whether Bout's operation was any more a threat than his rivals'. Frustration mounted among the few officials who felt Bout's network needed to be countered. "A U.S. intelligence person I know had been warning officials about Bout for years and no one listened," recalled Alex Vines. "He was quite disillusioned about it."[19] One of the officials deeply involved in the effort smiled wanly as he reflected on his early experience. "I've been eating and sleeping Viktor Bout the last couple of years," he said.[20]

Despite Clinton's insistence that his national security, intelligence, and legal experts coordinate efforts against transnational threats, Clarke's intrusion into fiefdoms traditionally guarded by the FBI, CIA, and State ran into resistance. Senior FBI and Justice officials balked at the NSC's involvement in narcotics and international organized-crime issues, openly vocal about what they perceived as Clarke's efforts to stage-manage counterterror and organized-crime strategy.

"As Dick Clarke assumed control over counterterror at the NSC, he was in position to plan and oversee terrorism ops," recalled Winer, who allied with Clarke's broad view of transnational threats. "Justice made strong objections. They simply didn't want to cede authority." And the FBI, under Louis Freeh, asserted its traditional watchdog role on any international organized-crime matters. "Freeh's attitude," Winer recalled, "was you can't get involved in that, don't do it, we have things under control." Clarke's backers chalked off much of the animosity to the hidebound reactions of territorial bureaucrats. But Justice officials and other internal critics also had raised cogent questions about whether Clarke and other NSC officials risked muddying national security priorities by lumping terrorism, organized crime, arms trafficking, and other international ills into one bulging portfolio. Was arms trafficking as ominous a peril as al Qaeda's Islamic terrorism? If not, did the NSC deserve the lead role in targeting such a wide range of transnational threats? Were traditional law enforcement and intelligence agencies being cut out of the decision loop as the NSC assumed dominance over transnational issues? These were essential questions of policy and government structure that could only be resolved from the White House.[21]

"Operationally, PDD-42 was supposed to be run by the FBI on the law enforcement side and the 'drugs and thugs' part of the CIA," acknowledged one of Clarke's supporters. "But at some point people either tow the line or you work around them. Some of both happened. We had an analysis capability at the NSC and a broader policy capability that they lacked. The question was whether they wanted to be involved in this effort. They had done the limits of what they could do in terms of looking at organized crime internationally. But they didn't have people from NSC and State going off to foreign countries and working the issues hard like Clarke did."[22]

It finally took Clinton's involvement and the intrusion of Congress to sort out the jockeying. In 1996 the National Security Act was amended by Congress to include formation of the Committee on Transnational Threats. The new entity was mandated to "coordinate and direct the activities of the United States Government relating to combating transnational threats."[23] Clinton objected to Congress's intervention, insisting he had already begun to institute the changes. But its creation jump-started his old objective of a unified approach to transnational threats.

In a final NSC realignment in the summer of 1998, Clinton expanded Clarke's authority as counterterror gatekeeper, appointing him to the new post of national coordinator for infrastructure protection and counterterrorism. At the same time, he created the new Office for Transnational Threats—under Clarke's authority. Its purview was broad and finally unambiguous: "Policies and programs on unconventional threats to the United States and Americans abroad; attacks on our infrastructures, cyber systems and government operations; terrorism; and attacks with weapons of mass destruction. This office also coordinates efforts to address other transnational threats such as international crime and narcotics trafficking."[24]

Clarke assembled a circle of hard-charging, accomplished young deputies to work as his transnational threats directors. Obsessed with cutting-edge foreign policy and mostly liberal Democrat by inclination, they shared Clarke's concern about al Qaeda and his urgency to root out similar global threats. The group grew to include Steven Simon, Daniel Benjamin, Roger Cressey, Michael Fenzel, Lee Wolosky, and William Wechsler—all key players in the secret chess moves against terrorism in the final years of Clinton's second-term.

After the 1998 embassy bombings raised Africa's profile as a key battleground against al Qaeda, Gayle Smith, the head of the NSC's Africa desk, also was drawn into Clarke's circle. Tall and animated, with a shock of spiky white hair, Smith would be one of the first senior officials to push for concerted action against Bout. A veteran of years of field work in Africa, she had seen firsthand the consequences of the continent's wars and its death spiral of small arms. "Viktor Bout almost leaped off the map," she said. "Meetings of principals and deputies on Sierra Leone always dealt with Liberia. Sierra Leone was spilling into Guinea. Things were not looking optimistic." At the end of one meeting, "one official asked: 'What about Viktor Bout? He shows up in all this stuff.'" Smith decided to approach Clarke to see if anyone on his staff could focus on Bout.

There was. It was Wolosky, a Russia specialist who had been steered into the transnational threats office by sheer accident. He would spearhead the American effort to bring Bout to justice.

Despite the absence of strong American interest in Bout's activities in Africa until late in the decade, it was only a matter of time before his nonstop cargo flights and massive arms shipments came under scrutiny from other quarters. All through the 1990s, the UN Security Council repeatedly imposed arms embargoes on African war zones, trying in vain to cordon them off from weapons flowing in from foreign sources. Liberia and Somalia were quarantined in 1992, Angola's UNITA rebels in 1993, Rwanda in 1994, and Sierra Leone in 1997. Rifles and ammunition were shipped in by the ton, and as Bout and other suppliers grew bolder, the killing power and sophistication of their weapons deliveries increased. East European helicopter gunships became a familiar sight in African skies. Land mines and mortars became standard issue. Armored vehicles and truck-mounted artillery and antiaircraft guns appeared in rebel arsenals.

As UN officials pressed their own experts to explain why the embargoes were so porous, they also began to rely on outside experts from the NGO community who had done much of the initial work on Bout. Chief among them were Johan Peleman and Kathi Austin.

Peleman's early investigation into Bout's activities had coincided with mounting concern about the massive worldwide supply of small arms, particularly in the Third World. By 1998 both the United Nations and other global security groups were calling for international summits to find ways to interrupt the weapons traffic. At a small-arms conference in Oslo that October attended by delegates from ninety nations, Peleman spoke about the issue of weapons flights from the Balkans in a speech, and in private conversations, cited Bout's prominence. He was surprised by the lack of interest. "Nobody heard of Bout or seemed much interested in him," Peleman recalled.

Despite its still-faint interest in Bout's growing operation, the Clinton administration had decided to push for more oversight. At the 1998 conference, U.S. diplomats lobbied European delegates to adopt versions of the tough new American law on arms brokering. They met with nearly total resistance. "This was a first-order issue of trying to get governments to own up to their responsibility," said one of the U.S. diplomats who pressed the issue. "But it's a real obstacle when governments don't want to do the right thing." Among the most hostile were Belgium, Portugal, Spain, and the East European bloc, led by Russia. Peleman was not surprised.

"The Europeans didn't see it as important and they each had private arms industries to protect," he recalled. "The French were not eager. The Belgians were already big arms producers. The British had introduced their own brokering law and weren't keen on changing it. Even if all the delegates agreed with the American position, they would have needed to persuade their national legislatures, and that was not going to happen. Their arms industries were too powerful."[25]

Despite the stony reactions, Peleman's work on Bout's network impressed UN officials desperate to learn more about how their embargoes were being circumvented. In 1996, when the UN Security

Council set up an internal panel to learn how weapons continued to flow into Rwanda, Security Council officials had approached Peleman for help. When the panel's term was extended, he turned over "everything I had." Three years later, UN officials again came knocking. This time, officials investigating arms embargo violations in Angola pressed for Peleman's latest records. He gave them a proof copy of *The Arms Fixers*, a book he was coauthoring on the weapons trade. He figured they would be back for more, and when they were, Peleman insisted he would only work under contract. The United Nations hired him to work for the Angola panel, and later, for another panel looking into Liberian arms violations. Austin was also hired onto the Liberia panel, and then worked in the DRC, spending several years on the ground, tracking weapons shipments.

Soon Peleman was flying to Luanda and Monrovia, retrieving yellowing end-user files and flight records, but this time under UN authority. In Sharjah, he and a team of UN investigators badgered reluctant emirati aviation officials to let them tour the airport and inspect Bout's planes. And as he shuttled between his monk's nook and the foreign capitals, Peleman found himself caught up in a bizarre "cat-and-mouse game" with the Bout brothers and their assistants.

The Belgian tried to set up interviews with the elusive Bouts, only to see the arrangements endlessly dashed. "Sometimes I give [Sergei Bout] a call inviting him to an interview. Then we agree to meet in Dubai. Subsequently, he does not show up and seems to have changed his mobile number once again. Sometimes I am talking to his associates, and in the middle of the conversation, Viktor calls. His brother asks whether he would to talk to 'our friend Johan,' and then he invariably answers: 'No.'"[26]

As the cat-and-mouse game kept on through the late 1990s, even the most dogged investigators had no idea how high the stakes had become.

Lee Wolosky was a latecomer to the Clinton administration. He had spent most of the 1990s immersed in Russia's turbulent economic and political transformation, first as an adviser and then as a New York attorney specializing in international law. Unlike Clinton loyalists who viewed Russia's democratic transformation as an essential American commitment, Wolosky was troubled by what he saw as the dark side of the process.

In the immediate years after the Soviet empire fell, Wolosky had a front seat on the shaping of the Eastern bloc's democratic future. Compact and cerebral, a Bronx-born intellectual with a pronounced skeptical streak, Wolosky graduated from Harvard in 1990 and jumped at the chance to work as a research assistant in Soviet political and economic reform with the university's John F. Kennedy School of Government. He had detoured from following his father's path into corporate law by painting and rehabbing houses. But the following year, he joined a group of young internationalists and headed for Moscow to help Russia's new leaders on their shaky trek toward the free-market system.

Between 1990 and 1992 Wolosky shuttled between Cambridge and Moscow, working with the Moscow City Council on political reforms. He met occasionally with former Communist general secretary Mikhail Gorbachev, then in his final months as the first president of Russia, and Grigory Yavlinsky, a liberal economist who was overseeing the rush to market reform. Yavlinsky and other Russian economists were still struggling to fulfill the ideals of perestroika, Gorbachev's effort to restructure the hidebound Communist economy, and some of The United States' top government and economic experts had joined them. Wolosky found himself working side by side with Graham Allison, the former dean of the Kennedy School who was advising Gorbachev, and Jeffrey Sachs, a Harvard economist who had made a career of advising emerging nations, from to Bolivia to Poland.

It was Allison who had hired Wolosky for the Kennedy School program, impressed by his "intelligence, diligence, and determination." Working with Yavlinsky on the "Grand Bargain," an ambitious Marshall Plan–scale proposal to pump Western aid into the Russian economy in return for radical market reform, Allison needed a supporting cast of promising young policy specialists to make it work. They worked around the clock for two months in mid-1991 to hammer out the details, but the ambitious plan was rejected by Gorbachev and President George H. W. Bush. Wolosky stayed on through 1992, working on other policy initiatives.[27]

It was a heady time for a young idealist. Moscow was overrun with Americans eager to teach democratic ideals to a new generation of Russians they no longer feared or hated. But Wolosky was also dubious about the grand talk of a rapid Russian transition to a free-market democracy, alert to signs of trouble behind the rosy scenarios. During one meeting with Gorbachev, Wolosky pressed for the former Communist leader's views of the "Grand Bargain." Instead, he noticed, Gorbachev kept grumbling about his inability to build a train to Siberia.

When he ventured away from the crowded meeting rooms where Americans and Russians talked confidently about the future, Wolosky noticed the detritus left behind by the Soviet state. Moscow was becoming a playground for a rising generation of economic hustlers. Their limousines prowled streets clotted with trash. On a road trip deep into former Soviet satellite states, he poked around to see what the big-name advisers missed. In Turkmenistan, close to the Iranian border, Wolosky drove out to an air base that had been a Soviet outpost for decades. Old MiG fighter jets sat rusting on the runways, exposed and unattended. They had once been the fearsome vanguard of Soviet military might; now they were silent markers of its decay. The image stayed with him. "I had the sense that this had been our enemy, but also that they were not as well put together as a society as the West was. It was the Second World. They had First World resources, certainly the intellectual resources and education of the First World, but Third World living conditions, especially outside of Moscow. Everywhere you went, there was deterioration. It didn't bode too well for instant democracy."

Wolosky returned to Harvard for two years of law school, then took up with a New York corporate law firm, handling mergers, acquisitions, and boardroom fights. He kept getting tugged back into Russian affairs, retained by big-money Western investors who had been burned in their dealings with Russia's new generation of corporate plutocrats. In one case he represented American industrialist Kenneth Dart in a lawsuit against Mikhail Khodorkovsky, the billionaire Russian banker who had taken over Yukos, the country's largest oil company.

Dart had complained that Khodorkovsky, the wealthiest man in Russia, had weakened his investments in Yukos subsidiaries by reorganizing the firm. A legal investigation discovered that Yukos shares controlled by Khodorkovsky had been scattered to distant offshore accounts, from Cyprus to the South Pacific island of Niue. Khodorkovsky and his henchmen were "bullies," Wolosky told reporters after Dart reluctantly sold his Yukos holdings.[28] The more he turned up evidence of financial scams and corruption for his private clients, the less sanguine Wolosky felt about Russia's chances for real reform. "It seemed like everything was for sale," he recalled. "Government assets, military assets, private assets, it was all being sold. The idea of minority rights, whether they were investors or Russian voters, were pretty much being trampled."

By the late 1990s, Wolosky had become an outspoken critic of the Russian political scene, worried that the plutocrats were hijacking the nation's struggling economy and co-opting its political leaders. He took a fellowship at the Council of Foreign Relations and began drafting an article for *Foreign Affairs*, the council's influential journal. Researching through early 1999, Wolosky aimed directly at Russia's new president. In "Putin's Plutocrat Problem," Wolosky predicted bleakly that Putin would do little to fight the culture of corruption long tolerated by his predecessor Boris Yeltsin. "In the face of such venality," Wolosky urged, the United States needed to withhold financial investment, treat Russia's oil oligarchs "like pariahs," and "vigorously prosecute" international cases of Russian organized crime and corruption. "In the battle against the oligarchs," he wrote, "Moscow and the West must rely on every weapon available. If they do not, the oligarchs will."[29]

Wolosky's cautionary warning did not sit well with the Clinton administration's top Russia experts. Clinton had bonded with Yeltsin and long talked approvingly of Russia's transformation. Clinton openly viewed the United States' role in promoting Russian democracy as one of his main historic legacies. Clinton's close friend and deputy secretary of state Strobe Talbott had accented the positive aspects of privatization, convinced that the culture of corruption stretched back through Soviet history and could only be overcome by democracy's deepening roots.[30]

But Wolosky's broadside struck a chord at the NSC. Unlike Talbott and other specialists on Russia at the State Department, Clarke viewed Russian corruption as a strategic threat to U.S. interests. In the summer of 1999, Clarke and Wechsler sounded out Wolosky about joining the NSC as a deputy in the Russian affairs section. But by the time he passed his government security check in the late fall, Wolosky had been steered over to the transnational threats office, where he was assigned as a director replacing Wechsler, who was moving over to the Treasury Department to oversee money laundering control strategy.

Wolosky plunged into preparations for a planned Clinton trip to Moscow in June 2000 to meet with Putin. Clarke wanted to make Russian corruption part of the agenda, and Wolosky began putting together the background for Clinton to bring up the issue with Putin. But by spring 2000 Wolosky had been diverted to a new project that dovetailed with his interest in Russian crime and corruption. He was given the Viktor Bout file.

Wolosky was intrigued from the start. Bout was the apotheosis of Russia's new wave of freebooting plutocrats, a personification of everything Wolosky had warned about in his *Foreign Affairs* essay. But while their corrosive influence was mostly confined to the chaotic Russian economic and political spheres, Bout appeared to be wreaking havoc on an international scale. "He wasn't just a flower trader," Wolosky said.

No longer a lone voice outside the government, Wolosky now had the authority to urge action about his concerns about Russian corruption—personified by Bout—at the highest levels of the Clinton administration. Bolstered by the bureaucratic clout of the National Security Council and newfound access to senior advisers at the White House, Wolosky turned his full attention to putting Viktor Bout out of business.

CHAPTER 7

The Taliban Connection

The mullah had a shopping list and money to burn.

In the winter months of 1996 and into the spring of 1997, Farid Ahmed, a young turbaned Afghan cleric, was a persistent visitor around the hangars and air freight offices at Sharjah International Airport. He had been secretly dispatched to the Persian Gulf emirate by senior mullahs of the new power in Afghanistan, the Taliban. Only weeks earlier, the puritanical mujahideen from Kandahar had swept into Kabul after their grueling two-year insurgency and routed the weakened government of Burhanuddin Rabbani. The missions given to Ahmed, a wispy-bearded, fervent graduate of Pakistan's fundamentalist Islamic madrassas, were to procure new supplies of weapons and airplanes for the Taliban and to set up a covert pipeline to transport arms back to Afghanistan.[1]

Sometimes alone, sometimes accompanied by other Taliban operatives, Ahmed went door to door through the airport's offices and hangars. He badgered flight directors and cargo shippers, flashing detailed lists of the lethal items sought by the Taliban's leadership. For the rogue state's foot soldiers, Ahmed sought massive quantities of Kalashnikov automatic rifles, shoulder-fired grenade launchers, ground rockets, mortars, antiaircraft batteries, and ammunition. For the Taliban's air force he wanted aviation supplies—tires, hydraulic fluid, spare fighter jet parts, and replacements for their ancient MiG-21 jet fighters. Most importantly, Ahmed told the air cargo executives he approached, the Talibs were willing to spend hundreds of thousands of dollars to purchase long-distance cargo planes capable of flying in the tons of military hardware their leaders craved.[2]

"He was all over the airport, in everyone's hair," recalled Victor Sherin, a stocky, blunt Russian who worked as managing director for Volga-Dnepr Gulf, one of several Russian-owned aviation firms that Ahmed pestered with offers to buy matériel.[3]

The Taliban's buying spree came at a crucial juncture for their armed forces. As the shock troops of true believers had waged their seesawing insurrection against the Rabbani government and forces loyal to his defense minister, Ahmad Shah Massoud, they had depended primarily on Pakistan's intelligence services and military for tanks, artillery, ammunition, and supplies. But their symbiotic relationship with the Pakistanis began to strain after the Talibs seized Jalalabad and marched into Kabul in late September 1996, forcing a ragged retreat by Massoud's forces to a safe haven in the Shamali plain. Eager to scatter the remnants of Massoud's holdouts, the Taliban's senior leaders began chafing at their dependence on Pakistani officials. Pakistan's military advisers and Interservices Intelligence directorate (ISI) agents had inflamed the Taliban's "mistrust and impatience" by parceling out weapons only after operations "were approved and cleared by the Pakistani Army."

At the Taliban's moment of victory, their senior leaders could not yet depend on the financial largess of their future patrons, Osama bin Laden and his cadre of terror operatives. Bin Laden would soon pool money, arms, and resources with the Talibs, but he and his forces had only recently arrived in Afghanistan after leaving their haven in Sudan in May 1995 and setting up a compound in the mountain redoubt of Tora Bora.[4] Not independent enough to break off from their Pakistani patrons, the Taliban's mullahs began to display "a vested interest in developing an independent procurement capability," Human Rights Watch analysts later concluded.[5] A U.S. military intelligence official later agreed with that assessment:

"Pakistan played a big role in weapons transfers, absolutely. They provided mostly the big stuff—tanks, trucks, heavy artillery. But the small arms that any army lives on, the Taliban needed a steady diet of that, and they would take it from whatever sources were available."[6] In late 1996 the Taliban regime looked to the emirates—with Farid Ahmed as their agent.

Ahmed set up shop in Sharjah that November, appointed as the new station manager for Ariana Afghan Airways—the nation's government-run airline. The baby-faced cleric had been selected for the post by a powerful patron among the Taliban's leadership—Mullah Akhtar Mohammed Mansour, the new head of the Afghan air force and later the Taliban's defense minister. An Afghan who worked as a senior executive with Ariana during the early days of the Taliban's rule said that Ahmed had an even more important patron—Mullah Omar, the reclusive, one-eyed Taliban leader who acted as apostle for Afghanistan's fundamentalist Islamic insurrection, and who remains to this day a fugitive from American forces. "He was under the direct control of Mullah Omar," the former Ariana executive said.[7]

To those who met him in Sharjah, young Ahmed seemed an odd choice to entrust such a clandestine mission. The newly arrived cleric saved money by sleeping in local mosques instead of renting. "He was basically a miser," recalled Samir Zeidan, general manager of Flying Carpet Express, a cargo firm that Ahmed later hired.[8] Ahmed brought his own tea to business meetings and was prone to bouts of sudden giggling. Only twenty-five when he arrived in Sharjah, the mullah was oblivious to the crucial details of plane routing, schedules, international air regulations, and cargo requirements that Ariana officials struggled with daily. He spoke little English, a staple among Ariana's pilots and senior staff, though he was fluent in Punjabi and Urdu and could hold his own in Farsi. A scion of a prosperous trading family with roots in both the UAE and Pakistan, he had worked briefly in Dubai before the Taliban came to power and had connections with the Afghan expatriate community there. Viktor Bout's business partner Richard Chichakli got to know Ahmed during his business trips to Sharjah and was unimpressed. "He knew nothing about the airplane industry," Chichakli said dismissively. "If he wanted to do business, he would send for someone else to help him."[9]

But Mansour had chosen Ahmed for other traits—his unwavering loyalty, his stealth and discretion, and his years of fundamentalist Islamic religious training. As Mansour's handpicked representative, the young mullah was given complete authority over Ariana's staff and bank accounts in the UAE. And he was entrusted by Mansour with the sensitive assignment of finding cargo planes for the Taliban's depleted air force. The minister informed senior officials of Ariana that Ahmed reported directly to him and that they were to follow his orders. In late 1996 Mansour quickly assigned the veteran Ariana executive to act as Ahmed's minder, helping him bolster Taliban flight routes to and from the emirates: "Mullah Farid is in charge of everything in the emirates," Mansour flatly told the executive.[10]

Until the Taliban takeover, Ariana had staffed only a few desultory flights through the UAE, mostly half-filled passenger routes back and forth from Dubai. Cargo flights laden with consignments of radios, refrigerators, and other prized appliances made runs into Afghanistan from both Dubai and Sharjah, but they flew fitfully, rarely on a standard schedule. That changed in short order. Passenger flights quickly grew to as many as five scheduled runs weekly, all routed through Sharjah. The volume of cargo activity rose dramatically, too, sometimes as many as three flights a day. Ariana's operation in Afghanistan swelled as the cargo volume rose, growing from a staff of eight hundred to nearly fifteen hundred by the late 1990s.

For both Ahmed and the older mullahs who oversaw his mission, Sharjah was an ideal location. The trade-obsessed UAE was one of only three nations in the world—along with Saudi Arabia and Pakistan—that had diplomatically recognized the new Taliban regime. The UAE's leader and founder, Sheikh Zayed bin Sultan al Nahyan, had spoken glowingly of the Taliban's new leadership. Both the elder Sheikh al Nahyan and the UAE's dynamic young crown prince and defense minister, Sheikh Mohammed bin Rashid al Maktoum, soon became visitors to Taliban-controlled Afghanistan, flying in with other wealthy Persian Gulf sheikhs to join in lavish hunting parties in the hills near Kandahar. Navigating the bleak terrain in Land Cruisers, they joined their Taliban hosts in releasing trained falcons to track down pheasantlike houbara bustards, a quarry prized in the traditional Bedouin hunting rites. The young crown prince returned several times in 1998 and 1999, mingling in well-appointed tents with his counterpart, Mansour, other senior mullahs, and on at least one occasion in 1999, reportedly with Osama bin Laden, who was known to fish at a nearby dam with Mullah Omar.[11] Warming to his hosts, Sheikh Maktoum agreed to suspend all landing fees for Ariana planes—a move that further aided the surge in air traffic to and from Sharjah.[12]

Sand-swept, arid, and overrun by legions of traders, shippers, moneymen, and smugglers, Sharjah's airport catered to the more than seventy airlines and air cargo firms based there. Loading bays hummed all day and well into the night with the propeller drone of antiquated, durable Antonovs and Ilyushins. Russian and Arab ground crews hefted off heavy pallets stacked high with appliances, construction materials, and military equipment. "The only reason to be in Sharjah was smuggling," the senior Ariana executive said. "In Sharjah, it was anything goes."[13]

Inspection was lax and regulations easily skirted. Planes regularly landed and took off at late hours. Ground crews were adept at whisking cargos on and off in the enveloping early-morning darkness without interference from airport security men. Abdul Shakur Arefee, an Ariana flight engineer who flew frequently through Sharjah in the late 1990s, watched puzzled as arriving planes taxied off to dimly lit nooks, where ground crews hustled shipments on and off without interference from airport inspectors. "In Dubai, all the cargo would have to be taken off near the gates. No exceptions," Arefee recalled. "But in Sharjah, there was not too much tight security. When the planes came, they would park in isolated places and unload there."[14]

Russian pilots and cargo shippers had been flocking to Sharjah's airport in growing numbers since the early 1990s, attracted by the facility's low overhead, paltry regulations, and close proximity to valued Third World capitals. Anxious to escape Russia's brutal winters and desperate to make a living, scores of Soviet air force veterans drifted to the UAE, taking whatever cut-rate opportunities they could find to fly. The Russians in Sharjah were a tough, freebooting bunch who maneuvered their aging freighters out on regular cargo runs to remote landing strips across the Middle East, Africa, and south-central Asia. Many were familiar with the region, having fought the Afghan mujahideen in the 1980s. But for some, memories of the brutal Afghan war and its bitter denouement were still too raw to contemplate doing business with the likes of Farid Ahmed. Alexei Inchuk, general manager of the Sharjah-based Phoenix Airlines, shuddered inwardly when Ahmed and "a whole pack of Talibs" entered his office that winter. The Afghans asked to buy an Antonov An-12 cargo plane. Inchuk turned them down flat. "They were ready to offer a very good deal on it," Inchuk recalled. "But I said no. I fought in Afghanistan in my time and I don't have much time for these people, especially for Talibs."[15]

Sergei Mankhayev, general manager of Republic Air Company, was approached by an unnamed Taliban broker who showed him a want list of "civilian aircraft and spare parts." The broker also waved a second list, detailing sought-after "weapons, ammunition, and MiG combat aircraft," along with several dozen armament varieties, from grenade launchers to ground rockets. Mankhayev refused the offers. So did Victor Sherin, waving Ahmed off when he proposed buying several heavy-duty Antonov air freighters for the Taliban's air force. "I have never met a more cunning and sly person in my life," an agitated Sherin recalled. "The word about him here was that it was nothing for him to cheat a *kaffir* (infidel). You could see how he was trying to catch every word that I said in Russian to my colleagues." The mullah was not deterred. He returned with his aides, pressing for aviation fuel, hydraulic fluid, and tires for MiG fighter jets. Again Sherin showed them the door. "I did not want to get hooked by them. You do something illegal and then they threaten to report you to the authorities and you will have to work for them for then on. So they left and went on looking around."[16]

For weeks, Ahmed made no apparent headway in his shopping spree for arms. Then he found the man who would fly for anything for the right price: Viktor Bout.

That winter, Ahmed met with two Russian businessmen in a hotel near the Sharjah airport. The former Ariana executive who had been assigned as Ahmed's minder flew in from Kabul after receiving hurried orders to join the mullah in Sharjah. He met Ahmed at the hotel and the two men went to a third-floor room, where they were met by the two Russians. One was a stout man with hooded eyes and a trim brush mustache who took the lead in the conversations.

The Russian did not give his name to the Afghan executive, who was excused by Ahmed after a few minutes, leaving the mullah alone with the visitors. But years later, the Ariana executive would identify the heavyset man as Bout—recognizing his stolid face from a color portrait of the arms merchant published in the *New York Times* in 2003. When the meeting was done and the Russians had departed, Ahmed told the Ariana official that he was "working with the Russian people to get supplies for the [Taliban] air force." Over the ensuing weeks, Ahmed divulged more, explaining that he had forged a deal with Bout's Air Cess operation "to get tires and other replacement parts for fighter jets. And it wasn't just tires," the Ariana executive recalled later. Ahmed confided that the Taliban was also getting "arms and ammunition," and explained that another Sharjah-based firm, Flying Dolphin, an allied company owned by an emirate sheikh, would handle charter flights for Ariana.[17]

Bout would vehemently deny that he had dealt with Taliban officials, and he has repeatedly maintained that he never dealt with al Qaeda or any other Islamic militants. "I haven't entered any contracts" with the Taliban or al Qaeda, he insisted during a 2002 Moscow radio interview. In a public statement released later the same year, Bout said, "I am not, and never have been, associated with al Qaeda, the Taliban or any of their officials, officers, or related organizations. I am not, nor are any of my organizations." In his flinty appraisal of world politics, Bout scoffed in his Moscow interview that U.S. officials had conveniently ignored their own historic role in arming Afghan militants, while using him as a scapegoat to "say that the Russians are to blame."[18]

It is not clear to this day whether Bout's arrangements with Ahmed were related to the Russian's negotiations over the previous year with the Taliban for his imprisoned crew and impounded Ilyushin Il-76. But his covert business relationship with the Taliban blossomed afterward. Though concealed from the outside world, Bout's clandestine deal became a turning point in the growth of his arms empire, providing weapons, cargo planes, plane maintenance crews, and even pilots to the Taliban in a relationship that would clinch his notoriety as the world's "gun runner extraordinaire," as the U.S. State Department later described him.[19]

Until that point, despite the growing global reach of his air fleet and business interests and his clientele of Big Men, guerrilla leaders, and warlords, Bout had remained a regional player in the international arms trade. He had dominated Africa's weapons pipelines, perceived as an integral threat to the continent's peace both by the British government and concerned activists such as Johan Peleman, and was only beginning to worry American intelligence officials who had finally started to focus on the continent's flaring internecine conflicts.

But Bout's secret deal with the Taliban showed just how far he was willing to go. By enabling one of the world's most fanatic and reviled regimes, Bout had taken the penultimate step of aiding a repressive government that was already shunned by most of the world—even by his own Russian government. But for Bout, the step was both logical and understandable. His operation needed to seek out the world's wars and chaos to flourish, and the ascendance of the Taliban had swept into power a dream customer—a warlike regime that required a steady supply of weaponry to maintain its hegemony and arm its jihadist al Qaeda guests.

Bout's arrangements with the Talibs were forged in secrecy and carried out covertly for nearly five years before their dimensions were revealed by press accounts and intelligence reports that emerged only after the September 11 attacks. Both Bout and the mullahs proved to be masters at operating in the shadows. As the Taliban's oppressive rule hardened, Western governments and the United Nations responded in the late 1990s with a tightening series of trade embargoes and even an international flights ban. But during the winter of 1996–1997, Bout risked only minimal sanctions by joining forces with the mullahs.

On December, 17, 1996, the European Union Council of Ministers imposed the first international arms embargo against the Taliban, banning the sale of "weapons designed to kill, and their ammunition, weapons platforms, nonweapons platforms, and ancillary equipment." The ban was tentative and porous. Just two weeks earlier, Bout had opened an Air Cess office at the Ostend airport—a move that left his Belgian operation in technical violation of the ban, which also covered "spare parts, repairs, maintenance, and transfer of military technology and contracts entered into prior to the onset of the embargo."[20] But Russia was not yet a member of the EU. And since most of Bout's planes were based in Sharjah and registered at various times during that period in Swaziland, Liberia, and Equatorial Guinea, it is not likely that the ban would have extended to his flights.

According to Bout's former pilot Vladimir Sharpatov, the Russian government had also issued a prohibition in 1995 on all flights by Russian-owned firms into Taliban-controlled territory in Afghanistan—a move that followed the militants' snaring of Bout's Ilyushin and his plane's crew. But because his firms and planes were based outside of his native country, Bout's operation again was likely exempted—and there is no evidence that any pressure was applied by Russian officials.[21]

The Russian government's attitude toward the Taliban was disapproving, but also hands-off and remote. Boris Yeltsin's diplomats had reacted stonily to the Taliban's seizure of Kabul, stating the move "only aggravates the crisis into which Afghanistan has been plunged."[22] Russia had been printing Afghani currency under a contract with the Rabbani government—shipments that were also ferried at times by Bout planes. And by early 1997, the Russian government also began openly selling some military equipment to Massoud and other rebel factions.

But the Russians still appeared reluctant to weigh in on Afghanistan's internal matters so soon after their late 1980s withdrawal, leaving an opening for entrepreneurs such as Bout.[23] There are even indications that despite Bout's clandestine relationship with the Taliban, he may have kept himself in good graces with Russia by still quietly supplying the regime's foe. In a February 2002 Moscow radio interview, Bout said he had continued to fly arms to the Northern Alliance "until the Taliban captured all the airfields"— a battlefield consolidation by Talib forces that was not completed until the United Front lost its airstrips at Mazar-i-Sharif in August 1998 and Bamian in May 1999.[24]

U.S. intelligence officials were impressed by the sophisticated arsenals that both the Taliban and the Northern Alliance displayed in the late 1990s. Both sides fielded T-54 and T-62 Russian-designed tanks, towed artillery, multiple-rocket launchers, and MiG-21 and SU-17 fighter jets—equipment that would have required foreign assistance to buy, maintain, and operate.[25] Russia's intelligence services also played a covert role in Afghanistan in aiding Massoud and his Northern Alliance allies. According to a former Russian intelligence agent who defected to the United States, Russian operatives helped in the clandestine movement of arms to both Massoud and General Abdul Rashid Dostum, a former Afghan army general who fought the Taliban but who also switched sides several times during the civil war. It remains unclear if Bout was part of that official Russian arms pipeline.[26]

"He was flying for the Taliban while flying for Massoud and the Northern Alliance," said a close Bout associate. "Of course he was. He was friend of everyone. They tolerated this because they had no alternative. No one else would deliver the packages."[27]

Bout's companies did more for the Taliban than merely deliver arms and supplies. Between 1998 and 2001, Bout's network and allied air transport operations in Sharjah secretly sold twelve heavy-duty cargo planes to the Taliban, enabling the militants' air force to bolster their air fleet and deliver tons of East European–issue arms into Afghanistan and ferry arms and thousands of jihad operatives inside the country. Some of the weapons shipments were eventually shared, U.S. officials later concluded, with the Taliban's sheltered guests, bin Laden and his al Qaeda fighters.

In June 1998 Vial, a Delaware holding company that Bout controlled through power of attorney and used to route arms profits to Belgium, transferred two Antonov freighters to the Taliban's air force. Two more planes from Air Cess were also transferred to the air force, in January 1999. A fifth Antonov was turned over to Ariana, a sale that netted Bout's network $100,000. That price, Afghan officials said, was more or less replicated in each of the other plane transfers—netting Bout's companies a minimum of $500,000 from the Taliban treasury.[28]

During the same period, the Taliban received seven other Antonovs from other companies working in concert with Bout's operation. During 1998 and 1999 the Taliban bought five Antonovs from Flying Dolphin and Santa Cruz Imperial, two

UAE-based air firms owned by Sheikh Abdullah bin Zayed al Saqr al Nahyan, an influential former ambassador to the United States who was named in a UN report as "a business associate of Viktor Bout."

The sheikh, a distant member of the UAE's ruling family and a diplomat who served as the emirates' ambassador in Washington from 1989 to 1992, boasted that he "got to know many of the Bushes" during his stay in the U.S. capital. But by the late 1990s, Sheikh Abdullah had joined the growing ranks of the UAE's air cargo haulers, basing most of his fleet in Sharjah. His flights, like Bout's, ranged into Africa and Afghanistan. UN investigators reported in a December 2000 report on arms embargo violations in Angola that a Flying Dolphin freighter had joined Air Cess in supplying arms to UNITA rebels. And a UN report issued that same month on arms ban violations in Sierra Leone asserted that Flying Dolphin and Santa Cruz Imperial planes had repeatedly used Liberian and Swaziland registries during African flights. UN investigators concluded that the sheikh's air operations worked in tandem with Bout's—although American and British intelligence officials downplayed allegations that his firms were directly controlled by Bout.

The sheikh had also been appointed during the late 1990s as a "global civil aviation agent" by Liberian dictator Charles Taylor. The posting gave the sheikh the authority to register foreign airplanes under the Liberian flag—in essence, giving him blanket authority to keep the freighters that he and Bout owned in Sharjah out of the range of international scrutiny. "The sheikh was operating abroad as an agent of the Liberian registry," Johan Peleman said.[29]

Sheikh Abdullah later acknowledged meeting both with Bout and with Farid Ahmed during that period. But the sheikh insisted he had not worked with either man. The sheikh claimed vaguely that former "Russian partners" of his had in fact owned the Flying Dolphin and Santa Cruz planes that were sold to the Taliban. He added that he had parted with the Russians after 1997—but he declined to identify them. Like Bout, the sheikh insisted he had never done business with the Taliban. He protested repeatedly about "the damage to my name" and how press reports about his firms' alleged arms smuggling had made him out to be "like Al

Capone, running this business for the Taliban. I am shocked at how they can say this, really I am."[30]

Another Antonov was sold in July 1999 to Ariana by Aerovista, a Sharjah-based cargo firm that worked with Bout's firms on occasion. Apandi Lakhiyalov, managing director of the firm, later admitted selling the Talibs an "old An-24 passenger plane whose service resources had been almost exhausted." Lakhiyalov said he had "a bad gut feeling" about the sale, but "what could I do? The economic condition was not quite good for our company and I don't think we could have sold it to anybody else." He insisted that he did not know Bout or coordinate business with him. But an official of KAS, a Kyrgyzstan-based firm that had joint rental contracts with Aerovista, said that Lakhiyalov's company "may have done some business with Bout's and Abdullah's companies. They were not affiliated, they were only partners." KAS was listed as a previous owner of the aircraft. Taliban records do not detail the seller of a seventh plane, an Antonov An-24 bought by Ariana in April 2001, but Afghan officials suspected that it, too, came from the orbit of Bout companies.[31]

Bout's work for the Taliban may have been hidden from the outside world. But the identity of his new customer was an open secret among aides and employees, one more rogue government joining his high-paying clientele. "Yes, he flew for the Taliban," said the Bout associate. "He flew *to* the Taliban, not *for* the Taliban. He was landing in Kandahar all the time. But it was people paying him from Swiss bank accounts to do those flights. I don't know who it was, but he was delivering packages to the Taliban. Not just weapons, but meat, food, all kinds of things." And just months before the September 11 attacks, Bout admitted to Belgian journalist Dirk Draulans that he had indeed done business with the mullahs—though he was careful to insist that he had never dealt directly with bin Laden's terrorist faction. "He said the Taliban were official, they were a government," Draulans recalled. "But he said he never met al Qaeda or flew for them."[32]

Bout's sweeping public denials also failed to reckon with a sheath of documents that sat in Taliban files. Senior officials of the Afghan coalition government that replaced the Taliban after the American invasion displayed the records to *Los Angeles Times* correspondent John Daniszewski in March 2002. The files documented the Bout network's plane sales to the militants. One top Afghan aviation official cited Bout by name. "He had a very upper hand in all these things," the Afghan said.[33]

South African intelligence reports also recounted a stream of profits from suspected sales of "heavy ordnance" to the Taliban, based on an informant inside Bout's circle of pilots. And in 2005, when U.S. officials moved belatedly to shut down Bout's global empire, the Treasury Department publicly stated that Bout and his firms had "profited $50 million from supplying the Taliban with military equipment when they ruled Afghanistan." Juan Zarate, who targeted Bout during his stint as assistant secretary of the treasury for terrorist financing and is now the Bush administration's chief national security official adviser on counterterror strategy, said that the Russian was "providing air cargo services to provide matériel to the Taliban, which was problematic at the time given the status of the Taliban as a sponsor of al Qaeda."[34]

During the American liberation of Afghanistan in late 2001 and 2002, U.S. troops uncovered massive caches of munitions that had been flown into the Kandahar airport during the Taliban's rule and hidden in vast storerooms ringing the field. Inside submerged bunkers, soldiers found mountainous stacks of Kalashnikovs and RPGs in termite-gnawed crates, mortar rounds piled by the "tens of thousands," and massive pyramids of ammunition boxes piled floor to ceiling. "It was clear the Taliban and al Qaeda shared the caches," said a U.S. Defense Department official who toured the stockpiles in early 2002 and interviewed Afghan residents and captured Taliban fighters. Weapons taken from some of those caches were likely deployed against American forces by al Qaeda and Taliban resistance during the U.S. invasion in late 2001, the official said—and the militants have continued using them while waging their guerrilla war from the hills.[35] "It was all intermingled," the weapons expert said.

By 1998, after his South African venture had imploded and Sharjah became the central hub for his Afghanistan work, Bout settled into a comfortable life the emirates. He worked side by side with his brother Sergei—who also spent a good deal of his time in Pakistan, tending Air Cess's operation in Islamabad.

Bout's Air Cess office near the Sharjah airport was well appointed, with a receptionist and a bar well stocked with liquor—despite the emirate's religious prohibition against alcohol. He moved openly in Sharjah's expatriate Russian circles, attending emirate functions with his wife, Alla. In January 2000 he joined the Russian embassy in the emirate of Abu Dhabi in sponsoring an exhibit of Russian art, followed by a cocktail reception at the Sands Hotel. He also spread out his business interests, carefully basing some of his planes in other emirates. He kept the workhorses of his fleet in Sharjah while circulating his more dilapidated planes into storage in sun-punished airfields in the remote emirates of Ras al-Khaymah and Fujairah.[36]

When one of his decaying Ilyushins in Sharjah became a candidate for the scrap pile, Bout faced a typical dilemma: he no longer wanted to pay steep storage fees for the useless plane, but UAE authorities prevented air firms from simply discarding their junkers. Ever the schemer, Bout came up with a novel solution. He sold the plane to a UAE advertising firm, promising to turn it into a roadside billboard along the bleak highway between Ras al-Khaymah and Fujairah. But he had to get the plane there. "He asked an ace pilot of his if he could do it," recalled a Russian air executive who worked in Sharjah. "The pilot examined the plane and found that it could only fly on three engines out of four. The pilot was about to say 'no,'" when Bout offered him $20,000 for this trick." After plastering the old plane with advertisements, the pilot managed to get the fraying hulk airborne. The plane shuddered aloft, engines sputtering, but the veteran airman managed to coax the old Ilyushin down to a soft landing in the sand along the highway. He walked away from the wreck and pocketed the $20,000—and Viktor Bout had wriggled out of another hole. "Bout loved this stunt and he bragged about it constantly," the Russian said. "Anything for money, anything for risk. The more risk the better."[37]

Bout also knew how to cover his bases. Like any foreign businessman in the UAE, he had been obliged by business custom to join forces with an agreeable emirati sponsor. "This is how the sheikhs spread the money around," said a U.S. diplomat based in the emirates in the late 1990s. "If you didn't play the game, you couldn't get visas, electricity hookups, phones, or anything you needed to stay in business. Clearly Bout had the right people working for him." Soon after he arrived in Sharjah in 1993, Bout joined forces with Sultan Hamad Said Nassir al Suwaidi, the influential brother-in-law of the sheikh of Sharjah. Suwaidi had held diplomatic and government posts for the emirate and was once Sharjah's police chief. Joining as Bout's partner in the Transavia Travel Agency, Suwaidi took a traditional cut of Bout company proceeds— the actual figure was not listed, but the American diplomat said UAE partners typically raked in as much as 40 percent of the profits. Still, it was a small price for Bout to pay for easing government oversight and for special access to the emirate's inner circles. Indeed, as his arms role in Africa became a diplomatic issue for American officials in the UAE, the arms merchant's emirate connections afforded him official protection.[38]

"We knew his planes were coming through Sharjah and we were concerned," the U.S. diplomat said. "I went out to Sharjah airport with request after request to shut him down. The airport people would say: 'But the aircraft aren't registered in Sharjah. We're afraid there's nothing we can do.'"

The diplomat went up the chain of authority to the sheikh of Sharjah, Sultan bin Mohammed al-Qassimi. The sheikh was an academic and an enthusiast of all things British, a visiting professor of Arabic history at Exeter who would jet off to London to spend his summers from June through September. The diplomat met the sheikh and his aides for tea in his royal business suite.

"Look, Your Highness," the diplomat explained as tea servers refreshed their cups, "you've got a problem here. This man is moving guns to Africa and his planes are in your airport. We need to have this man stopped." The sheikh nodded his assent, eyes distant. "He would say he understood, and then nothing would be done," the diplomat recalled years later. "Months would go by and we'd meet again over tea and I would mention Viktor again and the sheikh would smile and look at us as if he'd just heard the name for the very first time. After about the fourth time, we stopped asking."[39]

· · ·

As Sharjah's leaders averted their eyes, Bout's air operations for the Taliban proceeded apace. The clandestine arrangement with the Talibs was a poorly kept secret among the Russian air cargo workers and pilots at Sharjah and even among Bout's rivals back in Russia. Valery Spurnov, general director of SpAir Company in Yekaterinburg, learned about the arms flights in conversations with some of his pilots, who were hired in 1997 and 1998 as freelancers for Air Cess in Sharjah. After SpAir was idled following a crash of one of its Ilyushin Il-76s in Yugoslavia in late 1996, Bout lured nearly fifty of the firm's pilots to the UAE with promises of steady employment and $5,000 monthly paychecks, Spurnov recalled.

The pilots whispered openly about runs into Afghanistan, delivering arms for the Talibs on Air Cess freighters that had been leased by Ariana. Bout's ground crews at Sharjah also had unfettered access to the Ariana planes—and their cargo bays—as a result of Air Cess's maintenance work for the airline. The ground crews were adept at removing tail numbers—to obscure their provenance and make tracking more difficult. The tactic was an old standby—before the Taliban takeover, Western observers reported seeing Antonovs and Tupelovs in Tajikistani colors piloted by Russians and Bulgarians "offloading mortars, small-arms ammunition and missiles" to pro-Rabbani factions.[40] One Russian cargo executive familiar with Bout's Sharjah operation said that Air Cess ran so many flights into Afghanistan for the Taliban that members of his ground crews boasted they "changed numbers on the sides of their planes three times a week. They painted the numbers with water emulsion to make the work of repainting easier."[41]

The pilots were rarely told what they were delivering. But veterans familiar with the signs of arms transport work easily recognized their military cargoes by the telltale green wooden crates they carried and by the crews of Taliban soldiers who off-loaded the containers in Afghanistan. Said one pilot: "We carried stuff which was packed in green, oblong wooden boxes. The boxes were pretty heavy, too. We didn't ask questions. But what else could it be but weapons?" Bout's pilots also had to take part in the subterfuge. Many were issued false "Liberia-issued IDs" by Bout's executives, Spurnov recalled, which masked their identities as his employees. "No one asked about the nationality. For all they cared, the Talibs hired Liberian pilots."[42]

At least one other Sharjah-based air firm was approached to join in the weapons flights into Afghanistan. Igor Abdayev, general manager of Jet Line and a longtime acquaintance of Viktor Bout, said that "several people and companies came to us about this deal to deliver weapons from Albania to Afghanistan." Abdayev would not name them, but he said he was told "it was legal and the way that they put it, it looked like a pretty legal operation to us." Abdayev agreed to go in on the arms flights. But when he asked for "a whole package of necessary documents before we take this job," Abdayev's prospective partners never delivered them. "We did not do it," Abdayev said, adding: "But someone else could have."[43]

The routes into Afghanistan varied. Some flights went directly from Sharjah into Afghanistan, either to the main airport in Kabul, the Bagram air base near the Afghan capital, or the Taliban's favored airport in Kandahar. When weapons were shipped, Russian air executives said, the planes' cargo holds would have been loaded in Eastern bloc transshipment points before transiting in Sharjah. Other flights came southeast from the Pietersburg airport, in South Africa, and some reportedly arrived from convenient neighboring airfields in Central Asia. British intelligence officials also detected a pattern of flights through Islamabad, where Sergei Bout operated a Pakistani branch of Air Cess.[44]

At the same time, the Taliban's new Antonovs, acquired from Bout and Sheikh al Nahyan, were also pressed into service. Under orders from Taliban officials, the freighters under Afghan air force control were given false commercial registrations as Ariana planes. The use of spurious civilian registrations instead of the standard military designation was vital to the planes' ability to fly international routes. Iranian ground air controllers monitoring the planes' flight paths would not challenge their routes if they were assumed to be civilian planes. "If it was [known to be] air force, it could not overfly Iran or Pakistan," an Afghan government official explained in 2002, adding that each military overflight would have required permission from the Iranian foreign ministry—as well as UAE approval for each Sharjah landing. The Afghan officials had no choice but to comply with the false registrations. Several colleagues had been hustled off by the Taliban's secret police and held for months in Kabul prisons. "From the legal point of view we should not have done it, but what could you do? The minister [Mansour] ordered it, and we had no choice."[45]

To ensure that the new air force Antonovs were treated as Ariana planes on their covert arms flights, Taliban officials also ordered at least four of their planes disguised in the civilian airline's distinctive blue and white colors. "I understood that if it did not go under the color of Ariana, maybe Sharjah airport would [insist on] special permission," an Afghan official recalled. U.S. intelligence officials later surmised that Bout's large avionics operation in Sharjah may have played a role in repainting the aircraft. One official cast doubt on the Taliban air force's ability to properly disguise the Antonovs, saying they lacked adequate painting skills, experience, and tools to complete the task without threatening the planes' wing weight and aerodynamics. Bout's avionics crews, on the other hand, performed "a tremendous amount of painting work at Sharjah and Ras al-Khaymah. Bout's avionics shop had been certified by the Russian-based Antonov plane manufacturing company and was the premier service agency for Antonovs throughout Africa, Asia, and the Mideast. "It's a huge part of their business," the official said. "They're just about the only operation in the Mideast that would know how to properly repaint an Antonov."[46]

False Ariana identification cards were also printed for Taliban air force pilots who were assigned to fly the new Antonovs, posing as Ariana crewmen. Copies of fake IDs for at least four Taliban pilots ended up attached to several of the civilian Antonov registries.[47] Even the planes' bills of lading—mandatory cargo lists—were often altered to describe the military cargoes as "spare parts." Sometimes even that flimsy pretense was dropped. An October 23, 1998, waybill for an Ariana flight to Kabul cited "aircraft parts" for the Taliban air force—a shipment that originated with a now-defunct firm in Gaithersburg, Maryland.

U.S. and Western intelligence officials were never able to confirm the precise methods used by the Ariana planes and Bout's charters in moving weapons and other supplies into Afghanistan in the late 1990s. But American and Afghan officials and Russian aviation veterans said the hectic schedules of Bout planes provided enough information to detect likely patterns. The aircraft often flew at night, arriving in Sharjah and then flying out again under cover of darkness. The Antonovs would land briefly in Sharjah in the early morning hours for refueling and maintenance stops that Sergei Mankhayev described as a "so-called technical stopover" before heading for Afghanistan. Confiding an insider's view of an arms transporter's typical arrangements, Mankhayev said that "an airport station manager in Sharjah would of course come on board for inspection but all he would do is look at the papers, which would state that the cargo is TVs and spare parts. And he would leave without poking into it." Bout's planes had made similar stopovers during his early 1990s' arms shipments to the Rabbani government, Mankhayev said. "During the daytime, you could not see Ariana Antonovs landing in Sharjah. I never saw them then. They did it quietly, during the night.[48]

Russian air veterans theorized that in the case of Ariana planes, military cargo shipments were likely either transferred from the holds of other planes transiting in Sharjah, or from warehouses where arms had been stored from other flights or even from incoming deliveries dropped off by dhows plying the Persian Gulf. During a tour of Ariana's warehouse at the Sharjah airport in 1997, the former Ariana executive saw several massive military aircraft engines waiting for airlift to Afghanistan.[49] The planes would return to Afghanistan, landing again in darkness after each three-hour flight to disgorge new shipments of arms and ammunition at airfields in Kabul, Bagram, and Kandahar. Sometimes the planes were routed to Islamabad or Karachi, where they were loaded with heavy Pakistani matériel before returning to the Afghan airfields.

An Afghan air force brigadier who served for a brief period with the Taliban's air force was often among the military officials who waited for the weapons flights to arrive at the airport in Kabul. He sometimes supervised crews of soldiers hefting the familiar green crates. The official, who was later sacked by the Taliban during one of their purges, watched night after night as military crews removed crates of Kalashnikovs and aerial bombs, BM-12 and BM-40 heavy artillery pieces, and Russian-made Hurrigan (Hurricane) rocket batteries. "They were off-loaded in Kabul and then put on regular [An-32] military planes to go directly to Kandahar or to Konduz or Mazar, or wherever," the brigadier recalled in April 2002 during a tour of the Afghan air force's runways at the Kabul airport. The

Antonovs also made passenger runs into Pakistan, he said, returning two or three times a night to ferry squads of Arab, Afghan, and Pakistani jihad warriors to the front lines, where they were needed to reinforce combat operations against the Northern Alliance. The cargo planes carried as many as a thousand Taliban loyalists over the course of several hours, the brigadier recalled.

"Nighttime flights," the Afghan officer recalled tersely. "It was special aircraft and it was secret."[50]

CHAPTER 8

Black Charters

I n the summer of 1998, Jakkie Potgeiter, a security specialist with
SaferAfrica, a South African human rights group, began tracing a
batch of Air Cess flights from Pietersburg Gateway Airport to
Mauritius. Concerned that Bout's cargo airline was being used to
arm UNITA rebels in the southern Congo in their twenty-five-year
fight against Angolan forces, Potgeiter contacted Mauritian authorities, who informed him that some of the Air Cess flights were flying
on from Mauritius to Islamabad. Curious, he obtained flight
records from Pakistani aviation authorities for the Islamabad por-
tions of the flights.

Potgeiter was baffled by the Indian Ocean route taken by one
Air Cess plane, EL-RDK, an Antonov An-12, that had left Pietersburg on May 23. Oddly, the plane's tail number, he learned,
matched the registry of an old An-8 that had crashed years earlier.
Potgeiter grew even more suspicious when he discovered that the
Antonov had not landed as scheduled in Islamabad. He tried Air
Cess's South African handling agents, who refused to divulge more
about the plane's activities or what the Antonov listed on its cargo
manifests. "We couldn't find any records that the plane actually

landed there," Potgeiter recalled. "It seemed that it never showed up in Islamabad. Or if it did, they had no information showing that it had."

Finally, reaching out to his informal network of relief agency contacts in Central Asia to see what they could find out, Potgeiter stumbled onto one of Bout's arms routes into Afghanistan. A relief worker based in Kandahar relayed the news that the Air Cess Antonov had been spotted at the airport in the Taliban stronghold during the same period it had been scheduled to land in Islamabad. "The guy had no idea what it was unloading there," Potgeiter recalled in 2002. Unaware that Bout's planes were systematically helping the Taliban, Potgeiter filed the plane's diversion away as a curiosity, concentrating instead on Bout's arms pipelines in the Congo. "We were more interested in the Africa portion of the trip, so the Afghan landing didn't register as important to us at the time. After September 11 and all the talk about Bout working with the Taliban, it looked a lot more curious in retrospect, eh?"[1]

Potgeiter's early discovery about the Air Cess flight into Taliban territory was both a fluke and a portent. As early as 1998, the CIA's "thugs and guns" analysts had learned that Bout's ground crews in Sharjah were performing maintenance chores for Ariana airline planes flying into and out of Afghanistan. Michael Scheuer, the veteran CIA counterterrorism analyst who directed Alec Station, the Virginia-based unit that tracked bin Laden and al Qaeda, perceived the link as an ominous development that could aid al Qaeda's activities in Afghanistan. At the same time, the CIA was paying careful attention to a steady stream of intelligence reports that showed al Qaeda operatives moving furtively back and forth between the UAE and Afghanistan. Since Ariana was the primary transportation link between the two nations, the airline, Scheuer concluded, was being used as a "terrorist taxi service." If Bout's crews were involved in maintaining Ariana planes and loading cargo, Scheuer surmised, they were part of a clandestine system that aided in the movements of al Qaeda terrorists. "We'd see al Qaeda operatives in the emirates and then we'd see them later in Afghanistan," Scheuer recalled. "They were getting into Afghanistan either through Karachi, in Pakistan, or through the emirates. And when they were coming through the emirates, it was almost always through Ariana flights. Since

Bout's operation was working with Ariana, they were part of the same set of concerns."[2]

The movement of Taliban and Arab militants on Ariana was aided by a fraudulent document mill that had been set up by Taliban officials in Ariana's Kabul headquarters. Mullahs who needed quick passage to Sharjah were often handed false identification labeling them as Ariana employees. Flights that normally carried crews of five or six suddenly doubled or tripled in size, large enough at times to staff a 757 jet. "We would have planes going out with twenty mechanics on board," the senior Ariana executive said. "Do you think all those people were mechanics?" One Ariana flight from Kabul that arrived in Sharjah on March, 31, 2000, carried a "crew" of thirty-three. An outbound flight to Kabul the same day left with fourteen Ariana "staff" aboard, including pilot Captain Mohammed Wardak, a Taliban air force officer whose real identity lay hidden in Afghan aviation files. "The Taliban would always have lots of their own people on the planes and they always had Ariana cards," recalled former Ariana flight engineer Abdul Shakur Arefee. The engineer was unnerved to see mullahs sometimes carrying the same identification he did. "Sometimes they were soldiers. Sometimes there were Arabs, I guess bin Laden's people. They would come off the planes with heavy bags and nobody would dare ask them anything."[3]

At the time, American intelligence officials were unaware of the Taliban's widespread use of forged Ariana identification to provide easy passage. But in January 2003, U.S. troops captured a Taliban official, Janat Gul, who admitted that he had served as Ariana's president in the year before the September 11 attacks. Although Ariana's foreign flights had already shut down during his tenure because of the UN embargo, Gul was accused by U.S. officials of running the airline as a Taliban fiefdom. Gul, who also used the name Hamiedullah, was transferred to the U.S. detainment camp at the Guantánamo Bay Naval Base in Cuba, where he appeared on December 28, 2004, before an American military tribunal. During the hearing, Gul admitted to an unnamed U.S. Marine colonel overseeing his case that "there was a different facility for the Taliban themselves, other than where Ariana airline was serving the civilians. The Taliban had their facilities and there were gates and nobody else could go in there." Gul also testified that the airline "acquired help from aviation agencies to help us carry passengers." The Marine colonel cited evidence that Ariana had been controlled by the Taliban and used by the mullahs to transport their members and jihadists fighting the Northern Alliance. The colonel also said that "an active al Qaeda member and licensed pilot brought in other al Qaeda members to work for Ariana airline." Gul denied the charges, but he remains in U.S. custody at Guantánamo.[4]

American officials also grew alarmed in the late 1990s by the flight patterns of Bout's own planes into and out of Kandahar. The CIA's Afghan informants reported that shipments of light weapons and ammunition were being off-loaded from Bout-owned cargo planes on the ground at Kandahar's airport. "Our human intelligence said it was mostly small arms and ammunition, going to Kandahar and occasionally to Kabul," Scheuer recalled. Bout's flights into Kandahar brought arms and supplies directly into the heart of the militants' stronghold. The airport had long been the economic nerve center for the Taliban movement, and with the expansion of bin Laden's terror training camps at nearby Tarnak Farms in the late 1990s, the Kandahar airport became al Qaeda's logistics lifeline as well.

One former Ariana pilot who flew frequently into Kandahar said the facility constantly swarmed with Arabs—a sight Bout's pilots and crews could not have missed. "I would see Arabs with sat[ellite] phones walking around the terminal, in touch with Taliban officials at the highest levels," the Ariana pilot recalled. Mullahs and their al Qaeda contacts sometimes spread rugs out on the terminal floor for impromptu meetings. After one flight into Kandahar, the senior Ariana executive was stunned to see the reclusive Mullah Omar huddled on a rug with a rebel leader from Tajikistan, surrounded by their aides. "There they were, cross-legged on their mats, chattering into cell phones," the executive recalled. A Talib government official explained to him later that the supreme leader "likes to meet like this."[5]

Even bin Laden had reportedly flown on Ariana on his early travels in Afghanistan. After he was expelled in May 1995 by Sudanese officials under pressure from Saudi Arabia and the United States, the al Qaeda leader and nearly a hundred of his relatives and most trusted fighters flew into Afghanistan on a chartered plane. There was also a second flight from Sudan, also filled with al Qaeda loyalists. Later reports suggested the first plane that ferried bin Laden was a private charter; others suggested it was an Ariana plane. In one intriguing account, bin Laden's former bodyguard Nasir al-Bahari told the *al-Quds al-Arabi* newspaper that the flight that carried bin Laden was a Tupolev piloted by a Russian—an account also reported by FBI officials.[6]

Scheuer and some American counternarcotics officials were also intrigued by a curious dovetailing between the flight patterns of Bout's planes and the Afghan hunting activities of Persian Gulf royals. The pace of flights by Bout network freighters into Kandahar would suddenly pick up in February and March—the same period when emirati and Saudi princes were flying into Afghanistan on their private jets to join Taliban officials in the annual hunt of houbara bustards. In early autumn, the same flight patterns between Bout planes and Persian Gulf jets would twin again in Tanzania, where bustards migrated by the thousands before the hard Afghan winter set in. Officials at the CIA's counternarcotics center suspected that some of the Persian Gulf royals were using the hunting flights as cover to export Afghan heroin. And the presence of Bout planes enlarged the circle of suspicion. "They were very interested on the counternarcotics side about the patterns between Bout's flights and bustard-hunting season," Scheuer recalled.

British intelligence officials on the ground in the UAE and Pakistan had also relayed their own suspicions that Bout's planes were ferrying Afghan narcotics. "The British believed that a lot of their street crime was linked to Afghan heroin and they felt it was a major source of his income," Scheuer said. At one point the British broached a plan to approach UAE officials for permission to send in an undercover team of agents to search for evidence of Afghan heroin on one of Bout's planes. "They wanted to swab his planes for drugs," a U.S. official recalled. "They were confident if they were able to do a close microbiological inspection, they would find clear evidence of drug trafficking, presumably heroin." But the British never developed enough evidence to make the approach viable, and support for the scheme faded.[7]

Afghanistan's opium fields had been a steady source of Western

Europe's heroin supply throughout the 1990s, both during the Rabbani regime and during the ascension of the Taliban. Soon after the mullahs took power, U.S. diplomats and drug enforcement teams working in Pakistan learned that Taliban officials were being paid lucrative tithes from local drug lords to provide guards in the poppy fields and safe passage for drug rings as they transferred heroin shipments out of the country. "The Talibs were getting paid for safe passage of narcotics traffickers from Afghanistan into Pakistan and also for guarding the dope," recalled Jonathan Winer, then deputy assistant secretary of state for international law enforcement. Between 1998 and 1999, Afghan opium production doubled to forty-six hundred tons, accounting for more than 72 percent of the world's heroin trade.[8] Julie Sirrs, a Defense Intelligence Agency analyst who made four trips into Northern Alliance–held territory in Afghanistan between 1997 and 2000, heard frequent accounts during her travels that Ariana "planes would leave with opium and its derivatives. They used both cargo and passenger flights. The Taliban didn't make a differentiation."

Along with their suspicions of heroin trafficking, Scheuer and his CIA team also worried that Bout's deep connections inside the Russian government and military—and his alleged links to Russian organized crime—made him eminently capable of secretly flying contraband nuclear material into Afghanistan. "We paid particular attention to the WMD issue because of Bout's connections inside the Soviet military," Scheuer said. Counterterror officials knew that bin Laden's al Qaeda lieutenants had already tried and failed in the early 1990s to buy nuclear materials in Sudan, and they were anxious about the Eastern bloc's loose regulation of nuclear weapons and radioactive substances. The sudden appearance of Russian cargo planes deep in Taliban-controlled Afghanistan inevitably set off alarm bells.

The CIA never received credible reports of WMD material shipped on Bout planes. But intelligence officials briefly fixated on allegations from a senior Afghan official that the Ariana airline had moved shipments of chemical poison for al Qaeda. Citing Northern Alliance and American intelligence reports, Dr. Ravan Farhadi, then the Afghan permanent representative to the United Nations, said that cyanide, ricin, and other toxic substances were flown on clandestine cargo runs from Sharjah to Kandahar. Farhadi, who is the Rabbani government's UN ambassador and continued in that role through the Taliban era and the Karzai national unity government, told the *Los Angeles Times* in December 2001 that "many of these poison chemicals were bought from companies in Germany, Czechoslovakia and the Ukraine." The deliveries, Farhadi said, "were for bin Laden and his people." The diplomat insisted that U.S. intelligence officials were aware of the shipments, but CIA and military intelligence officials were unable to verify his claim.[9]

While intelligence reports on the Bout network's dealings with the Taliban continued to filter in through the end of 1998, the flurry of official interest in his activities quickly faded. Scheuer said he raised concerns about the Bout flights with several National Security Council officials but got nowhere. "I never got a sense that he was important," Scheuer recalled. "He was part of the problem we had with the terrorist infrastructure in Afghanistan, but there were so many parts we were dealing with." U.S. officials were already preoccupied with bin Laden, his al Qaeda organization, and their Taliban protectors, and "no one was going to fall on their sword to get Viktor Bout."

Scheuer and Richard Clarke had feuded repeatedly over counterterrorism policy and decision making during the late 1990s, and their acrid relationship has not eased over time. Clarke has not spoken publicly about his involvement in the U.S. effort to scuttle the Bout network, but former colleagues insist he would have moved forcefully if there had been ample intelligence in 1997 and 1998 showing the extent of Bout's dealings with Islamic militants. "If we had known then that Bout was working with the Taliban, it would have gone right up the flagpole," said Jonathan Winer. "Dick Clarke would have ginned that up in his terrorist working group. We would have looked hard at using a designation under IEEPA [International Emergency Economic Powers Act] to freeze Bout's assets. If we had facts showing him working with al Qaeda, definitely—the Taliban, probably."

The team of U.S. officials that began targeting the Bout organization in early 2000 was aware of the sparse reports about its flights into Afghanistan, but Bout was considered primarily in his "African context," Lee Wolosky recalled. "There was a lot of activity but it required people to connect the dots." Soon after he was given the Bout file, Wolosky had a "gut feeling" that Bout's operation had some sort of dalliance with militants in Afghanistan. "There were red flags—doing aviation work out of the emirates, flying into Kandahar, flights through Islamabad, flights to certain African areas. This was a logistics network that was linking up with people in caves who had powerful, dangerous ideas." But strong suspicions were not enough to trigger action.

When Ariana Afghan Airways was brought up in mid-1999 at NSC and State planning meetings as a possible target for a flight ban as part of a stiff series of sanctions against the Taliban, Bout's clandestine relationship with the airline was not raised. "His name didn't come up," recalled Thomas Pickering, State's undersecretary for political affairs, who was overseeing the planning sessions.

Instead, senior Clinton administration officials concentrated on shutting down Ariana. The tipping point had been al Qaeda's devastating embassy bombing operation in East Africa. Al Qaeda cells in Kenya and Tanzania had plotted for five years and obtained bin Laden's personal approval, laying low until August 7, 1998. In a coordinated strike, the two bombing teams set off powerful truck-mounted explosions in Nairobi and Dar es Salaam, killing 220 people and wounding more than 4,000. The Clinton administration responded with a barrage of seventy cruise missiles on bin Laden's terror camps in Afghanistan and a purported chemical agent factory in Sudan. The same day as the cruise missile strikes, NSC and State Department officials began high-level discussions to impose a quarantine on the Taliban regime aimed at forcing the mullahs to turn over bin Laden and his terror fighters.

There was already a trove of actionable intelligence showing Ariana's use as a terror conduit by al Qaeda, and Taliban officials clearly controlled the airline's operations. "One airline was servicing Afghanistan at the time and that was Ariana," recalled Steven Simon, then one of Clarke's chief counterterror deputies and the senior director for transnational threats at the NSC. "It gave them the flexibility they needed [to deliver arms and carry militant operatives]."[10] Despite the easy movement of Ariana planes from Sharjah, federal emirate officials had begun quietly cooperating with

U.S. intelligence, tipping them off to the travels of terror operatives. "We would give them names on a watch list and they would tell us who was moving through the emirates," Sirrs said. During one excursion into Northern Alliance territory, Sirrs also heard first-hand accounts of al Qaeda's use of Ariana flights. A captured Yemeni who had joined bin Laden's jihad fighters in 1997 told of "being flown from Yemen to Afghanistan and then flying back home [through Sharjah] on an Ariana jet. That was an easy way for bin Laden's fighters to get into Afghanistan."[11]

Although Clarke and other NSC officials were unaware at the time how thoroughly Taliban officials manipulated Ariana to move weapons and terror operatives, they knew enough to press for a tough policy initiative aimed at designating the Taliban regime as a state sponsor of terrorism. Under the plan, the United States would use the threat of embargoes and an international flight ban against Ariana as tools to pressure the Taliban regime to hand over bin Laden. At first the State Department was divided over whether to pursue that aggressive approach or try a new diplomatic effort to end the still-simmering Afghan civil war and persuade the Talibs to accept a national unity government. But by the summer of 1999, the Pickering-led effort to gin up sanctions had begun making headway in the UN Security Council for an arms and financial embargo against the Taliban.[12] The idea won swift support from a surprising ally: Russia. "The Russians were out front because of their problems with Chechnya," said Karl "Rick" Inderfurth, then assistant secretary of state for South Asian affairs. Inderfurth met several times with Russian officials and found them eager to cooperate. "They saw bin Laden as contributing to their problems back home. The attacks we suffered in Africa worried them as well."

Even before the Security Council had a chance to take up the proposed embargo, the United States moved unilaterally against Ariana. On July 6, 1999, President Clinton signed Executive Order 13129, imposing a ban on economic transactions between Americans and the Taliban government. On August 10, the United States froze $500,000 in Ariana assets in American banks after Treasury agents scoured the airline's accounts. Ariana, an American official said tartly, "has supported, or is linked to, the bin Laden network."

The mullahs shrugged. Approached by a Reuters correspondent

in Dubai, Farid Ahmed sneered at the American pressure tactic. "This is nothing for the airline—$500,000 is nothing," he said. Ariana's five weekly flights between Kabul and Sharjah were running unaffected, he boasted. "Up to now there have been no changes. All operations are normal." And he insisted that Ariana had no stake in his government's dismal relations with the West. "This is an airline. This is not in any politics. This is an airline working for civilian people."[13]

There was more punishment in the works. Aided by the Russian delegation, the U.S. lobbying effort at the United Nations met with no resistance. On October 15, the Security Council unanimously voted for a freeze on Taliban assets, a sweeping arms embargo, and a ban on all international flights operated by the Taliban leadership— a measure that effectively shut down all of Ariana's international flights and allowed only humanitarian routes. Sergei Lavrov, Russia's ambassador to the United Nations, condemned the mullahs for allowing the "sheltering and training of terrorists and the planning of terrorist acts" and demanded that they "turn over Usama bin Laden to the appropriate authorities."[14] The United Nations also issued a list with fifty-nine suspect Ariana and Taliban air force aircraft that were subject to the ban. At least three of the planes on the list were Antonovs that had been sold to the Talibs by Bout-orbit firms in Sharjah.[15] But like the earlier sanctions in Africa, the UN embargo was porous. It made no mention of the Air Cess charters that still slipped into Kandahar.[16]

By October 2000, after urgent pleadings from Taliban officials for medical and humanitarian supplies, UN officials relented and allowed a single airline to fly between Sharjah and Kandahar for humanitarian supplies and to Jiddah for the annual hajj pilgrimage. The choice pleased the Talibs: Sheikh Abdullah's Flying Dolphin. "I went to them [UN officials] and said, 'Gentlemen, I want to fly,'" the sheikh recalled. "It was not a major business. The planes were about half-full, maybe 50–60 people in a big 727."[17] The flights were supposedly restricted to humanitarian aid cargo, relief workers, and Afghans who were being deported from the UAE. Taliban officials touted Flying Dolphin on their official Web site, urging travelers to Afghanistan to use the new service. When U.S. and UN counterterrorism learned that a company linked to the Bout orbit was flying with official sanction into Afghanistan, they immediately grew suspicious, concerned that Flying Dolphin's cargo might be carrying contraband and militant passengers. "Flying Dolphin was suspected of arms shipments," a former U.S. official said flatly. "The Brits were convinced of that. They'd come over and brief us about Dolphin's movements."[18]

In December 2000, two months after Flying Dolphin's flights began, the United Nations tightened the noose. All nonhumanitarian flights into and out of Afghanistan were banned, and all Ariana international offices were ordered shut down. In January 2001 the Security Council ordered Flying Dolphin to halt its Afghan service. The sheikh fumed. "These arms flights did not happen," he insisted, adding, "Any time they wanted to inspect, they could have come. But they never looked." [19]

Even after the last scheduled Flying Dolphin plane flew, on January 21, reports persisted that "black charters" still penetrated into Afghanistan. A panel of UN experts led by British military veteran Michael Chandler warned in May 2001 that "no means currently exists for observing and verifying illegal flights in and out of Taliban-controlled Afghanistan, which is one possible way by which arms, terrorists and cash are moving in contravention of the embargoes." Afghanistan's harsh mountainous terrain made it "almost impossible," the experts added, for Iranian air traffic controllers "to spot aircraft on their radars, when they are flown low by experienced and able pilots." [20]

With all air traffic into Afghanistan effectively grounded, Farid Ahmed lowered his profile in Dubai. When the American invasion of Afghanistan started in November 2001, he went underground. Ariana officials suspected that Ahmed had gained access to a company vault in Sharjah where Afghan currency printed by the Russian government had been stored. As the Taliban's top man in the emirates, Farid also controlled an Afghan account that contained $400,000 in International Air Transport Association fees paid to Afghanistan by other countries for flyovers. Officials of the Afghan coalition government that replaced the Taliban believe that some of the money had been used by the Taliban to buy the Bout network Antonovs.[21]

Ahmed briefly surfaced in April 2002. He answered a call to his

Dubai cell phone, telling a *Los Angeles Times* interviewer: "I am not Taliban." Ahmed conceded that "Russian companies helped us, yes, but only in fixing the planes." He added that "I have nothing to do with guns." He then turned over the phone to a companion, who insisted, in quick succession before hanging up, that Ahmed was unavailable, away in Sharjah, living in Kabul, and, finally, unknown to him altogether. Ahmed's current whereabouts are unknown.[22]

Viktor Bout and his brother Sergei remained based in Sharjah, where their planes continued to ply a tidy business, even after the September 11 attacks. Jakkie Potgeiter tracked Air Cess planes flying into the DRC that fall, carrying ammunition to Jean-Pierre Bemba's rebels and departing with precious metals and timber from the airfield in Bunia. The Bouts also were laying the groundwork to replace Air Cess with a new company, Air Bas, which had a Texas branch incorporated by Richard Chichakli.[23]

By the time al Qaeda unleashed its air attacks on New York and Washington, D.C., on September 11, 2001, the cargo planes that Taliban officials had acquired from Victor Bout had long been rendered useless. Spare parts were hard to find after the embargo. Aviation fuel supplies dwindled. Afghan airports were reduced to ghostly, open-air warehouses where once-busy Antonovs sat rusting beside vacant runways. When American B-52s and fighter jets seized control of Afghanistan's air corridors two months later, the old Antonovs lay prone, stationary targets for the devastating bomb lines that pinwheeled down. The thunderous explosions that decimated Taliban airfields from Herat to Kandahar left the Russian planes in flaming, metal shreds.[24] The charred hulks lay exposed in the sun for months afterward, the tattered remnants of the secret fleet that Viktor Bout assembled for the Taliban.

CHAPTER 9

Gunships and Titanium

I brahim Bah was furious. He was accustomed to being whisked in to see presidents and ministers at a moment's notice. Instead, on a sweltering evening in November 1999, he sat in his black Toyota jeep, stalled at a roadblock on the outskirts of the crumbling city of Monrovia. The car was blocked by a group of thugs armed with AK-47s. Even a special driver's pass signed by the president himself did not help. "Mr. Vic," a personal guest of Liberian president Charles Taylor, had not informed them that anyone was coming to his residence—and without Mr. Vic's permission, the goons said, shrugging, no one was allowed through.

Bah was accompanied by a group of senior commanders of the Revolutionary United Front (RUF), the violent rebel group that operated in neighboring Sierra Leone. The RUF leaders knew little of the world beyond their bush battle zones. But accustomed to getting what they wanted by threatening execution or mutilation, they, too, squirmed at being told to wait, unhappy at being on the business end of the guards' assault rifles.

The head of the RUF delegation who sat with Bah was General Sam "Mosquito" Bockarie, a former hairdresser who had been credited with turning the RUF from an ineffective, ragtag rebel group into a disciplined and effective force. His troops believed he was endowed with magical powers that made him bulletproof during combat. Bockarie was an enthusiastic proponent of the RUF tactic of hacking off the arms and legs of civilians. He had personally overseen several amputations. Reed-thin and easily excitable, Bockarie was sometimes hard to understand, speaking a rapid-fire, British-accented mixture of English and Krio, the regional dialect spoken among different ethnic groups in the bush. A fine-featured man with a thin, scraggly beard, Bockarie was a publicity hound who regularly used his satellite telephone to call the BBC's *Focus on Africa* program to give long and unsolicited interviews and share his thoughts on the war. The program was required listening across the continent as one of the few that dealt exclusively with African news, and Bockarie's appearances spread his reputation far beyond the RUF.

Finally, Cindor Reeves, Bah's aide-de-camp and Charles Taylor's former brother-in-law, reached Bout's chief of security by phone from the car. The guards allowed them through, but more indignation awaited inside the roadblock. Mr. Vic's personal Russian bodyguards, dressed in black and wearing earpieces, insisted on frisking Bah and his companions before they could enter Villa 31—Viktor Bout's Liberian home.

Bout kept the group waiting in his living room for almost an hour before he descended from the second floor. He offhandedly apologized to Bah and Bockarie and their entourage. The forced wait was the final act of a Bout power play. Bout himself blithely barged in on presidents and ministers without waiting for permission. But he often kept other VIPs waiting, demonstrating that in the pecking order of the African imperial court, he was too important and well protected for anyone to storm out or threaten him. Even alpha males such as Bah and Bockarie had to wait until Mr. Vic was ready.

Bah alluded tartly to his poor treatment, but Bout dismissed the complaints with a tight smile. There were many people, he told Bah, who wanted to kill him. This put his Russian security men in a perpetually bad mood, Bout added, laughing. The trouble at the roadblock, he said offhandedly, was the fault of his Liberian security detail, a simple lack of communication. Then Bout changed the subject. He had a proposition, he told his visitors, that would make them all rich.[1]

Bout had reached the height of his power and influence in Africa at the time of the meeting. After several years of building from the ground in Liberia, he was operating on a scale grander than anything he had tried before. His venture into South Africa had failed, but it had not adversely affected his business in the rest of Africa. Many of the planes in his Sharjah-based air fleet were now registered in Liberia, a result of well-placed friends running the registry. Other aircraft had been tied to pliant registries in Swaziland, the Central African Republic, and Equatorial Guinea. There were enough wars and legitimate deliveries to keep the money flowing. His affairs in Afghanistan were booming, too, as both the Taliban and the Northern Alliance continued their arms buying sprees. His air cargo fleet was so large—now more than sixty planes—that Bout could afford to spin off a small flotilla to the Talibs. He was constantly on the move, looking for new opportunities.

Although his main African base was now Liberia, Bout still amassed new opportunities farther east and south, in Uganda and Rwanda. Both nations were enmeshed in the intractable fighting in the DRC. After initially helping to install Laurent Kabila as the successor to Mobutu, the two nations turned on the hapless rebel-turned-president and sent troops to occupy large swaths of territory where they began extracting caches of diamonds, timber, and other resources to finance their military occupations.

Ignored by the outside world, the armies gouged rudimentary airstrips out of the bush. Airlift capacity was essential both to keep the troops supplied far from their home bases and to fly out the natural resources being plundered. The most prized resource was coltan, a rare mineral suddenly valuable for its use in the manufacture of cell phones, computers, electronic goods, and even the U.S. stealth bomber. The boom in coltan would later go bust, but the mineral was in great demand at the time, but only within reach of the rugged cargo planes operated by the Bout network.

A UN investigation found that about 70 percent of the coltan exported from the DRC was mined by the Rwandan army near Kigali and Cyangugu and that "Rwandan military aircraft, Viktor Bout's aircraft and small airline companies were used in the evacuation of the coltan."[2] Shortly after leaving South Africa, Bout bought a large compound in Kigali, the capital of Rwanda. Soon there were so many Russian pilots coming and going from the large, heavily guarded house with heavy iron gates that locals referred to the place as "the Kremlin."[3]

In Uganda, too, Bout's business was thriving, and he occupied another large house there. A UN investigation labeled his aircraft and flights in Uganda as part of a "transnational criminal group." In early 1998 Bout bought a dormant Ugandan airline company called Okapi Air, a move that gave him the right to use Okapi's landing licenses and routes across the continent. He quickly changed the airline's name to Odessa and was again flying virtually undetected. Entebbe's airport became one of his chief hubs for refueling and transshipping weapons to his other African customers. Bout's aircraft also flew as Planet Air, a company that frequently filed flight plans for Bout's aircraft as its own. Planet Air was owned by the wife of a senior Ugandan military official, ensuring that Bout's activities were not detected.[4]

Air crews would regularly drop off weapons in the DRC, then fly east, to Lake Tanganyika, one of the Great Rift Valley Lakes bordering the DRC and Tanzania.[5] There his crews would load their aircraft with fresh fish and fly the cargo to Europe for a handsome profit. UNITA rebels in Angola kept Bout's planes flying regularly between Burgas, the center of Bulgarian weapons production, and Lomé, Togo, for transshipment to the rebels, or else straight into Savimbi's remote strongholds. In return, Bout reaped packages of diamonds worth millions of dollars. Savimbi had a safe in his office with seven shelves in it, mostly filled with the precious stones. When his weapons were delivered, he would open the safe and take out a handful of diamonds, place them on a scale, and pay the merchant by weight of the stones. A few paces away, two Lebanese working for Savimbi would offer to buy the diamonds for cash.

"You would get a bag of stones and you can sell them for dollars, or you can take them with you," said Gary Busch, who was an acquaintance and competitor of Bout in Africa. "That is how you got paid, and Viktor Bout flew many flights for Savimbi."

Among all the deals that Bout cinched in Africa in the 1990s, none loomed as outlandish as the rapacious proposal that Bout unveiled to Ibrahim Bah and Mosquito Bockarie at his Monrovia villa in November 1999.

Bout's proposition was simple and astonishing: he would supply the RUF with badly needed weapons and ammunition at no cost if the rebels used the arms for a specific military mission that would benefit the Russian and his partners. Bout wanted the rebels to launch an attack across the border into southwestern Sierra Leone and take over a group of abandoned mines.

It was a drastic new step for Bout, a crossing of a moral Rubicon that augured ambitions far beyond weapons deals. He was urging direct military action that would bring him an economic windfall, offering his military wares as compensation for the seizure of foreign territory. As with his willingness to supply the Taliban two years earlier, his effort to launch a strike into Sierra Leone marked another defining passage in his amoral business dealings and his grandiose dreams.

The Sierra Leone mines produced rutile, a titanium ore used in paint pigments and welding rods. It is relatively rare, but easy to extract, making it a lucrative commodity. In the 1980s the owners of the mines, the Sierra Rutile Company, had been the largest U.S. investment in West Africa outside of the petroleum industry. The mineral ore generated half of Sierra Leone's foreign export earnings and often outpaced diamond profits.[6]

The mines were about eighty-five miles southeast of Freetown, outside an area where the RUF normally operated. The RUF had attacked the facilities in 1995, then withdrew. But the attack had led the company to evacuate its employees and suspend operations. Now Bout saw an opportunity to restart the vacant mines and reap a healthy profit. He told Bah that he had investors lined up from Russia. But production could not start unless the RUF took over the mines and provided the necessary security afterward.

Bout was confident he could get what he wanted from both Bah and Bockarie. Since at least 1995 Taylor had been reluctant to let Bout deal directly with the RUF, preferring to control all the deals himself. Bout had repeatedly raised the issue of the rutile mines with Taylor, only to be told that patience was needed. Finally, Bout had convinced Taylor to allow him to make his proposal directly to the RUF leadership.

The day before meeting Bout, Bah had arranged for his aide Cindor Reeves to fly by helicopter to the border town of Foya, a RUF stronghold near the Liberian border. There he picked up Bockarie and the others. The RUF delegation then visited Taylor at his White Flower residence on the outskirts of Monrovia. Taylor told Bockarie, whom he treated as a son, to go ahead with whatever Bout asked. His reasoning was that the deal would make them rich, allowing them to acquire all the weapons they needed to finally end the lingering military stalemate and United Nations–imposed cease-fire in Sierra Leone.

Taylor confided that the move would speed his ultimate goal of creating "Greater Liberia," a stretch of real estate that encompassed the diamond mines of eastern Sierra Leone and bauxite reserves in southern Guinea. Bout drove a hard bargain and his lack of respect was bothersome, Taylor told Bockarie, but the payoff was huge.

But when Bockarie and Bah sat down with Bout, they cautioned that the RUF did not have enough troops or weapons to both penetrate deeply into Sierra Leona and then hold the mines. UN peacekeepers had begun to deploy in Sierra Leone to enforce a tenuous cease-fire between the RUF and the government, a presence that made large-scale military activities more hazardous.

Bout asked Bockarie how long it would take the RUF to take over the mines if he had *all* the weapons he needed. If that were the case, Bockarie replied, they could carry out the mission in three to four weeks.

Bout seemed pleased. He was anxious to get started as soon as possible. He asked for a list of the matériel needed and, as a parting gesture of goodwill, gave $10,000 for the "boys," as the RUF troops were universally known. Within a few weeks, several Bout-supplied helicopters landed in RUF territory and unloaded the first down payments on the deal. Not only did Bout arrange weapons, he also supplied rice, shoes, uniforms, and communications equipment.[7]

Bout could not have done what he did in Africa without reaching into the highest echelons of the continent's governments and militaries. Access required relying on an international cast of fixers. Some of them were as nominally powerful as the heads of state they courted, bullied, enriched, and fleeced. But Bout remained at the top of the pyramid of African influence because he had access to guns and the ability to deliver them. Bout may have needed fixers to get to the Big Men, but both the fixers and the Big Men needed him even more.

Bout first met Ibrahim Bah, perhaps West Africa's most accomplished fixer, in Burkina Faso in the early 1990s. Bah had been a star alumnus of Muammar Gaddafi's terror training camps and came to the fore in Jonas Savimbi's rebel structure. Those origins provided Bah with a long and checkered career in combat and deal-making.[8]

Bah, who also used the alias Balde, was a Senegalese whose birth name was Bocande. Born in 1957, Bah fought in the Casamance rebellion in Senegal when he was in his early twenties, then made his way to Libya for special forces training. A handsome, soft-spoken man with a deeply cleft chin and small ears, Bah had studied Islamic theology in Egypt, and in the mid-1980s joined the mujahideen in Afghanistan for almost three years. He returned to Libya in 1985, then fought for two years with Hezbollah in Lebanon before returning to Libya to help Gaddafi train the future leaders of West Africa's failed revolutions. The RUF of Sierra Leone gave Bah the rank of general, and he led an RUF column on its first combat operation. He also became one of the few people Charles Taylor trusted.

Bah had access to clients Bout needed. Bah retained close ties to Blaise Compaore, the president of Burkina Faso, and a host of other government leaders on the continent. "I have traveled with presidents, but I have never seen someone treated with the respect and fear that Bah was treated with," said a business associate who traveled with Bah to several West African capitals in the late 1990s. "He could get an interview with any president or minister just by picking up the telephone. He would fly into a capital city, go straight to the palace, and walk right in."

Intelligence reports listed Bah as a native of Burkina Faso, Niger, and elsewhere. Because of his vast experience in the world outside of West Africa and his gift for languages (he speaks French, Arabic, English, and several African languages), he often handled diamond sales for both Taylor and the RUF. Bah also had one of the few government-granted diamond licenses in Liberia, allowing him to sell gems on his own. By late 2000 he had brokered a deal with al Qaeda operatives to sell them diamonds from RUF-controlled territories. Those sales ended abruptly on September 10, 2001. Like Bout, Bah operated out of the public eye and had a deep aversion to having his picture taken. When the *Washington Post* ran Bah's picture on its front page on November 2, 2001, linking him to al Qaeda diamond sales, Bah was more upset about the photo than about the allegations.[9]

Bah also played several different sides of the complex game of survival in West Africa. He had ties to the U.S. intelligence community and provided intelligence reporting for the Special Court for Sierra Leone, a United Nations–backed court set up to try Taylor and others for crimes against humanity.[10] And Bah's relationship with Bout, which would later turn into a partnership, would pay off handsomely.

Bout also worked with Sanjivan Ruprah, another of Africa's well-connected fixers. The two men met in Burkina Faso, where Ruprah, a Kenyan British citizen, was an operator with ties to a variety of mercenary groups politely known as private military companies (PMCs). Ruprah also had a host of mining interests, particularly in the DRC, and dabbled in civil aviation. He was married to the sister of one of the leaders of a Rwandan-backed rebel group in the DRC, a relationship that gave him, and later Bout, access to that market. Ruprah was also an acquaintance of both Bah and Taylor, and an accomplished tennis player who loved to read John Grisham novels and Deepak Chopra self-help books.[11]

Described as an "arms broker" in a UN report, Ruprah managed to work several sides of African conflicts for profit. He directed the Kenyan office of Branch Energy, a company that had, in the early 1990s, negotiated to obtain control of diamond mining rights in Sierra Leone. According to a UN investigation, the company also introduced a private military company, Executive Outcomes (EO), to the Sierra Leone government in 1995.[12] EO was largely made up of white, former Special Forces troops from South Africa and Zimbabwe, and was a pioneer in offering soldiers for hire in African conflicts. The group often operated in mineral-rich areas and used subsidiary companies to take over the concessions that were used to pay for their services.[13]

Ruprah, like Bah, operated in the shadows of different networks that pumped diamonds and other commodities to Europe and the United States in exchange for weapons. After brokering deals with Branch Energy on behalf of anti-Taylor forces, he then worked with Taylor when the opportunity arose. His joint work with Bout was extensive, but Ruprah also separately hatched his own deals. In 2000 a UN investigation into the DRC found that Ruprah was involved in a massive counterfeiting operation to print new notes to finance diamond deals.[14]

Several of Bout's African associates say it was Ruprah who introduced Bout to Taylor in Burkina Faso in the early 1990s. Ruprah has given different times for his first meeting with Bout and insisted that he had no role in introducing Bout and Taylor.[15] Ruprah told the FBI that he first met the Russian in 1996, hiring Bout to fly diamond-mining equipment for him from South Africa to the DRC. He later changed his story, saying he met Bout in April or May 1998 in Johannesburg. Ruprah also said he "literally ran into Bout" in Entebbe, Uganda, in 1999 and saw him socially several times that year. But he also told the FBI that he had worked with Bout in 1996, 1997, and 1998 in Zaire and Rwanda. He described himself as a "business friend" rather than a partner of the Russian.[16] While Ruprah now staunchly denies having a close personal relationship with Bout, eyewitnesses in Liberia said he was constantly at Bout's villa when Bout was in town and occasionally spent the night there.

In addition to working together in Liberia, Bout and Ruprah had extensive contacts in the DRC, where Ruprah had mining interests. They jointly exploited and moved coltan and other minerals under the protection of Rwandan forces.[17] Ruprah said that Bout was reluctant at first to discuss his weapons deals, but soon came to talk about them openly. In his interview with the FBI, Ruprah rattled off the models and the prices of weapons ($195 per AK-47) that Bout supplied to Taylor. Over time, Ruprah also became a primary source of UN investigators, and spoke on the record to them about Bout's operations.

Ruprah was vital to Bout's operation for several reasons. Besides knowing his way through the political jungle of much of Africa, he was Bout's entrée into another circle of powerful economic brokers—the Lebanese community that runs a large swath of businesses across West and Central Africa. Members of this merchant community of several hundred thousand, which is largely Shi'ite Muslim, dominated the illicit diamond trade in Sierra Leone, Liberia, Angola, and the DRC. The Lebanese merchant class retained strong ties to Lebanon, and all sides of Lebanon's recent civil wars have been funded in part through the sale of the diamonds they moved.[18]

Almost as soon as he arrived in Monrovia in 1999, Ruprah was given an official commission that also made him valuable to Bout. Ruprah was made an official agent of the Liberian civil aviation registry, a government post.[19] It seems highly unlikely that he could have obtained such influence in a matter of weeks after arriving in Liberia for the first time and meeting Taylor just once, as Ruprah has claimed.[20] Taylor's Liberia was open for business, and just about anything, from protection to diplomatic passports and aircraft registrations, were up for sale.

Ruprah was also was given a Liberian diplomatic passport under the alias of Samir M. Nasr. And he was awarded with the title of deputy commissioner of maritime affairs, working under Benoni Urey, an Israeli Liberian who was a close Taylor crony. The maritime position gave Ruprah a central role in overseeing the Liberian International Shipping and Corporate Registry (LISCR), a Vienna, Virginia-based company that handled the flags of convenience registrations of ships from around the world. The Liberian registry is second in the world only to that of Panama in ship registrations. The company also handles the registration of some forty thousand offshore Liberian companies. Throughout Liberia's traumatic wars the registry, under different managers, kept generating a steady stream of some $20 million a year in government revenue, one of the few reliable sources of income the country depended on.[21]

Ruprah would not say directly how he came to be involved in the aviation registry. But in November 1999 he was authorized in writing to act as a "global civil aviation agent worldwide" on behalf of the Liberian Civil Aviation Regulatory Authority.[22] Ruprah said he got involved because "I was asked by an associate of Victor's to get involved in the Aviation registry of Liberia as both Victor and him wanted to restructure the same and they felt that there could be a financial gain from the same."[23]

That associate was Michael Harridine, a British citizen to whom Taylor had given control of Liberian aircraft registry in 1997, which was operating out of Kent, England.[24] Harridine also ran the air registry of Equatorial Guinea, another favorite place for Bout aircraft registration.[25] Taylor, Bout, and Harridine cast their net even wider in hopes of attracting aircraft to the Liberian registry. Another "registered agent" for the registry was Sheikh Abdullah bin Zayed al Saqr al Nahyan, the UAE royal whose air firms had joined Bout's companies in selling planes to the Taliban. The sheikh registered aircraft from two firms, Flying Dolphin and Santa Cruz Imperial, in Liberia. UN investigators found that the sheikh was "a business associate of Viktor Bout," and both of al Nahyan's air firms had also registered aircraft in Swaziland, where Bout's aircraft were also registered.[26]

Well positioned in Africa, Bout moved to expand his operations across the Atlantic Ocean. In late 1998 Bout branched his arms delivery operation into South America, aiding an entirely new terrorist group—the Revolutionary Armed Forces of Colombia (FARC). The former Marxist army was the oldest insurgency in the Western Hemisphere, but it had devolved into a violent criminal organization that thrived on its increasing involvement in the cocaine and heroin trades that had made Colombia infamous.

As the group's ideological drive withered at the end of the Cold War, the FARC's leaders embraced the dark side of capitalism's law of supply and demand—the drug trade—with a vengeance. By the late 1990s the FARC was collecting hundreds of millions of dollars a year for protecting the coca plantations and cocaine laboratories that were run by Colombia's drug cartels. Able to field a force of some seventeen thousand combatants, the FARC also raised millions of dollars a year through kidnappings and extortion. The guerrillas controlled few urban areas, but their supremacy was almost unchallenged in the thousands of square miles of Amazonian jungle in the southern and western sections of Colombia. The government seldom had a presence in the rural areas of the country, and the FARC protection of the coca fields that were planted under the jungle canopy offered peasants a chance to make a tidy living. The guerrillas watched over jungle laboratories that turned coca alkaloid to pure cocaine, and they patrolled the airstrips used by the sophisticated, high-speed aircraft that carried the white powder to addicts on several continents, from the United States to Russia.

Because of their criminal activities the FARC was routinely condemned by human rights groups and hoisted onto the U.S. State Department list of terrorist organizations. In the immediate years before al Qaeda surfaced with catastrophic results, the Clinton administration embarked on a multibillion-dollar program called "Plan Colombia" to combat drug barons and the FARC. With their huge cash reserves, the leaders of the FARC responded by shopping for weapons across the globe. By 1998 they were on a major spree to upgrade their arsenal.

It is not clear how the FARC's leaders found Bout's transportation network, but between December 1998 and April 1999 an Ilyushin Il-76 belonging to one of Bout's front companies flew at least four circuitous flights from Jordan to Peru, carrying some $78 million in weapons that appeared to be legitimately purchased by the Peruvian government.[27] The AK-47s were East German in origin, but they had been purchased by Jordan in the mid-1980s and kept in storage.

En route over the FARC-controlled jungle in the southwestern corner of Colombia, the Bout planes would dive to three thousand feet, dumping out cases of AK-47s. The crates were equipped with two main parachutes and two emergency parachutes to ensure a soft landing. The boxes were also equipped with GPS devices so they were easy for the guerrillas to locate in the dense jungle near the Peruvian border. All told, the flights dropped about ten thousand weapons to the rebels, enabling them to greatly enhance their military capabilities.[28]

"Suddenly the FARC has new AKs, courtesy of those airdrops," recalled State veteran diplomat Thomas Pickering. As the department's number two person at the time, Pickering was responsible for monitoring the situation in Colombia. "We traced them [the weapons] to East Germany. We wondered who was giving the FARC new weapons and suspected Bout. It was unbelievable."

The operation was audacious because the jungle drop zones were blanketed by United States–supplied radar. Yet the flights were never interdicted. Investigators in Peru alleged that after dropping the weapons, the planes were loaded with cocaine and flown back to Russia, where the narcotics were then shipped throughout Europe. The investigators eventually threw suspicion on Peru's police chief, Vladimiro Montesinos, for providing fake Peruvian EUCs to Jordan that were used to make the arms purchases. Montesinos was a longtime CIA asset, and for years he had successfully cultivated the image of a staunch antiguerrilla hard-liner. But as later investigations revealed, Montesinos was also one of the most successful con men on the continent, taking money from anyone who would pay for his protection. Only a fraction of the arms Montesinos bought were for the FARC. The rest appeared to have been diverted to his own security forces and other armed groups on the continent. Montesinos is currently serving thirty years in prison for a variety of drug and weapons trafficking charges.[29]

Even as his flights stretched from the jungles of Colombia to the crags of Afghanistan, Bout's primary focus remained Africa. Nowhere on the continent was his influence greater than in Liberia under the despotic rule of Charles Taylor.

Bout's villa in Monrovia was at his sole disposal during frequent week-long visits to Taylor to discuss weapons sales. Five elite guards of the Liberian Special Security Service and ten from the Antiterror Unit (ATU) manned the two roadblocks on the rutted road to the villa. Bout kept his own security forces in a separate villa, an almost unheard-of privilege. Bout's pilots were housed in the main buildings of a nearby run-down hotel that was owned by Gus Kouwenhoven, a Dutch national and Taylor confidant who would later be imprisoned in Holland as the first person convicted of breaking a UN arms embargo.

Taylor was the ideal partner for Bout. Bout had stayed close to Taylor as the warlord's fortunes waxed and waned, sometimes leaving the future dictator small gifts of several thousand dollars. When Taylor campaigned for Liberia's presidency in 1997, the relationship deepened. Taylor became the odds-on favorite because Liberians were terrified that if he were defeated, war would flare again. The mordant slogan that carried him to victory was "He killed my ma, he killed my pa—I'm going to vote for him." According to eyewitnesses, Bout traveled with Taylor to kick off his campaign in Nimba County.

Once in office, Taylor accorded Bout the highest possible accolade for a business partner—he dubbed Bout his "pepper bush," a colloquial expression meaning something dear to the heart that no one else could touch. "Taylor would say that Bout was the root of his pepper tree and that without the roots, the tree dies," recalled Lawson Plaque, who helped with Bout's security. Taylor told his guards that their job was to "keep the insects and parasites from around the pepper tree," Plaque said. That meant that even those close to Taylor, such as Bah, were not allowed past the security men, whose meager salaries were supplemented by monthly donations from Bout.

By January 1999 Bout's aircraft were running circuitous routes from the Balkans and East European countries into Monrovia, the Liberian capital. From there, the planes would fly on to Taylor's rebel clients in Sierra Leone, the RUF. One U.S. intelligence official reported that a Bout aircraft, in conjunction with planes from Skyair and Occidental Airlines—a partly Belgian-owned by United Kingdom–run charter company—was used "to ferry arms from Bratislava, the Slovak capital, via Liberia and Gambia to bush airstrips" for the RUF. The report added that "Victor BUT has usually leased his freighter aircraft to other operators so he could claim ignorance of such dealings."[30] Two months later, another consignment, of sixty-seven tons of weapons for the RUF from Ukraine, arrived via Burkina Faso.[31]

Taylor controlled access to Roberts International Airport, Liberia's only international airfield. The field's battle-scarred cluster of air traffic control buildings oversaw a fitful spate of regional flights each week. The main airport building had been burned to the ground during the civil war. But Roberts International had several advantages for Bout's planes. It was almost thirty miles from Monrovia, so it was far from the prying eyes of diplomats and others in the capital. More importantly, it had been built by U.S. forces in World War II to help ferry troops and supplies for the North African and Italian campaigns. Because it was built to handle heavy transport aircraft, it was ideal for Bout's Il-76s and other large air freighters. Taylor could keep prying eyes off Bout's operations, provide security, and make sure there were no repeats of unpleasant incidents like the raid on the Russian's home in South Africa.

Still, Taylor was uneasy with the minimal scrutiny Roberts International received. In 1999, Taylor took Bout to his private farm in Gbanga, an estate that was lit gaudily like a Christmas decoration all year long while neighboring peasants went powerless. Taylor showed Bout a partially finished airstrip and said he was hoping to finish its construction soon so he could switch Bout's landings to the more remote field. Hard beside Taylor's farm was the main training camp of Taylor's infamous Antiterrorism Unit.

Taylor paid either in diamonds, which Bout accepted without hesitation, or in cash or wire transfers. In turn, Bout slaked Taylor's insatiable appetite for weapons, night vision equipment, and other matériel. The sophisticated equipment was vital to ensuring the military viability of the RUF and the loyalty of Taylor's own troops. Taylor was so pleased with the supplies that he regularly offered Bout young women he had slept with. The meaning was not lost on the Taylor's Liberian aides—trifling with Bout was tantamount to offending the president himself.

By 1999, eager for a strategic advantage in firepower and mobility against his enemies, Taylor told his arms connections that he wanted combat helicopters. Worried about a looming invasion of the rebel troops from neighboring Guinea, Taylor ordered Sanjivan Ruprah to find gunships that could be delivered quickly. Ruprah contacted a group of Israeli arms merchants and bought two civilian helicopters that were not in violation of the arms embargo. But Taylor wanted the copters converted for combat, and found to his dismay that they could not be reconfigured to mount guns. Taylor demanded two more helicopters that could be easily converted.

Ruprah turned to Bout. The Russian recommended Soviet-built helicopters, good for both transport and easily equipped with machine guns and rocket launchers. The cost would be $500,000 each. Ruprah's share would be 10 percent of the deal, or $100,000 if both helicopters were acquired.[32]

Taylor had a long list of other weapons he wanted Bout to acquire, including machine guns, mortars, rocket-propelled grenades, and millions of rounds of ammunition.[33] Ruprah claimed that these requests were routed through him. But it is unlikely that Taylor needed a middleman to make arrangements with Bout. Cindor Reeves and other eyewitnesses say Taylor met regularly with Bout and passed on his weapons request in direct meetings in a private sitting room at his White Flower residence. Lawson Plaque, Bout's chief bodyguard, took notes, in part to make sure that the RUF shipments were kept separate and billed separately from Taylor's Liberian requests.

While Bout went in search of the helicopters, Ruprah set up a front company in Abidjan, Ivory Coast, that served as a non-Liberian destination for lethal cargo. The company, Abidjan Freight, would be used for several weapons movements that ended up in Liberia. In June 2000 Ruprah also set up an airline called West Africa Air Services, which leased planes from San Air, a Bout company in Sharjah, and from Renan, a Moldovan airline that used Bout planes.[34] West Africa was an airline set up for "smuggling operations only," a UN investigation found. Pilots said the person overseeing its operations as its aircraft flew in tons of weapons and ammunition in subsequent months was "Mr. Sanji."[35]

Bout found helicopters for Taylor and several tons of spare parts in the remote republic of Kyrgyzstan. Tons of weapons were found in other former Soviet bloc countries. After purchasing fake EUCs from Guinea and Côte d'Ivoire, Bout's planes began to haul the goods to Liberia in a series of flights in July and August 2000.[36] The plane he used for the main transportation was an Il-76 that had been registered in Liberia in 1996, then subsequently reregistered in Swaziland. When it was decertified there, Bout reregistered the craft in the Central African Republic as part of Centrafricain Airlines.

However, the same plane often flew with a registration from the Republic of Congo.[37] With the Il-76 tail number TL-ACU, it registered its flight plans as "Entebbe–Robertsfield–Abidjan," with the final destination to be Ruprah's fictitious company. Instead, the deadly cargo was left in Liberia.

"This aircraft and an Antonov made four deliveries to Liberia, three times in July and once in August 2000," a UN investigation found. "The cargo included attack-capable helicopters, spare rotors, anti-tank and anti-aircraft systems, missiles, armored vehicles, machine guns and almost a million rounds of ammunition. The helicopters were Mi-2 and Mi-17 types."[38] Viktor Bout had delivered again.

A separate investigation noted wryly that "It is difficult to conceal something the size of an Mi-17 military helicopter, and the supply of such items to Liberia cannot go undetected by customs authorities in originating countries unless there are false flight plans and end user certificates, unless customs officials at point of exit are paid to look the other way. The constant involvement of Bout's aircraft in arms shipments from Eastern Europe to African war zones suggests the latter."[39]

Bout insisted on payment as the helicopters and weapons were delivered. This forced Taylor to dip into the only cash he had on hand—the LISCR shipping registry funds that were normally paid into specific government accounts.

On June 21, 2000, LISCR, at the written request of Benoni Urey, transferred $525,000, via Standard Charter Bank, to San Air General Trading, Bout's main holding company in Sharjah. This coincided with the delivery of the first helicopter. Two weeks later, on July 7, another transfer of $400,000 was put through the same route.[40] LISCR officials were later formally reprimanded by the UN investigations for lack of "due diligence" in making the payments to a non-government bank account, contrary to normal practices.[41]

The pace of the weapons deliveries accelerated as the year progressed. Ruprah kept a running tally for Bout on what each weapon cost, how much each pilot was paid, how much their insurance coverage cost and what it covered, and how much Taylor owed Bout. The files outlining these payments were among the trove of documents found on Ruprah's hard drive when he was arrested by

Italian police in early 2002. The Italian authorities in Monza, near Milan, printed out reams of incriminating documents showing how close the business relationship between Bout and Ruprah had become.[42]

Despite Bout's continued success, there were gathering clouds. Old African ties that once eased access for his business deals were starting to turn acrimonious. One hint of trouble came in January 2000, during a summit of African presidents held in Libreville, Gabon.

When the president of the Central African Republic, Ange-Félix Patassé, made his entrance, several of his fellow heads of state congratulated him on his fine new presidential jet. They were impressed by the Ilyushin Il-62 they had seen sitting on the runway. It was painted with the flag of Patassé's nation, and its tail carried the number TL-ACL, a Central African Republic registration. There was only one problem: the plane was not Patassé's. The aircraft had been used by the delegation from Gambia. Deeply embarrassed, Patassé ordered an investigation into the origins of the plane as soon as he returned home.[43]

The investigation found that the Il-62 belonged to Viktor Bout and was operating on a forged "temporary" airworthiness certificate. On January 24, 2000, the Central African Republic ordered Bout's arrest and also the arrest of Bout's local manager and the CAR's civil aviation director. Bout was in Bangui, the capital of the republic, when the arrest warrant was issued. But he managed to escape, resurfacing shortly afterward in Liberia.

The investigation found that Bout and his local partner had fabricated airworthiness certificates, air operator permits, and certificates of registration for several aircraft. Among the illegally registered craft found were the two helicopters Bout later used to buy beer for rebel leader Bemba in the DRC. Most of the aircraft holding the false registrations had been decertified by Swaziland a few months before.

The Il-62 that set off the investigation had been purchased by a company called Gambia New Millennium, run by a man named Baba Jobe. Baba Jobe, in turn, was a close friend and business associate of Ibrahim Bah, the RUF liaison for Taylor. Jobe had also been trained in Libya when Bah and Taylor were there. The papers of the transaction showed the aircraft was sold by Mr. Victor Bout, general manager of Centrafricain Airlines. The money was paid into the Standard Chartered Bank account in Sharjah of Transavia Travel Agency, a Bout company.[44] Gambia New Millennium would later run significant amounts of weapons for the RUF.

But Bout's luck, while shakier, still held. On June 16, 2000, Doungovo, the director of civil aviation, was sentenced to a year in prison. Bout was sentenced in abstentia to a two-year prison term, and the Central Africa Republic issued an international arrest warrant for him. But suddenly, on June 28, the court reversed itself in Bout's case, acquitting him of all charges. No official explanation was ever given for the sudden change of heart of the judicial authorities.[45]

In April 2000 the RUF finally launched the major offensive that Bout anticipated, a strike aimed in part at taking the rutile mines. But in early May, after several units of the RUF broke camp and marched toward the rutile mines, the rebels made a colossal mistake, impulsively taking more than five hundred UN troops hostage. The blunder drew immediate condemnation and global media attention. But much worse for Taylor and the RUF, it also provoked the intervention of soldiers from Great Britain.

British prime minister Tony Blair sent British navy ships to the coast of the former colony, carrying several thousand elite paratroopers, along with helicopters and Harrier fighter jets. The force had carte blanche to use whatever means necessary to keep the RUF at bay.

Taylor, uncharacteristically, had misplayed his hand. Anxious to recover and earn international goodwill, he offered to mediate the dispute between the rebels and the United Nations, while denying any direct ties to the RUF. The bid was accepted, and soon the Reverend Jesse Jackson and others were leading delegations that Taylor hosted with great fanfare. The UN hostages were released in small groups. But at the same time the British, with U.S. support, began an unprecedented effort to electronically monitor Taylor's communications with the RUF.

Directing satellites at the Liberia–Sierra Leone border, British intelligence officials soon heard Taylor personally directing RUF operations and timing the release of UN hostages. The British also obtained photographs of Liberian military trucks moving weapons to RUF allies in Sierra Leone, unmasking Taylor's lie that he had no formal relationship with his proxies next door. The information was shared with the United States, with its interests in Liberia, and with the French, who monitored Guinea. For the first time the super-powers had learned the full extent of Taylor's involvement with the RUF, weapons trading, and the illicit sale of diamonds.[46]

Like Taylor, Bout had misread international and local conditions. He had placed too much faith in the RUF and in Mosquito Bockarie. The RUF general had tried to prepare the assault sooner, but not long after his 1999 meeting with Bout, Bockarie lost control of his troops after a major rift with Foday Sankoh, the RUF's supreme commander.

Sankoh, who had trained under Gaddafi, was a short, pudgy, demented former army corporal and photographer who had commanded the RUF child soldiers before Bockarie. A wild-looking figure with matted hair and a tangled beard, Sankoh was an ineffective field commander who claimed to receive military instructions from mysterious voices audible only in his head. Sankoh's 1997 arrest in Nigeria had allowed Taylor to promote Bockarie, giving him day-to-day control of RUF combat operations. But in early 2000, as a result of the United Nations–brokered peace talks, Sankoh was freed. Deeply jealous of Bockarie, Sankoh suspected his one time protégé of cheating him out of his share of the diamond revenue generated by the RUF's slave labor. Bockarie, who claimed to have magic strong enough to cause bullets to bounce off his head, was scared enough of the old master's threats that he fled to Monrovia, where Taylor gave him a well-appointed compound.

Without Bockarie at the head of the invasion force, Bout's plans for the mine raid collapsed. As the UN troops were freed and British peacekeepers solidified their presence, Taylor's iron hold on Liberia weakened—as did Bout's. But Taylor's setbacks in Sierra Leone in early 2000 actually proved to be a short-term boon for Bout. With tactical support from the British, tacit agreement from the United States, and the blessing of the French, a group of rebels in neighboring Guinea calling itself Liberians United for Reconciliation and Democracy (LURD) began a military campaign to oust Taylor. Led by some of Taylor's former commanders, the LURD was little better than the regime it sought to replace. But the growing strength of the rebels forced Taylor to go on a buying spree to rearm his own forces. As always, Bout was willing and able to help.

On July 7, 2000, senior U.S. diplomat Thomas Pickering flew to Monrovia to meet Taylor and formally express the displeasure of the Clinton administration with his meddling in Sierra Leone. As he landed at Roberts International Airport, Pickering noticed a plane on the far side of the tarmac. It was a large Il-76, one of Bout's cargo planes. As long as Taylor intended to keep his iron grip on Liberia, he would need the services of the ultimate fixer.[47]

CHAPTER 10

"Get Me a Warrant"

Lee Wolosky joined the Bout task force in March 2000, not long after a group of National Security Council and State Department officials met in the Old Executive Office Building to discuss the eroding situation in Africa. Wolosky did not attend, but Gayle Smith, the NSC's director for African Affairs, who was in on the session, followed up with an e-mail to Richard Clarke, asking if he had someone on his transnational threats staff who could coordinate the effort to tackle unimpeded weapons flows into the continent. Clarke chose Wolosky.

Smith felt the effort needed a fresh set of eyes. Still haunted by the 1993 ambush of Special Forces peacekeepers in Mogadishu, the Clinton administration remained gun-shy about committing American troops to Africa. But Smith was keen on providing other means of assistance to UN peacekeepers in Sierra Leone who were struggling with a violent resurgence by RUF rebels. A New Year's lull had given way to sporadic violence, and UN monitors had reported that RUF units were refusing to disarm and had begun mining contraband diamonds at an unprecedented pace. In February the UN Security Council decided to double the size of its multinational mission in Sierra Leone from 6,000 to 12,000 troops; the total would eventually reach 17,500.

Despite promises to disarm under a United Nations–brokered peace agreement, the RUF was stocking up with new and better weapons and openly challenging UNAMSIL troops. Some of the weapons came from hijackings of truckloads of guns and mortars from UN troops, but that did not account for the bulk of the RUF's massive new arsenal. As the weapons flowed in, hundreds of RUF combatants went through the surreal motions of leaving their old weapons at United Nations–led disarmament areas and then picking up new guns back at their bases. Witney Schneidman's team suspected that Bout's operation provided many of the weapons, emboldening rebel leaders in their refusal to abandon their lucrative diamond fields. Ground reports were just as gloomy in Angola, where human rights groups warned of a rising toll in civilians executed by both Jonas Savimbi's UNITA guerrillas and government forces.[1]

Near the end of the Africa meeting, Smith and Witney Schneidman raised the Bout network's role in keeping violence in the region at the boiling point. Their comments were almost afterthoughts, but as the officials sifted through possible policy options, they concluded that targeting the Bout organization might prove effective in squelching the flow of weapons into the battle zones.

"We raised the issue of Viktor Bout and connecting the dots in terms of arms sales," Smith recalled. "It would be hard to imagine even any temporary stability with the steady supply of arms coming in." They had a receptive audience. Susan Rice, who headed State's Africa desk, was already convinced of the perils Bout's operation posed from the status reports she had heard from Schneidman. Rice viewed the growing effort to target Bout as a "no-brainer. He was a bad guy doing bad stuff in a volatile region. His fingerprints were everywhere." Undersecretary of State Thomas Pickering, who chaired the meeting, agreed that Bout's activities had to be countered. Pickering and the other senior officials present decided "it would make sense to try and shut down his operation," Smith recalled.

Smith wanted the NSC to add muscle to State's diplomatic heft. She figured she would get a receptive hearing from Clarke, whose access to the White House and law enforcement, she felt, could jump-start the process.[2] "Can't we do something about this guy?" Smith messaged.

Clarke summoned Wolosky and, showing him the e-mail, assigned him to join the effort to counter Bout's arms operation. Wolosky got an even stronger nudge during a follow-up meeting of top NSC officials chaired by Lieutenant General Donald Kerrick, the deputy to National Security adviser Samuel R. "Sandy" Berger. Kerrick also wanted Bout put out of business, and emphasized his interest to the gathered officials. "When Kerrick mentioned it to us at the deputies meeting that reinforced it," Wolosky recalled. "It quickly got out in the bureaucracy that Kerrick was behind it, and that really strengthened our position."

Wolosky had been only vaguely familiar with the spiraling chaos in West Africa. But Bout's Russian background and the long tentacles of his worldwide logistics network intrigued the new NSC hire. The rapid expansion of Bout's business empire mirrored the rise of Russian plutocrats that Wolosky had warned about in his *Foreign Affairs* essay. Wolosky felt instinctively that Bout, like the oligarchs, had to be confronted by strong American countermeasures.

The question was how to do it. There was no evidence in the spring of 2000 that Bout's network was operating on U.S. soil or illegally trading in American weaponry. To shut his organization down in Africa, the United States would need cooperation from foreign allies. Schneidman and his small team of intelligence analysts had already begun to lay out the groundwork for one possible policy option, pursuing Bout with help from South African authorities. The Russian's short-lived effort to fly out of South Africa in 1997 and 1998 had ended abruptly after his gated estate was allegedly invaded by grenade-wielding thugs. Bout had fled Johannesburg and shut down his Air Pass cargo airline. But U.S. officials had learned that South African intelligence agents and members of the government's elite anticorruption "Scorpions" unit were investigating Bout's Africa operations.

Bout and his planes were gone, but the South Africans' aborted 1998 attempt to charge his Air Pass operation with 146 civil aviation violations suggested that Pretoria had the political will and the investigative resources to take further action. Schneidman had extensive contacts in the South African government and felt they would be receptive. Starting in spring 2000 he began setting aside time during diplomatic stops in Pretoria and Johannesburg to consult with officials there about mapping a strategy against Bout.

For much of the spring and summer, Wolosky boned up on the classified stores of material that Schneidman and his intelligence team had amassed. During the mornings Wolosky often wandered into Clarke's office, where he and other NSC deputies swapped tips from their respective fiefdoms. The Bout effort was only part of Wolosky's portfolio. He had joined Clarke's operation expecting to spend much of his time working on money-laundering cases tied to Russian organized-crime groups. Bout's case provided glimmers of that issue, but he also juggled other aspects of transnational crime, from drug trafficking to financial offenses. While Clarke had other deputies who specialized only in counterterror affairs, Wolosky found his cases often overlapping with theirs.

The Bout network's arms flows concerned him, but what alarmed him more was the logistics threat posed by the Russian's air fleet. He had been briefed about the Bout planes sighted in Kandahar and Air Cess ground crews working on Ariana planes at the Sharjah airport. "We couldn't directly link him to al Qaeda at that point, but there were red flags that concerned us," Wolosky recalled. "He was dancing around the edges." Bout's global reach gave him a capability that no other private air force rivaled. "They could almost run certain airports and essentially did. They carried men around on their aircraft with guns. They moved armed helicopter gunships, and they did this as an organization. That is not a thing you see every day. When you see photos of those activities, you typically equate them with governments, not private organizations. That becomes very compelling. This is not the government of Ukraine, this is a private organization that will work for whomever hires them."

Wolosky did not have Schneidman's deep knowledge base in African affairs, but made up for it with his insights into Russia's free-market tumult and its shadow oligarchs, mobsters, and apparatchiks-turned-capitalists. The two men took turns chairing the task force's strategy and informational meetings with intelligence analysts and officials from other agencies. Wolosky tended to the national security arena and to the action-oriented corners of government—Justice, Treasury, Commerce—that worked with the NSC on transnational threats. Schneidman concentrated on diplomatic realms, making the case to British and South African officials that an aggressive, coordinated approach against Bout could pay off for their interests. Wolosky's impatience sometimes flared, but his occasional differences with Schneidman had more to do with the divisions among agencies than personality shadings. "We were at loggerheads at times, but we had a good working relationship," Wolosky recalled. "I wanted things done right away and done aggressively."

Schneidman, too, moved urgently. He had acted early on to contact the international police agency Interpol, about U.S. concerns over the Russian's organization. And he had quickly passed word to State officials to place Bout's name and his multiple aliases on the department's international watch list. The warning went out to customs and immigration agents working in border posts and airports and to diplomats abroad who handled travel documents. If Bout tried to enter the United States for any reason, the alert was designed to raise alarm bells before he could slip into the country.

The contacts were made quietly. The task force's work remained strictly classified, an enforced silence aimed at keeping Bout in the dark about the sweeping electronic surveillance aimed at him and the growing American effort to scuttle his empire.

By spring 2000, Bout was no longer operating in anonymity. In March the UN Security Council publicly singled out him out for his extensive involvement in supplying weapons and matériel to UNITA forces in Angola, flagrantly violating a seven-year-old arms embargo. In assessing why the sanctions were so weak, a panel of UN experts headed by Robert Fowler, a former Canadian diplomat, placed the blame on air cargo firms that repeatedly loaded up with weapons in East European airports. Planes had made repeated clandestine runs into African landing zones, using forged or unauthorized transshipment documents to escape scrutiny by aviation and security officials.

Bout's air firms were not the only exploiters. The panel also named several other suspected European arms dealers. But the report went to great lengths to detail the outlines of Bout's operation, from its Sharjah hub to its satellite landing points stretching from South Africa to Bulgaria. "Victor Bout is known to operate with a number of partners, some of whom are also believed to be involved in sanctions busting activities on behalf of UNITA," the UN report warned. "Further investigation and exposure of these connections should be a high priority for future sanctions enforcement actions."[3]

Much of what the Fowler panel knew about Bout had been supplied by Johan Peleman. He was brought on under contract in the fall of 1999 to help the UN experts learn more about how air cargo firms were evading the embargo. Hired as a consultant to deliver a "profile of Bout," Peleman went on a whirlwind tour of the far-flung capitals where the arms network had laid down roots. He dug up transit documents in Luanda, Angola. In Switzerland he pressed for banking records. In the UAE he badgered aviation officials to learn more about Bout's plane holdings. The emirates' director of civil aviation claimed to be surprised about the presence of Bout's fleet and promised answers. None came. As his circle of informants grew, Peleman learned that Western intelligence agencies were on the Bout trail. Belgian and Dutch agents were employing wiretaps to learn more about the arms routes in the Great Lakes region, in the DRC and Rwanda, while British intelligence officials, concerned about the United Kingdom's mounting plans to deploy paratroopers in Sierra Leone, had done the same in West Africa.[4]

Peleman went to London early in 2000 to sound out British officials on what they could confirm about Bout's operation. Three men in suits met him in a small room at the Foreign and Commonwealth Office. When he tried to exchange business cards, the men had none to offer, but they acknowledged working for MI-6. Hoping to swap information, Peleman noticed they carried copies of *The Arms Fixers*, a book he had coauthored on the arms trade. But the MI-6 agents insisted they had little to offer and seemed skeptical when Peleman summarized his research showing the Russian's prominence in Africa. "They assumed I was an amateur," he recalled later. He returned to Antwerp with few new leads.

The British had reasons for keeping their cards hidden. By spring 2000, the Labour government under Tony Blair was seriously considering sending a contingent of peacekeepers to Sierra Leone, a former crown colony, to augment the United Nations' six thousand troops—a force supplied by Nigeria, Ghana, India, Kenya, and Guinea. Britain had already backed Sierra Leone's previous efforts to counter the RUF, first using African peacekeepers, then relying on Sandline International, a mercenary force, to reinstate the government by force after a 1998 coup. Neither effort had blunted the RUF's growing strength. By spring 2000 the UN bastion was nearly overwhelmed, and both MI-6 and Defence intelligence officials were analyzing security issues that troops might confront on the ground in Sierra Leone. Viktor Bout's weapons pipelines were a prime topic.

"He was institutionally sexy because he was a force protection issue," said the analyst familiar with British intelligence work on the Bout organization. "That meant the military was on board. And the [diplomatic] problems also meant the foreign office was interested as well. On Bout, the British government was ahead of the curve." [5]

But foresight had not led to action. While MI-6 kept tabs on Bout's organization through the late 1990s, British diplomats took no policy initiatives against him or even mentioned his name. That changed with the involvement of Peter Hain, the minister of state for Africa at the Foreign Office. Hain was a veteran Labour Party politician who was active in the 1980s and the early 1990s as a campaigner against the separatist apartheid policies of South Africa's white-dominated government. Soon after Hain joined the Foreign Office in June 1999, he learned that MI-6 and the Defence ministry had compiled extensive files on the Bout network's role in ferrying in weapons into Africa. "I was very aware we had all this intelligence and nothing was being done," Hain recalled. "Why do we have it," he asked the analysts, "if we are not going to use it?"

As discussions intensified over whether to send British troops to Sierra Leone, Hain worried that Bout's arms deliveries to the RUF could put them at risk. "What galled me particularly was that the guns could be used against British soldiers," Hain recalled. "I was outraged that he was doing this with impunity, fomenting wars that destroy countries. And on top of that his arms could be turned on our soldiers."

Hain seized on the notion of publicly targeting Bout as a way to crystallize the remote conflicts of Africa—both to the Blair government and to world opinion. There was immediate resistance from some quarters. "No one had done this before, and no one would have done it if I hadn't pushed the envelope," Hain said. "The alternative was to do nothing. We had all this information. We knew when he was flying, where he was flying. But nothing was being done."

Hain won the backing of Robin Cook, Blair's foreign minister, to go public. On January 18, 2000, during a House of Commons debate about the growing problems in Africa, Hain mentioned Bout publicly for the first time. Calling him a menace to British foreign policy, Hain said Bout "has flown in arms to UNITA. It is also believed that Bout owns or charters an Ilyushin 76 aircraft, which was impounded in Zambia en route to Angola last year."[6]

In early May, Sierra Leone erupted. As violence choked Freetown, Blair's government announced that a thousand British paratroopers were being shipped into the capital to protect British and European nationals. Britain was now fully engaged, and Hain and other officials believed that weapons supplied by Bout and other arms dealers were being used against the peacekeepers.[7]

In November, during a later House of Commons discussion, Hain amplified his grim imagery. "Sanctions-busters are continuing to perpetuate the conflict in Sierra Leone and Angola, with the result that countless lives are being lost and mutilations are taking place," Hain said, rising from his bench. "Victor Bout is indeed the chief sanctions-buster, and is a merchant of death who owns air companies that ferry in arms and other logistic support for the rebels in Angola and Sierra Leone and take out the diamonds which pay for those arms. All the countries that are allowing him to use their facilities and aircraft bases to ferry that trade in death into Sierra Leone and Angola are aiding and abetting people who are turning their guns on British soldiers, among others, in Sierra Leone. It is important that they stop doing that."

American officials were quietly nervous about Hain's public campaign, worried it would spur Bout to lower his profile, making it harder to track his operation. "We weren't happy about it," Wolosky said, "but it did cause us to coordinate more [with the British] so we weren't working for different objectives." As part of the joint effort, the United States broadened its electronic surveillance of African warlords and militia leaders in Central and West Africa. At the same time, British intelligence operations on the ground in West Africa were in full swing. Both agencies shared the gleanings of their efforts. "Every day I knew what Viktor Bout was talking about the day before," said a Bout team member. "This was mostly courtesy of the British."[8]

Hain's "merchant of death" tag stuck, a dark sobriquet that became synonymous with Bout's growing perch atop the international arms trade. The Fleet Street press parroted the phrase repeatedly as British investigative reporters began to nose into Bout's background and business operations. Web bloggers, too, picked up on the mocking title to the point where Internet searches for the phrase "merchant of death" invariably led straight to "Viktor Bout."[9] Hain's one-man "name and shame" campaign proved as effective in its own right as the United Nations' painstaking efforts to document the Bout network's arms routes. Hain's rhetoric demonized Bout as the enigmatic fueler of Africa's ills, while Johan Peleman and his UN colleagues provided the damning evidence.

As Sierra Leone disintegrated through the summer of 2000, Peleman found new work as a member of a second Security Council panel of experts researching arms embargo violations there. Now wielding the authority of a full-fledged UN staffer, Peleman jetted off on another grinding world tour, this time chasing the Bout network's pipelines into West Africa. Among his stops were Freetown and a side trip to Sierra Leone's diamond trading center of Kenema, and to Guinea, Liberia, South Africa, Switzerland, and once again, the UAE. Emirati officials stalled politely, then abruptly insisted that Peleman and his UN team had to leave the country. But when the UN team held their ground, demanding a tour of the Sharjah airport, the UAE officials suddenly relented. Peleman and the other UN officials observed the Bout fleet at close range. But they were still kept away from airport workers and Bout's employees. "We were puzzled," Peleman said. "Were they helping us or trying to get us out of the way?"[10] A senior UAE official later confided that emirate federal officials and Sharjah's local leaders were deeply divided over how to deal with the growing controversy over the Bout planes.[11]

During a summer visit to UN headquarters in New York, Peleman also detoured to Washington, where he briefed State Department officials and met with analysts for the CIA and the Defense Intelligence Agency. When Peleman sounded them out about Bout's operation, the Americans had little to offer. "Either we don't know or we can't tell you," Peleman was told repeatedly. When the Americans offered a few scant details, Peleman was surprised by how inaccurate they were. "The CIA had names spelled wrong," he recalled. "They had nothing on the connections between the companies. They knew who Bout was but they had companies listed that weren't part of the network."

The world's superpowers had finally come around. But their reluctance to share information left Peleman skeptical about their commitment to make the tough compromises necessary to work together against Bout's organization.[12]

In mid-August Wolosky, Schneidman, and four other officials from the Bout task force trooped into Richard Clarke's suite in the Old Executive Office Building. Taking seats around a large conference table, they spoke for twenty minutes, briefing Clarke about what they had learned about Viktor Bout. From monitoring provided by both American AWACS planes operating over West Africa and ground surveillance by British intelligence, they knew that the Russian talked openly on his satellite telephone about weapons shipments. There had been extensive tracking of the flight paths of his planes, from Africa to Sharjah and even into Afghanistan. As they ran down their options, Clarke sat at one corner of the conference table, peppering them with questions. Finally he cut to the chase: "Get me a warrant."[13]

The ramifications of Clarke's blunt challenge were clear. If the Bout team could find an amenable foreign ally willing to press charges against the Russian, Clarke would leverage the resources of the U.S. government to have him detained and brought to trial. The United States would persuade cooperating police officials to arrest Bout abroad, most likely in the UAE, where Clarke had close ties with emirati officials, or else in a consenting African or East European country. Then, sidestepping cumbersome international extradition procedures, American officials would whisk Bout to the nation that had issued the arrest warrant, where he would stand trial.

The plan was an early version of "rendition," the controversial technique of arresting suspects and turning them over to a third country for questioning and custody that has become a hallmark of the Bush administration. During the discussions, "Clarke raised the possibility of sending in a plane and doing a rendition," one participant recalled. "It was definitely an option." Another participant said that if Bout was seized "in the UAE, they would have to be willing to enforce that warrant. You can call it rendition or whatever you want, but it was one country choosing to enforce a warrant issued by another country without an extradition process."[14]

Since the September 11 attacks, the practice has been a common—and legally questionable—maneuver used by the CIA against scores of suspected al Qaeda operatives. During the Clinton administration, a number of Islamic terrorist suspects were seized by American intelligence and law enforcement officials in foreign countries and flown to the United States without extradition. Clinton officials referred to the seizures as "international enforcement actions." But Bout was among the first foreign suspects targeted for capture abroad and trial in a third country.

In the days that followed, the Bout team turned to the immediate next step—figuring out how to get the warrant. They began mulling over a short list of countries that might be willing to put Bout on trial. The UAE was considered and rejected—Bout was too entrenched with Sharjah's rulers, and U.S. Justice and Treasury officials saw no evidence of a clear criminal case that could be built there. They considered Angola, but were well aware that Bout's planes were delivering to both UNITA rebels and government forces. "It would leak in a nanosecond," Schneidman said. They thought about Uganda, but too many weapons coursed through Uganda into the DRC and other war zones. But South Africa was a strong option, Schneidman felt. And there were positive signs that Belgium's secret investigation into allegations of Bout network money laundering might also produce an arrest warrant.

Before they could settle on likely candidates, word arrived in August from the embassy in Abu Dhabi that Bout was trying to enter the United States. He had applied for a visa to travel to an address in Richardson, Texas. The address was matched to the office of Richard Chichakli, the former Sharjah free-zone manager who had worked with Bout in South Africa. Chichakli worked as an accountant in Richardson, a suburb of Dallas, and in June 2000 he had registered with the state of Texas as the agent for a newly incorporated Bout-orbit company, San Air General Trading LLC. The firm was a mirror image of Bout's Sharjah-based San Air cargo airline, and one of Bout's associates, Sergei Dennisenko, was listed as an officer.[15]

Chichakli later explained that he had "set [San Air] up for Viktor" and that Bout had intended to fly to the Dallas area to scout out a location where he hoped to build a factory to manufacture plastic parts for Russian cargo planes. Those plans were scuttled, Chichakli said resentfully, after the UN arms embargo inquiries named him as a Bout associate.[16]

The Bout team learned that Abu Dhabi embassy officials had quickly turned down Bout's visa request. But some officials on the task force questioned whether it might be a better idea to let him into the United States. The Russian could be tailed by law enforcement agents and might even be caught in the act of a crime on U.S. soil, they suggested. In his monitored phone conversations, Bout had been overheard talking about coming to the United States to buy sophisticated telecommunications equipment that was restricted for sale outside the country under State Department trade laws. "He was looking for certain equipment, very advanced and secure," said a Bout team member. "We assumed it was for his use but we couldn't be certain." Bout had been taking more precautions in his phone conversations, a sign that he suspected he was being monitored. He moved around often between calls, frequently discarded his phones, and spoke in veiled code, ordering "items" instead of specific weapons.[17]

The embassy's decision to bar Bout's visit seemed to have settled the issue. But the realization that Bout had a toehold in Texas raised uneasy questions about what other United States–based operations existed. The Bureau of Alcohol, Tobacco, and Firearms (ATF) was assigned to put together a profile of Bout's holdings, both inside the United States and abroad. The ATF discovered a "clear pattern" of contacts between Chichakli's Richardson office and Bout's shifting phone numbers. Authorities also learned that a branch of Air Cess, Bout's Sharjah flagship, had been incorporated in Miami in

September 1997, and a Gulfstream jet linked to Bout given a U.S. registry. The agent who set up the firm, a Floridian named Jerry Dobby, later declined to say who had hired him. But Dobby explained that the aviation registry was sought "for leasing purposes." Dobby added cryptically: "It's not good to haul arms in. A Gulfstream doesn't do too well on those remote desert airstrips. It can tear up the landing gear." [18]

With Bout now a top priority at the NSC, surveillance and intelligence data poured in. At almost the same time that the task force was grappling with Bout's visa request and mounting hints about his work for the Taliban, Wolosky learned of another possible terror connection. Roger Cressey, Clarke's chief counterterrorism deputy, pulled Wolosky aside one morning and showed him a cable about a sudden move by Libyan dictator Muammar Gaddafi to send a negotiating team to the Philippines to help free twenty-one European hostages held by Abu Sayyaf, an Islamic terror group linked to al Qaeda. "Guess who's flying in to take out the Philippine hostages?" Cressey asked. "Your friend Viktor."

American intelligence had learned that Bout had provided an Ilyushin Il-76 to Gaddafi to fly a Libyan negotiating team to Manila. At the time, Gaddafi was still considered a main sponsor of international terrorism, and any aid to his isolated regime raised suspicion. Abu Sayyaf, who would later be hunted down and killed by Philippine forces, had been schooled in terror techniques at Gaddafi's Libyan training camp. The Libyan negotiators flew to Manila on the Ilyushin, reportedly carrying as much as $21 million—in answer to Abu Sayyaf's demand for $1 million per hostage. On August 28, the cargo plane flew back to Tripoli with the Libyan negotiators and the first six freed hostages. Over the following weeks, the others also would be released.

Bout's ties to the mercurial dictator turned out to be more extensive than the single flight. On August 8, a plane belonging to Jet Line, a Sharjah-based firm linked to the Bout network, was registered in Tripoli for Sin Sad, an airline tied to the Gaddafi government. Western intelligence agencies also learned that Bout ground crews had been servicing Gaddafi's government planes, and that on several occasions Bout's pilots flew Gaddafi himself. "One of his businesses was that he flew around African heads of state," Wolosky said. "It was just another of the services he provided. It got him in good standing with heads of state and it was good for business."

Bout's planes also had flown Zaire's Mobutu and Liberia's Taylor. The Bout team learned in late 2001 that U.S. aviation officials had even cleared one of the Russian's planes to fly the wife of Gambian dictator Yahya A. J. J. Jammeh into Dulles International Airport in Virginia. Because it was an official visit, State Department officials were leery of provoking an international incident.

Beyond the Africa desk, senior State officials were divided over how hard to press foreign allies, particularly Russia. Pickering felt that Bout was "a total rogue" and supported his capture. But Pickering was skeptical that Putin's government would respond to a direct approach. "We assumed he was operating out of their control since he was not based in the country any longer," Pickering said. "We figured an appeal wouldn't have much effect." Susan Rice said the matter was "on the bilateral agenda with the Russians, but I don't know how far up. It is fair to assume it was a talking point, but not a focal point." The Americans learned that British diplomats had been talking with Russian officials about Bout, but they expected little movement. Wolosky had no use for dialogue "just for the sake of chatting." Besides, he felt that the details of any talks with the Russians would filter back to Bout. "I figured a guy with his background and organization would have lines into the Russian government."

Late in the year, the Bout task force went on high alert again after British intelligence relayed a tip that a courier working for the Russian was on a flight bound for JFK International Airport in New York, carrying a large contraband diamond. The Bout team notified customs officials, and agents rushed to the gate as passengers exited the plane. But the courier was not found. "They had a name but they couldn't find the guy," a Bout team member recalled. "Either he never showed up or he got through."[19]

In the tense hours before the plane arrived, officials in Washington were caught up in a frenzied bureaucratic tussle. NSC officials had to wrestle with the elaborate process of declassifying top-secret intelligence about Bout and his courier to provide key information to the customs agents. The snafu was typical of interagency roadblocks the Bout team encountered when they dealt with Justice,

FBI, and Treasury officials. In turn, law enforcement officials felt the Bout team was treading on their turf. International organized crime was a fief traditionally handled by the FBI, and Justice officials were openly skeptical of Bout's sudden prominence as an international target.

"There were people who said: 'Why are you obsessed with this guy? If you take him out, there are other people who will fill his shoes,'" Wolosky recalled. "My response was that I'm not obsessed with the guy, we were in charge of implementing a presidential directive [on transnational threats]. And Viktor Bout is the first major guy on the agenda."

On the morning of November 8, 2000, it was no longer clear whether the Bout team would be able to carry out Clinton's directive. After an extraordinary night of electoral chaos, the 2000 presidential race between Vice President Al Gore and Texas governor George W. Bush was deadlocked. Florida's close vote count was under protest. Lawyers and political operatives from both campaigns were descending on the state for an unprecedented legal battle.

On December 9, Secretary of State Madeleine Albright met in Pretoria with South African president Thabo Mbeki and raised U.S. interest in seeing Bout brought to trial. Susan Rice, who was traveling with Albright, briefed the South African leader, and when she finished, Mbeki agreed to forward the case to his special prosecutor.

But the next step was departure. On December 12, the U.S. Supreme Court halted a Florida vote recount sought by Al Gore's campaign, allowing the certification of Bush's win in the state and sealing his victory as the forty-third president. With a Republican administration looming, the Bout task force was operating on borrowed time.

Still hoping for a breakthrough in the final days of the Clinton administration, Schneidman decided to use a trip to an AIDS conference in Nairobi as a jumping-off point for a final bid to persuade the South Africans to move against Bout. He had been consulting for months with South African diplomats and legal officials. On one trip he had taken along several intelligence officials to make the case. The South Africans were sympathetic but made no commitments.

With a flurry of international phone calls, Schneidman set up a last round of meetings in Johannesburg, hoping to persuade the South Africans to refer the Bout case to their special prosecutor, Jan D'Olivera. Arriving in early January, Schneidman met with Aziz Pahad, the deputy minister of foreign affairs. Pahad listened, but was still hesitant. Exhausted and frustrated, Schneidman headed home. He flew back to Nairobi first, where he planned to call Susan Rice on a secure line and tell her that the effort was a bust. "I figured I'd failed, I'm giving up," he recalled.

A message was waiting for him at the embassy. Pahad had changed his mind. He would refer the Bout case to the special prosecutor. Elated, Schneidman returned to Washington convinced that Bout's arrest was only a matter of time. "I came back feeling there would be a next step," he said.

He would not be around to see it. On inauguration day, Schneidman, Susan Rice, Gayle Smith, and other senior Clinton staffers packed their files and left. "We just ran out of time," he said.

Wolosky and Clarke decided to take their chances in the incoming administration. Clarke was a bureaucratic survivor who had prospered under Bush's father. Wolosky was easily identifiable as a Democrat and had privately disagreed with most of the new administration's statecentric foreign policy impulses. But he had been impressed during the 2000 campaign by Bush's tough talk about taking on Russian organized crime. If the new national security team showed interest in extending the Bout hunt, Wolosky decided, he would stay on until the Russian was under arrest.

CHAPTER 11

Now or Never

Shortly after the inauguration of George W. Bush in January 2001, Condoleezza Rice, the new national security adviser, joined counterterrorism chief Richard Clarke and several NSC deputies for a classified briefing in the White House Situation Room. Lights dimmed and an overhead projector flashed a series of slides on a large screen. Each click brought up a satellite photograph showing dozens of aging Soviet aircraft parked on an airfield tarmac. An expert in Soviet studies and arms control issues, Rice instantly recognized the Soviet-era aircraft. One by one, she neatly identified a succession of Antonovs, Ilyushins, and military helicopters with each new image pulsing onscreen.

Clarke, who had invited Rice to the briefing, asked his new boss if she knew who owned the massive armada of planes. They belonged to the Russian air fleet, Rice answered. No, Clarke explained. The planes *had* been part of the Russian fleet. Now they belonged to Viktor Bout's air armada.

The briefing had been designed to enlist Rice's support for continuing the top-secret effort to obtain an international warrant for Bout's arrest. Clarke, Wolosky, and other NSC officials were convinced they were closing in on the Russian. They hammered home two simple points to Rice: Bout's air fleet and global logistical network rivaled that of many NATO nations—an image made starkly clear by the Russian planes parked wing to wing in the satellite photographs. And the United States could no longer afford to let him rent that network out to the highest bidder, continuing its gunrunning activity in a volatile world.

"She immediately saw what the problem was," said one participant in the meeting. "The visuals were compelling. We got her support by showing her the logistics."[1]

The impact of Rice's support was immediate. In the early days of the Bush administration, White House officials had little interest in following up on old Democratic initiatives, an "anything but Clinton" mind-set that openly scorned the priorities of Bush's predecessor. But despite the Bush administration's return to a traditional foreign policy agenda dominated by states instead of nonstate actors, Rice was persuaded that the NSC should continue the Bout hunt. She authorized Clarke and Wolosky to forge ahead.

Wolosky's first move was to request Rice's permission to pick up where Schneidman had left off. He wanted to meet with the Belgians and the South Africans and develop support for an arrest warrant against Bout. The Bush White House, seeking to reshape the flow of power in the executive branch, had sharply curtailed NSC staff travel, limiting trips only to those flying with the president or in direct support of a presidential meeting. But Rice again agreed.

Wolosky was the first NSC staffer allowed to independently take an overseas trip in the Bush administration. His plan was simple. He wanted an arrest warrant for Bout from anyone who would give him one. What happened after the warrant was uncertain, but consultations between Clarke and his contacts in the UAE left Wolosky with the strong impression that the emirates would honor a commitment to arrest Bout if there were a legal basis.

"There was a limit to what the United States could do," Wolosky recalled. "We couldn't hold people for three years at Bagram Air Base, like they do now. We knew eventually we would have to have him in a court somewhere and make the case against him. That is why Belgium and South Africa were the best opportunities."

Their case that Bout was a key figure in the international arms trade had been strengthened by two public reports issued by the United Nations in late December 2000. The separate reports, issued by experts hired by the Security Council to monitor arms embargo breaches in Angola and Liberia, contained a wealth of new details on the Bout network's air operations. The reports not only named Bout but also listed his associates and allied firms and identified some of his aircraft. One Bout-linked air firm cited in the Angola report for suspected arms flights was Flying Dolphin, the Sharjah-based cargo airline that was the only firm allowed by the United Nations to continue flying to Taliban-controlled Afghanistan in late 2000. Barely a month after the Angola report's release, the United Nations halted the air firm's Afghan routes, raising further suspicions about Bout's dealings with the Afghan Islamists.[2]

Wolosky flew first to Belgium, where there was an open investigation into reports of massive money laundering by Bout firms. But during meetings in Brussels, negotiations quickly went off the rails. Wolosky had invited the local Belgian prosecutor handling the Bout case, Dirck Merckx, to the U.S. embassy for the initial discussions. A small man with a wandering eye, Merckx arrived alone and seemed surprised to find himself facing several U.S. officials across a long conference room table, sitting in front of a large American flag. The U.S. officials encouraged Merckx to "think big," but then proceeded to rapidly fire off questions about the prosecutor's knowledge about Bout and his activities, front companies, and money movements. Merckx spoke carefully, reluctant to compromise his inquiry. And when the Belgian asked the Americans what information they would be willing to provide, Wolosky and his team were equally cagey, declining to open up about intelligence and sources because they doubted the sensitive information could be adequately protected.

"I think we scared the crap out of him," Wolosky recalled ruefully. "In retrospect it may not have been the best way to handle it." There were more desultory American contacts with Merckx and other Belgian diplomats over the following weeks, but the two sides never recovered from the strained first meeting. "Ultimately, he wasn't willing to open his books to us, or us to him," Wolosky said. "It is too bad because we had a commitment from the UAE to execute the warrant if it were issued."

The Belgians later broached the idea of a secret multinational meeting in London with officials from Britain and the United States to share current information on Bout's operation and coordinate their separate offensives. But intelligence-sharing remained an insurmountable hurdle, and Wolosky had no interest in the proposal. The Belgians soon soured on the idea when unnamed officials suggested that the meeting include Russian and East European officials. The Belgians and the Americans worried that word would get back to Bout. "It was, how shall I say, a question of trust," a senior Belgian foreign officer said. "We were not prepared to share our files with all of these governments."[3] The fears that Bout had his own intelligence channels proved justified. Within a week of the first Brussels meeting between the Americans and Merckx, U.S. officials later learned, Bout had been informed of the session.[4]

Wolosky still had hope for South Africa, where special prosecutor Jan D'Olivera was looking into the possibility of charging Bout with either immigration violations or offenses under a newly passed antimercenary law. U.S. officials believed they could establish a case based on Bout's alleged criminal intent while operating there. But in meetings with legal officials in Johannesburg, Wolosky sensed that they, too, were nowhere close to delivering a warrant. Without overwhelming evidence, South African officials were reluctant to act. "We did take it seriously, but it needs to be within our law," D'Olivera explained in 2002. "If someone says that Viktor Bout landed at a certain airport, can you connect it with a certain offense? Without concrete evidence, there's nothing one can do."[5]

There was one bright moment. In February, the same month Wolosky went abroad, the government of Slovakia, aided by U.S. and British intelligence, halted the Bout-sponsored shipment of a combat helicopter from Slovakia to Liberia. Using a complicated scheme to circumvent the embargo against Charles Taylor's government, Bout-controlled front companies had arranged for two grounded Mi-24 helicopter gunships to be purchased from the government of Kyrgyzstan, then flown in an Il-76 to Slovakia for repairs. On paper, the helicopters were then to be shipped to Guinea, a neighbor of Liberia in West Africa. The company ostensibly ordering the helicopters was Pecos, a paper entity that frequently served as a front company for Bout's West African operations.[6]

In both cases the helicopters were picked up in Kyrgyzstan and delivered to Slovakia by Il-76 aircraft belonging to Bout's Centrafricain Airlines. The same aircraft was to fly the repaired helicopters to their final destination: Liberia.[7] The repair and delivery of the first helicopter went off without a hitch, but with U.S. and British intelligence monitoring the movements of Bout's aircraft, the second delivery soon hit snags. Slovak authorities, checking the paperwork of the Centrafricain aircraft requesting permission to pick up the second helicopter, found numerous irregularities in the registration and insurance. With the encouragement of the U.S. embassy, Slovakian officials denied the aircraft permission to land. On February 22, after several days of desperate attempts by Bout associates to obtain landing permission by presenting papers from several different companies controlled by Bout, including San Air, the airplane was allowed to land in Bratislava. But the Slovak authorities, having determined the EUC for the helicopter was a forgery, refused to allow the helicopter to be loaded.[8]

Wolosky was ecstatic. He went out of his way to meet with the Slovakian defense minister when the minister visited Washington shortly after the incident. "I wanted to thank him for his help and encourage him to keep doing things like that," Wolosky said. "It took a lot of moxie for the Slovaks to do that."

Obscure as the incident seemed, for those who were tracking international conflicts, bringing down Bout would be a big win for the United States and its allies, and for the first time it was starting to look truly possible.

In the late spring of 2001, after the Slovak interdiction of the helicopter, other smaller weapons shipments also were interdicted or delayed. The mood among those in the U.S. government following Bout was still hopeful.

A member of the intelligence community decided to host a Viktor Bout party to acquaint people from different government agencies with each other, given their common interest in the elusive Bout. Several dozen people turned up for the gathering, which took place under cover of a weekend cookout in a Virginia suburb south of Washington, D.C. The mood was festive. Spouses and children were invited, and as the burgers and hot dogs sizzled in the fading light of dusk, those working on Bout clustered into small groups to discuss the latest developments in their hunt for the arms trafficker. With the NSC interest spearheaded by Wolosky, government resources for the operation had expanded and key policymakers had been won over. To this small but dedicated group that included officials from the CIA, DIA, NSA, and NSC, the wind seemed to have shifted in their favor.

"The idea of thirty or forty people showing up on this one issue was remarkable," said one attendee. "Our spouses had no idea why we were there, but there would be little cliques of people off in the corner who talked about Bout. It was fun."[9]

On March 30, 2001, Richard Clarke chaired another interagency meeting on Bout in the Situation Room. The topic was how to quietly press the UAE to crack down on Bout's aircraft and target his larger organization. Because there were so few regulations in the UAE relating to weapons trafficking and aircraft registration, his flight and ground operations operated with near impunity. One option was to ask UAE officials to require all aircraft operating out of Sharjah to install expensive communications and emergency response equipment. Some officials felt that Bout had so many aircraft based in the emirates of Sharjah, Ajman, and Ras al Khaymah that he would be forced to pack up and leave because of the prohibitive cost of installing the equipment—more than $10,000 per aircraft. The strategy had been proposed and accepted by the UAE two years earlier, but never implemented in a serious way. The UAE also had failed to move on promises to enact legislation outlawing at least some of the most egregious gunrunning. A new push on both fronts was ordered.[10]

At the same time, the growing evidence against Bout compiled by the UN experts had finally spurred the Security Council to go beyond its "name and shame" campaign and restrict Bout's movements. On May 21 the Security Council formally placed him on a mandatory international travel ban list, aimed at punishing senior members of Charles Taylor's regime in Liberia. Along with Taylor and Bout, others on the list included Bout's American partner Richard Chichakli; Ibrahim Bah, who had introduced Bout to the RUF; and Bout's partner in weapons shipments to Liberia Sanjivan Ruprah.[11] The United Nations' move gave legal standing to any country willing to try to stop them on entrance, but few countries ever tried to stop anyone on the list. Bout continued to move at will.

In January 2001 his San Air General Trading company in Sharjah signed a contract with the Ministry of Defense of Côte d'Ivoire for the sale of two Mi-8T helicopter gun ships. At the time, the government of xenophobic president Laurent Gbagbo had launched the traditionally stable West African nation on a long, downward spiral of civil war, fanning ethnic and religious hatreds. As opposition in the Muslim-dominated north mounted toward Gbagbo, the beleaguered president turned to Bout to bail him out.

An invoice for $2.6 million, dated January 16, 2001, for the two gunships, equipped with C5 missile launchers and bomb launchers for 100-, 250-, and 500-kilogram bombs, was signed by Bout's longtime San Air business manager Sergei Denissenko on behalf of San Air. The price included a training crew to train three Ivorian crews for four months, as well as $450,000 worth of bombs and missiles for the gunships.[12]

San Air also concluded a separate deal on the same day for Bout's more standard deliveries: AK-47s, millions of rounds of ammunition, mortar bombs, and grenades, for a total of $1.6 million. The invoices instructed that payment be made to San Air's Dubai account number 01-5712572-01 in Standard Charter Bank and promised delivery of the merchandise within fourteen working days of receipt of payment.[13]

The sanctions noose might be tightening, but Bout seemed to feel no need to answer to anyone. He refused to talk to the UN panels investigating him, and neither he nor his lawyers or associates responded publicly to their reports. Johan Peleman and fellow investigators on the Liberia sanctions panel finally managed to photograph the Sharjah fleet at close range and interviewed Sergei Bout and a few of Bout's lieutenants. But the boss always remained unavailable.

When one company was outed, Bout and his associates nimbly avoided sanctions by reorganizing, changing the names of companies, creating new firms, or reviving old ones that had been in mothballs. In August and early September a new company, Air Bas Transportation, set up offices in the old Air Cess building in Sharjah. Air Bas, unknown at the time to UN investigators and intelligence operatives, effectively replaced Air Cess, Centrafricain and Air Pass, all of which had ceased operations.[14] Air Bas officials did not even bother to change the old Air Cess phone number. The aircraft were transferred without hassle.

In Washington, attention was waning in the absence of concrete results. Bureaucratic inertia had set in. Despite Condoleezza Rice's earlier interest, the NSC's activist role developed under the Clinton administration was being reshaped to a narrower policy-coordination role. Clarke's influence had faded, and he was no longer allowed to sit in on the "principal's meetings" with cabinet secretaries and directors of the various intelligence agencies, access that enabled him to focus attention and resources on Bout. The Clinton administration's late-blooming interest in transnational threats had rapidly given way to the Bush administration's more traditional state-centric view of the world.

By August, in a last-ditch effort to keep the Bout operation going, Wolosky transferred from the NSC to the State Department's Bureau for International Narcotics and Law Enforcement Affairs (INL). He had already received two extensions for his stay at the NSC, and was told no more would be forthcoming. Rand Beers, a longtime intelligence and security officer, headed the INL office, and was willing to give Wolosky a home, at least for a short time. Beers would resign from government in May 2003 after leading the NSC's counterterrorism office and then work as a national security adviser for the presidential campaign of John Kerry.

"It goes without saying that the new administration came into office with a sense that nation-states remained the primary actors in the world and transnational threats were not as important to deal with," Beers said. "It was not like the administration wanted to stop anything we were doing. They just weren't interested."

The British continued to push the State Department and others in the U.S. administration to take more aggressive action, but the Bout hunt was losing momentum. "We were stuck between the FBI not having an investigation open, and not particularly energized to do anything, and the Brits, who were very concerned and were trying to get our attention on it," Beers recalled. "The Africa bureau continued to be worried by Bout. But nothing happened."

In late spring Wolosky briefed Stephen Hadley, Rice's deputy at the NSC, on Bout and global organized crime. He had received the go-ahead to present a full-fledged presidential briefing, but no date was set. Wolosky was scheduled to go to the White House to make final arrangements for the briefing on September 11. But in the chaos of the morning's catastrophic events, his meeting was canceled.

Soon afterward, Wolosky left the Bush administration, no longer convinced there was any desire to bring Bout in and scuttle his operation. "We knew we were being phased out," he said. The government's most determined Bout pursuer saw no future in the chase. The U.S. hunt for Viktor Bout was essentially over, lost in the rubble of September 11.

As American intelligence and law enforcement officials ranged across the world trying to unravel the terror plot, a cryptic correspondence of letters and e-mails began in November 2001 between a U.S. agent in Washington and Viktor Bout's Africa partner Sanjivan Ruprah, who had immigrated to Brussels. Ruprah wanted the American, an FBI agent working on loan to the CIA, to help overturn the recent UN ban on his international travel.

In return, Ruprah broached a series of ambitious proposals. In a November 12, 2001, e-mail he offered to set up a team of operatives to deliver information on al Qaeda and militant Islamic terrorists across the Third World. Ruprah said his staff would "do their part properly only knowing that I require this info but not why, as they work with me on that basis always."

"There will be no other person in this loop with me and I would be your only contact," Ruprah wrote. "It would be fairly easy to for me to deliver data weekly at several points in Europe/MidEast/CIS [Central Asian republics] depending on what you suggest."

Ruprah pegged his team's minimum expenses at an exorbitant $252,000 per month. This included $60,000 for "expenses for purchases of info from third parties," and $30,000 per month for "my personal travel." He insisted the money would be well spent because the "effectiveness will be very high." He offered the deal on "an evaluation basis, if you are satisfied at the of the 2/3 month period, then my priority is to proceed to the next phase as per our conversation." [15]

As the correspondence continued, Ruprah made an even more astounding offer. In an undated letter believed to be written to the American at about the same time, Ruprah said that he and Viktor Bout would secretly help the United States arm Northern Alliance forces to battle against the Taliban and Osama bin Laden's al Qaeda forces in Afghanistan. "Victor and I have discussed various aspects of cooperation with yourselves regarding Afghanistan, the main area being support of the group opposing the Taliban regime as well as collecting information on O [Osama bin Laden] and his people," Ruprah wrote.[16]

Ahmad Shah Massoud, the Afghan warlord whom Bout armed and then betrayed by working with the Taliban in the late 1990s, was dead. He had been assassinated by a team of al Qaeda suicide bombers inside his Afghan hideaway two days before the September 11 attacks. But despite Bout's earlier arms and cargo flights for the Taliban, Ruprah wrote that "we have very good relationships with the group headed by the late Gen. Massoud, who was a personal friend of Victor's, also this group is probably known to you is capable of achieving a lot against the Taliban given the right support, logistics and guidance."

Ruprah had been in contact through much of 2001 with Western intelligence officials, first with the British, then with the FBI. Johan Peleman also met with Ruprah frequently during the period in Belgium. Peleman was aware of Ruprah's efforts to barter with Western officials, but he was suspicious of what he described as Ruprah's habit of hyping his information to suit the mind-set of his questioners. "I happened to have a picture of a bottle made out of tin or nickel with uranium or plutonium in it and he became increasingly fascinated with that," Peleman recalled. "He told Belgian police some tales about radioactivity. Every day I would speak to him he came up with something new."[17]

Ruprah had first approached Peleman in May 2001 because of his UN connections, then began dealing with the British and the Americans later in the summer. Ruprah's relationship with Bout was well documented and should have been known in the U.S. intelligence community, which is what made Ruprah's efforts on Bout's behalf so brazen. Yet the contacts were not coordinated or reported to Wolosky or other Bout team officials at the White

House, where the effort to have Bout arrested was still under way.[18]

The correspondence between Ruprah and his FBI contact, who alternately used a pseudonym, "Waters," and his real first name, "Brad," proceeded in surreal Alice in Wonderland fashion. It was a looking-glass universe in which the hunted proposed to join forces with his pursuers. Ruprah mentioned nothing of Bout's previous work for the Taliban and indirect aid to al Qaeda as he touted his Russian partner's ability to aid the United States in its gathering war in Afghanistan.

Ruprah insisted that he and Bout "could make the necessary arrangements through Dushanbe and Iran for logistical purposes." With Bout's help, Ruprah boasted, the Northern Alliance could "advance rapidly & cover 40–50% of the country within 3–4 months given the necessary logistical & technical support, they could also reach Kabul, Herat, in a short time span," Ruprah wrote. "Importantly they could rout out most of [Osama's] hideouts as they claim all the known hideouts have been deserted in the last 7–8 days, this would be the most systematic way of locating [Osama] as being on the ground they will get the most accurate info on his movement unless he leaves the country."[19]

Such an undertaking, Ruprah explained, would entail a significant amount of weapons and other logistics needs. Ruprah wasted no time proffering an ambitious, multimillion-dollar shopping list that he and Bout would be eager to provide—and Ruprah indicated that one had already been developed in consultations with leaders of the Northern Alliance. The list included: "80–100 6X6 trucks, 6,000 AK47 + 5 million rounds; 1,000 PKM + 2 million rounds; 3,000 RPG7 + 18,000 PG7/OG7; 100 122mm Gun + 8,000 shells; 50 Concurs anti-tank launchers; 40 Igla Anti Aircraft Launchers + 160 missiles; 4–6 Mi-24 V [helicopter gunships] fully equipped & Crewed; 8–10 Mi-17 [combat helicopters] Equipped and Crewed; 3 An-24/26 cargo/Personnel aircraft crewed; 120 Comms [communications] sets; 40 PortaClinics."[20] It was an impressive arsenal for the first major battle in the war against terrorism.

There was no way for the Americans to know whether Ruprah was telling the truth about his assertions that he and Bout could quickly arm the Northern Alliance. As Peleman had described, Ruprah seemed to have an instinctive ability to adapt to what his questioners wanted to hear. At one point in the correspondence, Ruprah appeared to play on the Bush administration's suspicions of Iraq. "Tajik/NA [Northern Alliance] believe Iraq partly bankrolled the US Bombings & is currently providing funds to Zawahiri," Ruprah wrote, referring to bin Laden's chief deputy. U.S. officials later confided that during one point in the extensive contacts with the FBI, Ruprah also claimed to have details about business dealings between Bout and his Islamic militant clients in Afghanistan. Ruprah's lawyer Luc de Temmerman later insisted that Ruprah had not made those claims.[21]

Ruprah did not confine his inside information to terror-related material. Perhaps feeling the need to curry favor to be removed from the travel ban list, he also sent Brad a paper detailing the inner workings of Charles Taylor's Liberian finances. In a November 11 fax marked "urgent," Ruprah listed banks, account numbers, and account holders from Riggs Bank in Washington, D.C., to Emirates Bank International in Dubai.[22] His level of information and promises of additional insight showed an intimate knowledge of the Taylor regime's financial structure—contrary to Ruprah's later public statements that he hardly knew Taylor and had no financial dealings with him.

The communication with the FBI was not a one-way street. There were hints from Brad that a deal was in the works. The FBI agent replied cryptically on November 14, 2001, to one Ruprah missive: "Have received message. Will take for consideration. Meet Friday to discuss. Business should be good for you under current circumstances. Don't expect an answer before next week re your proposal." The American agent also said "we're still interested in specific associates you may have in this country . . . if YOU are familiar with unseamly [sic] business practices. In such a case, we may be interested in working with YOU independent of other associates. Interested? Regards, Waters."[23]

There is no clear evidence that the American government ultimately took Ruprah—and Bout—up on the offer to aid in the invasion of Afghanistan. But Western government officials and intelligence agents have talked openly in the intervening years about Bout's role as if it were well understood that Bout had provided assistance to the U.S. efforts either before, during, or after the invasion.

Several European intelligence officials claimed that Bout's aircraft were used by U.S. Special Forces and the CIA to fly into Afghanistan in preparation for the landing of Special Forces and CIA teams in October 2001. Bout's air fleet was well positioned in Sharjah and frequently flew to neighboring Central Asian airfields.

"We know Bout had his aircraft near Afghanistan and made them available to the U.S. efforts almost immediately," said one European official. "They needed him and he had the only airlift capacity in the region. Why not? Anyone else would have done the same. The deal was, if he flew, the U.S. would leave him alone."[24]

Richard Chichakli would later boast that during the Afghan invasion, Bout had organized three flights ferrying U.S. personnel to Afghanistan. Chichakli declined to elaborate on their purpose or when the flights occurred—and later, he disowned the remarks.[25]

Brian Sheridan, who served as assistant secretary of defense for special operations in the Clinton administration, flatly dismissed the idea that military officials would have hired Bout planes to fly in Special Forces units into Afghanistan. "We would never trust putting our special ops people on anyone else's aircraft," Sheridan said. And Michael Scheuer, who had left the CIA's bin Laden task force before 9/11 but returned immediately afterward, said that to his knowledge, the U.S. intelligence teams that were inserted into Afghanistan before the invasion were flown in on Northern Alliance Mi-8 helicopters operating out of Uzbekistan.

Lee Wolosky, who was still working out of the State Department in the weeks after the terror attacks, said he had been aware that Bout "offered himself up after 9/11, as did many of his ilk, who crawled out of the woodwork, viewing this as a tremendous opportunity to ingratiate themselves to the Americans." But Wolosky said he never saw any credible information indicating Bout's overtures were acted on. "I'd be curious to know what his intelligence value could be in the war against al Qaeda. It would require that someone made the determination after 9/11 that he might be helpful in the war against terrorism. We knew he had a relationship with the bad guys so my question is what would his value be and what could he deliver that would be worth setting him up in business with us? From our vantage point, you would have to know those answers in order to justify a trade-off—and I'm not sure that anyone in the

U.S. government was in a position to know that. You would only work with him if you knew he had something to offer. But how would we truly know that?"

Even if he did not fly for U.S. forces, Bout and his pilots had other types of assistance they could offer in exchange for forging a future relationship. They had, from years of dealing with all sides in Afghanistan, unique and detailed knowledge of the landing strips and air approach routes inside a country where the United States had virtually no presence for decades. His pilots were among the only ones who regularly flew the terrain, kept detailed maps, and knew how to negotiate the treacherous mountain passes, even at night. It was vitally important intelligence that could aid the United States in its assault on the Taliban. Navigational aid may have been part of a deal with Bout, with the promise of other jobs in the future. "The GRU and DIA people have a working knowledge of each other's assets," said a private contractor with intelligence ties. "On both sides they know how to make the approach."[26]

Yet soon after hostilities ceased in Afghanistan in January 2002, U.S. Defense intelligence experts were sent to Afghanistan to root through seized Taliban and al Qaeda weapons caches, searching for any evidence that militant arsenals had been provided by the Bout organization. "Everyone's looking for it," said one U.S. official involved in the hunt. "Everybody wants the proof. But how do you find it?"

They left without it. When the U.S. experts poked into Afghan caves and storerooms crammed floor-to-ceiling with Kalashnikovs, grenade launchers, and shells, they found few traces of identifying paperwork or records. The caches were little more than dusty, first-come, first-served warehouses where Taliban and al Qaeda fighters grabbed what was available. Many of the guns were of East European issue, but there were Chinese and North Korean copycat models as well. None bore any markings that could lead the Defense experts back to the Bout network.

In the end, the searchers had little choice beyond turning the weapons over to the Northern Alliance or disposing of them. "We just blew them up mostly," the official said.[27]

A UN panel charged with monitoring the flow of weapons into

Afghanistan, however, found flows of new weapons into the Taliban and al Qaeda remnants in early 2002. Led by Michael Chandler, a no-nonsense retired colonel from the British army, the panel was aggressively seeking to keep the Islamic radicals from gaining access to guns and, even more worrisome, weapons of mass destruction. Chandler, who had come across Bout's network in Bosnia in the early 1990s and knew of his operations through British intelligence, was receiving information on Bout's ties to Afghanistan. In January Chandler's panel wrote that it had "reliable information" that caused concern that "certain individuals, including Victor Bout . . . could have been involved or may be tempted in the future to become involved, in the illegal supply of arms and ammunition to the Taliban, their sympathizers and elements of al Qaeda."[28]

On January 25, 2002, Sanjivan Ruprah flew again to Washington, granted a secret waiver by U.S. Immigration to travel despite being on the UN travel ban list. He was hustled over to the FBI's Washington field office headquarters for an interview. The debriefing was voluntary, and Ruprah still hoped for American help in being shunted off the UN sanctions list.[29] The interview lasted more than an hour, and FBI agents asked surprisingly few questions about Bout, although that was the ostensible reason for the interview. More time was spent asking Ruprah about his business activities before he got involved in the arms trade. Even so, Ruprah showed a detailed understanding of Bout's businesses, giving the name of his air companies, front companies, and methods of payment. He pressed the FBI again for help in getting off the travel ban list and help for his family. No commitments were made.

The FBI kept its contacts with Ruprah secret from the Bout task force. The agency also later declined to release copies of its interviews to other federal agencies that had begun looking for information on Bout's corporate structure in order to freeze his assets. But a transcript of the January interview turned up on Ruprah's hard drive in Italy, becoming part of the case file.

Soon after Ruprah's return to Belgium, the net of Belgian justice finally caught up with him. On February 2, he was arrested and his house was raided along with seventeen other offices and homes, including those of four Bulgarians. Among the items found in the raid, according to local press reports, were records of payments from the UNITA rebels in Angola, "passes from Bagram airport in Afghanistan, which could indicate that Bout had done businsess with the Taliban," and maps of Afghanistan detailing the nation's military facilities.[30]

Luc de Temmerman, a lawyer hired by Ruprah, put out a garbled statement in Ruprah's defense. The lawyer acknowledged Ruprah's contacts with U.S. officials and said that Ruprah had been asked to obtain information on al Qaeda. While saying that Ruprah had a "privileged relationship" with Liberia's Taylor and that he knew Bout, De Temmerman maintained his client had done nothing illegal. He said Ruprah had provided authorities with information about his "conversations with Victor BOUT concerning unpaid debts of [Rwandan president] Paul Kagame and DRC rebels. These debts amount to more than $21,000,000 for the lease of airplanes in the rebel areas and pillaging of the Congolese soil. KAGAME refuses or cannot pay these debts."[31]

Responding to accounts in the *Washington Post* and the *Los Angeles Times* quoting federal officials that Ruprah had offered information about Bout's aid to Islamic militants in Afghanistan, De Temmerman insisted that "at no time Sanjivan Ruprah could give any usefull [sic] information about a possible relation between AL QAEDA and a RUSSIAN ARMS DEALER (BOUT)." He added that Ruprah "was approached by the FBI-CIA and the UNITED NATIONS and given the assignment to obtain information about al QAEDA through his own network."[32]

Ruprah was jailed in a bleak Belgian federal prison in downtown Brussels. His only visitors were De Temmerman and Ruprah's sister, Simi, who came from London to support him. Ruprah kept up his correspondence with Brad, pleading for aid in getting released. In a May 2002 handwritten letter, Ruprah told the FBI agent that "I am receiving news very regularly on matters we discussed last when we met. I will continue to do so. I would appreciate any form of formal/informal pressure from you and your people if possible on the authorities here, should you feel comfortable with that."

The whole affair was a giant misunderstanding, Ruprah complained to the agent. "I have only been questioned once on my association with Victor (and that was the first time I was questioned)," Ruprah wrote. "Subsequently there has been no further questions regarding Victor as there is no evidence of any association between us in the year (94–96) that Victor was living in Belgium when he is meant to have broken arms laws here."[33]

Ruprah asked if he could cite Brad to Belgian authorities as a "concerned friend" to speed the U.S. official's visit to him in prison. It is not known if the agent agreed, but Ruprah was suddenly freed on bail two months later, on the condition that he report regularly to the authorities. Ruprah took off to Italy, where he was rearrested on August 2, only to be again freed on bond in September. He fled to Africa, where he remains.

Ruprah's arrest was only the first phase by Bout's European pursuers, who had been angered by his extensive U.S. contacts. Fearing the Americans might move to protect him, the Belgians said nothing to Washington about their next step.

On February 18, 2002, the Belgian Foreign Ministry quietly issued an Interpol red notice accusing Viktor Bout of money laundering and illegal weapons trafficking. The four-year investigation led by Dirk Merckx had finally led to an arrest warrant charging Bout's organization with funneling more than $32.5 million in laundered payments through Belgian corporations between 1994 and 2001. But there was no immediate American response; the task force once headed by Wolosky and Schneidman had been disbanded.

The Interpol notice required officials in any country where Bout was residing to apprehend him and turn him over to Belgian authorities. Bout was presumed to be still based in Sharjah, but to ensure that he was not tipped off, the Interpol action was not announced publicly. European intelligence officials scrambled to come up with a plan of action to nab him before he could slip back to the safety of Russia and its cozy official krisha protection.

The British joined the Belgians in a plan dubbed "Operation Bloodstone." In the aftermath of the September 11 attacks, Hain had sharpened his campaign of rhetoric against Bout. In Febuary 2002 Hain told the *London Sunday Telegraph* that the Bout organization had been "supplying the Taliban and al Qaeda. He must be put out of business." From British intelligence reports, Hain recalled later, he had been aware that Bout's network was "supplying the Taliban on a commercial basis quite early on."[34]

European intelligence networks were already monitoring Bout's movements in Moldova, Cyprus, and other countries he visited in flagrant violation of the UN travel ban. There was solid intelligence in late February that Bout was going to be on an aircraft flying from Moldova, one of his new hubs, to Greece. When Johan Peleman got wind of the operation, he put a bottle of champagne on ice for the moment that Bout's arrest was announced.

An encrypted message was sent by British intelligence field agents as soon as the aircraft took off, alerting superiors in London that the plane was on the way, in order to prepare for the arrest in Athens. But shortly after the message was sent, the aircraft suddenly veered off its flight plan and disappeared into nearby mountainous terrain. About ninety minutes later it reappeared on the radar screens tracking its movements and landed in Athens. Greek and British special forces and intelligence agents boarded the aircraft, only to find it empty except for the pilots and a few other passengers. Less than twenty-four hours later, Belgian intelligence reported a confirmed sighting of Bout in the DRC.

"There were only two intelligence services that could have decrypted the British transmission in so short a time," said one European intelligence official familiar with the operation. "The Russians and the Americans. And we know for sure it was not the Russians."[35]

Bout returned to safety in Moscow, where he could count on the protective eaves of his krisha in the intelligence apparatus. It was the closest he had ever come to being caught.

CHAPTER 12

"We Are Very Limited
in What We Can Do"

T he public leaking of the Belgian arrest warrant sparked an immediate spate of media coverage. Several newspapers had already linked Bout's air network to the Taliban, and the Belgian criminal case against him launched a new wave of stories.[1] Besieged, the Russian finally broke his long silence. On February 28 he appeared for a live interview at Radio Echo Moskvy in Moscow, one of the city's most popular stations. Sitting down with an interviewer for two hours, Bout strongly denied any ties to al Qaeda and the Taliban.

He compared the accusations against him to the cartoonish plot of "Lemonade Joe," a Czech cowboy parody film popular in the Eastern bloc. In Bout's eyes, he was the quarry, hunted by a Western "cowboy who rides around the African jungle, through prairies and deserts in Afghanistan and pulls off anything he wants. And every day I am amazed at this plot, like a thriller. What else will they come up with? Which terrorist organization have I not yet helped?"[2]

In his wounded tirade, he launched into elaborate conspiracy theories, depicting his predicament as part of a larger anti-Russian agenda driven by old Cold War rivalries. "You see, in relation to

Russians there is always bias and double standards," Bout said. "For example if a Russian businessman works somewhere abroad he is very easily labeled Russian. Next comes the word mafia, then weapons, then something else. It is very difficult to fight off. . . . They can't catch bin Laden. Naturally they have to come up with another idea, to say the Russians are to blame. Here is Viktor Bout. Let's catch him."[3]

During the interview, a bulletin from the Interfax news service arrived and was promptly read on the air by Bout's interviewer. "The Russian bureau of Interpol has announced that it has been seeking Viktor Bout, suspected of having supplied weapons to the Al-Qa'ida organization, for four years," the announcer said. "[Interpol] spokesman Igor Tsiroulnikov declared: 'Today we can say with certainty that Viktor Bout is not in Russian territory.'"[4] Then the interviewer returned to Bout, whose presence had just been denied by his own government. Embarrassed Russian officials later backtracked from the denial. A new statement claimed "there is no reason to believe that this Russian citizen has committed any illegal actions."[5]

In the days afterward, Bout kept up the pace, appearing from Moscow on CNN and other TV stations, the only times he has ever gone public on television to defend himself. He declined to answer most direct questions about the specifics of his business dealings, preferring sweeping denials of all charges and bristling when pushed to answer specific points. On March 4 he released a statement through Chichakli, his U.S. partner, saying that he had remained silent for years in the face of the "barrage of allegations" because he felt responding would only legitimize them.

"I have been silently watching my family, friends, associates and the countries that provided me with an opportunity to conduct honest business, hurt and harassed and the cargo business I spent years to build dissipate into dust," Bout said. "All of this occurred without a shred of evidence other than the questionable testimonies of thugs and untrustworthy characters that directly benefited from having a scapegoat."[6]

"For the record, I am not and never have been associated with al Qaeda, the Taliban or any of their officials, officers or related organizations," Bout wrote. "I am not nor are any of my organizations, associated with arms trafficking and/or trafficking or the sale of arms of kind [*sic*] anywhere in the world. I am not, nor is any member of my family, associated with any military or intelligence organizations of any country."[7]

Bout painted himself as an honest businessman hounded by news organizations that "have recklessly and intentionally fabricated stories which continue to snowball away from reality. . . . I appeal to you to reexamine the story and use nothing more than common sense to separate fact from fiction."[8]

In a subsequent interview Bout maintained he had only one passport, from the Russian Federation, and that Russian intelligence had never questioned him about his activities. He deflected questions about his business, including where he obtained his original aircraft. "Are you conducting an investigation or a journalistic inquiry?" he bristled when asked about how he started. "You shouldn't intrude in the area of relations that I don't have the right to reveal according to my contracts and my obligations."[9]

Asked about Afghanistan, he replied: "Afghanistan? Yes, we delivered large quantities of freight before the Taliban arrived," Bout said. "According to 1997 figures, we were second only to Lufthansa in freight deliveries. We worked with the legitimate and internationally recognized Rabbani government. We delivered consumer goods—90 percent were textiles, various types of equipment, bearings, furniture."[10]

In the post–September 11 world, the Bush administration had little interest in involving itself in Belgium's efforts to arrest Bout or in media investigations into Bout's prior ties with Islamic militants. Russia was rapidly emerging as a key country to be courted in the administration's efforts to build a global consensus to fight al Qaeda. Russian Federation president Vladimir Putin himself was immersed in a bloody war in Chechnya, where the independence movement was led by al Qaeda-affiliated Islamic groups. Whatever Bout's past misdeeds, even his deals with the Taliban, Bush officials felt they were not worth jeopardizing the chance to build a counterterrorism alliance with Russia. The perception within the intelligence community at the time was that Bout was protected by senior Russian officials, possibly even Putin himself. Making Bout an issue could damage the chance to advance other issues higher on the bilateral agenda.

In late May there was a direct opportunity for U.S. officials to raise the issue of the Bout network during Bush's state visit to Moscow for a series of talks with Putin. But Wolosky was no longer around to provide a thorough briefing, and Condoleezza Rice was more concerned with lining up Russia's support for the war on terrorism. Even if Bout had been the militants' enabler, bringing his name up at the summit risked provoking Putin at a moment when Russia was needed as a stalwart ally, senior Bush administration officials felt. "We are very limited," a U.S. national security aide to Rice explained, "in what we can do."[11]

As U.S. and British intelligence assets that once monitored Bout were redirected to other targets, Bout was relatively free to go about his business, including recementing his ongoing ties to the tottering Taylor regime in Liberia. The loss of former partners such as Ruprah barely seemed to slow Bout down.

The only real scrutiny came from journalists and the UN panels, which continued to monitor the movements of Bout's aircraft with brutal efficiency. But with no enforcement mechanisms other than the globally mandated but rarely used travel bans, the UN could be easily ignored.

From June 1, 2002, to August 25, six large weapons shipments totaling 210 tons arrived at Roberts International Airport in Liberia. They fueled the last gasp of Taylor's crumbling rule, allowing him to hold out almost another year before being driven to seek asylum in Nigeria. Most of the weapons were flown by an Il-76 owned by a company named Jetline, registered in Moldova, which in turn had leased the aircraft from the Bout-controlled Aerocom, also based in Moldova.

The shipments originated in Belgrade. Most of the flights refueled in Libya en route. The sellers used a series of fake EUCs from Nigeria procured by a Yugoslavian company called Temex to make the shipments appear to be legal. The pilots filed false flight plans, indicating the Nigerian Ministry of Defense in Lagos, rather than Liberia, as the final recipient of the cargo. The cargo was often labeled "mining equipment" rather than weapons. Front companies such as Waxom in Liechtenstein were used to further confuse the trail.[12]

Slobodan Tesic, one of the infamous weapons brokers in the Balkans, organized the sales for Bout's network, even flying to Monrovia to meet with Taylor to set up the deal.[13] The companies he used, Temex and Waxam, were not unknown in the world of international sanctions busting. For several years Tesic, through the same two companies, had quietly been working with Saddam Hussein to update Iraq's military arsenal, including technology to build cruise missiles, in clear violation of UN sanctions.[14]

The Liberia shipments contained million of rounds of ammunition, thousands of rifles, missile launchers, antiaircraft guns, spare parts for helicopter gunships, and countless other weapons. Bout was still interested in maximizing his profits as well. The return flights in several cases included stopovers to pick up lucrative loads of fresh fish to deliver in Slovakia.[15]

Bout also was expanding his activities in two of his previous haunts, Sudan and Libya, where he had companies and carried out charter businesses. His brother Sergei opened several businesses in Sophia, Bulgaria.

But even as Viktor Bout was issuing the new denials, elite European intelligence units were picking up ominous indications that Bout's network had not completely severed his ties with the radical Islamic groups in Afghanistan. As the Taliban fell, its holdouts and al Qaeda stalwarts had sent waves of couriers to move their jeopardized treasury of gold ingots and other valuables across the border for safekeeping in Pakistan. Some of the gold, as well as new stores acquired by trading opium, were quietly shipped by air from Pakistan to the UAE and Iran, and then on to Sudan. At least some of the aircraft being chartered to fly the gold shipments and other products belonged to Viktor Bout's companies.[16]

The militants' use of gold as a currency was not unusual. Gold had a special place in the financial architecture of the Taliban and al Qaeda, as well as among the general populations of the Arabian Peninsula and Pakistan. The metal was a traditional measure of wealth, and a stable holding in the face of the often volatile currency fluctuations in the region. The Taliban collected much of its taxes and donations in gold, and bin Laden offered rewards in gold for killing his enemies. On May 6, 2004, in an audiotaped message, bin Laden had offered "a reward equaling ten thousand grams of gold to he who kills the occupier [Paul] Bremer or his deputy or the commander of Americans in Iraq or his deputy . . . and five hundred grams of gold to he who kills a military or a civilian from the slaves of the General Assembly in Iraq. . . . Due to the security situation, the payments of the rewards will be at the earliest opportunity, by leave of Allah."[17]

The gold supplies were the takings of what one Pakistani businessman knowledgeable of Taliban financing called a "commodity-for-commodity exchange," with the Taliban and al Qaeda trading opium and heroin for gold. When the Taliban ruled Afghanistan, according to Pakistani intelligence officials, it actively engaged in opium and heroin production, and allowed al Qaeda to raise funds through taxing the cultivation of poppy, the raw material for heroin.[18]

The reports of Bout company aircraft involved in aiding the flow of gold for narcotics heightened suspicion among European officials monitoring Afghanistan that Bout's enterprises had long been involved in drug trafficking—an allegation they were never able to prove, but one they could not dismiss. Further concerns of a drug connection surfaced in 2003 when an Antonov 26B aircraft, later traced to Bout's Aerocom company, landed on a remote jungle road in the sleepy Central American country of Belize and later was found abandoned.

A report by the Drug Enforcement Administration revealed that on August 29, 2003, the aircraft landed one and a half miles from Belize's remote border with Mexico, a favorite cocaine trafficking route for Colombian drug cartels. "After landing, the aircraft's landing gear became stuck in the mud and it was unable to take off," the report said. "Before the aircraft was abandoned, several individuals arrived at the landing site, and picked up the crew and 10 bales of suspected cocaine, and departed for Mexico."[19]

Belgium, the Netherlands, and other European countries, all with small intelligence services and dedicating most of their limited resources to tracking terrorist threats and supporting the U.S. occupation of Afghanistan, had little ability to run down the continuing reports of Bout's activities. But the Belgian Foreign Ministry doggedly continued to press Russia for a formal response to the Interpol arrest warrant. In December 2002, almost a year after the arrest warrant was issued, the Belgians were stunned by the Russian response. The Russian Foreign Ministry formally stated that Viktor Bout was not a Russian citizen, despite the fact that he had applied successfully for Russian nationality as an ex-member of the armed forces of the Soviet Union.[20] Despite the preposterous Russian claim, the Belgian government could get no further explanation or clarification.

In Washington, official interest in Bout's network was little more than dormant. Frustrated by the Bush administration's inattention, Lee Wolosky had returned to the life of a corporate lawyer in New York. Richard Clarke had been sidelined to the position of national cyber security adviser, his broad authority over transnational threats diminished. The Bout portfolio was shifted to Joseph M. "Jody" Meyers, a Clinton holdover who had worked on terror finance at Treasury before taking over international threats at the NSC.

In the weeks after the Belgian government and Interpol circulated the red notice for Bout's arrest in February 2002, there was a brief uptick of attention at the NSC. Meyers found himself at the center of a flurry of "papers and phone calls" and proposed letters of démarche to the Russians requesting their cooperation in handing Bout over to the Belgians. But with the lack of interest from Rice and other senior NSC officials, the unsent démarches were filed away. "After 9/11, things changed with Russia," Meyers said. "Suddenly, they were our best friends. Anything having to do with Russian organized crime was swept under the rug."[21]

A small working group of State and NSC officials was thrown together to mull over new directions against the Bout empire. During several inconclusive meetings, officials recited the latest collated intelligence on the Russian's network. But by mid-2002, the meetings petered out.

In July, Wolosky and Will Wechsler wrote a stinging op-ed essay that ran in the *Los Angeles Times* and the *Moscow Times*, faulting the Bush administration's silence and inactivity on Bout. "To date, Putin has not touched him. And why should he? Neither President Bush nor any senior administration official has asked him to." Bout's "continuing impunity," Wolosky and Weschler wrote, "sends the wrong message" from international partners who "need to address post–Cold War threats together. A good way to start would be to take down Victor Bout."[22]

There was no reply from either nation. But one enterprising U.S. official had grown intrigued by the Bout empire's global reach, fascinated enough to start gathering his own private files with the hope that he might prod government action.

Andreas Morgner read all the press stories he could on Viktor Bout, adding them to a growing collection he had started in the weeks before September 11. Middle-aged, sandy-haired, and slightly paunchy, Morgner had spent ten years in the CIA as a counternarcotics specialist before moving over to the Treasury Department's Office of Foreign Assets Control (OFAC) in the spring of 2001. The OFAC, created in 1950 to block all Chinese and North Korean assets during the Korean War, originally had the job of enforcing economic embargoes on sanctioned countries such as Cuba and Iraq. But as the war on drugs snowballed in the late 1980s, the small office had become increasingly important because it could designate an individual or a business as dangerous to the United States and freeze their assets. The threshold for taking such action was high and had to pass through numerous interagency and judicial reviews. But it had proved to be an effective method of freezing the assets of Latin American drug barons inside the United States and was much quicker than building a criminal case.

Morgner started out as part of the OFAC team looking to seize drug money. Both at the CIA and the OFAC he had specialized in Latin American drug trafficking and the money movements of the criminal syndicates. He well understood the importance of aircraft in illicit enterprises and had become something of an aviation buff on the side.

In August 2001, while reading an aviation magazine, he came across a photo spread of dozens of Russian planes on the runways of Sharjah, including some belonging to Bout. The story noted that "these aircraft are destined to fly again in Africa irrespective of their certificate of airworthiness status."[23] The story planted the germ of an idea—why not target the assets of Viktor Bout for seizure by the OFAC? He tore out the pages and kept them for future reference.

When Morgner mentioned it to his superiors, they expressed no opposition. It was a low priority, but Morgner was free to pursue the idea as long as he took care of his other business.

Morgner was not aware, however, that the NSC, the State Department, and the CIA already had a long-standing program under way. He knew nothing of Ruprah's contacts with the FBI agent "Brad." Morgner did not even have access to an unclassified report on Bout that the Treasury Department's own Bureau of Alcohol, Tobacco, and Firearms had written in December 2000 and circulated to UN investigators and European intelligence services. Because of the incompatibility of databases and the lack of shared information among government agencies, much of the classified information gathered on Bout's operation by the task force headed by Wolosky and Schneidman had been stovepiped into hidden bureaucratic compartments that Morgner, even with his high-level clearances, could not find.

In the aftermath of September 11, the OFAC's role suddenly changed. Terrorist charities, banks, and money-changing hawalas—informal money remittance services—had suddenly become key targets in the war on terror, and the OFAC was thrust into the forefront of investigative efforts to unravel their structures and freeze their assets. Morgner's nascent interest in Bout remained a back-burner item. Morgner's primary job was to pitch in on various OFAC investigations into Islamic charities alleged to be supporting al Qaeda and other terrorist groups

But as Morgner read the growing barrage of media stories on Bout in the spring and summer of 2002, he realized that he was not the only one with an interest in the shadowy arms merchant. He was summoned to join the working group that met several times after Bout surfaced in Moscow. But without direction from above, the group treaded water. The meetings stopped. "Basically, everybody was trying to figure out what everyone else knew. There was no sense of urgency," Morgner recalled.

Only as the crush of terrorism cases eased was Morgner able to devote his attention to Bout, who had by then become linked publicly to the Taliban. Morgner felt that the OFAC might be able to designate the Bout network as a terrorist-related target, based on the media reports of its airplane sales and logistics support to the Taliban and its gold shipments for Islamic militants. Using the

OFAC was a new approach and would prove to be one of the effective government weapons against Bout's freewheeling operation.

Morgner began reaching out to old friends in the intelligence community and the State Department, then to Johan Peleman and other UN investigators. But even as the informal network fed him updated information, Morgner realized he was only gathering string. The Bout issue was no longer a high enough priority anywhere in the government to command serious interagency cooperation, and there were no policymakers asking for information. Morgner tried couching his official requests for information under the rubric of "counterterrorism," but his efforts went unanswered. No one waved him off the Bout case, but it was not a pressing interest higher up in the OFAC or at the main Treasury Department.

After September 11, a senior Treasury official explained, the Russian's network was only "one in a fertile field of targets. Yeah, he was a bad guy, but there are a whole lot of other bad guys out there."[24] Given the OFAC's limited resources and the labor-intensive nature of each designation, the official said, Bout's indirect ties to al Qaeda did not immediately make him a top-tier terrorism target.

Still, the more Morgner learned, the more passionate he grew in his pursuit of Bout. He felt that Bout was something more than a typical criminal. "Viktor Bout supports people who absolutely slaughter people," Morgner concluded. "No one else has the ability to pour that kind of stuff into wars. He is a vulture, basically profiting on other people's misery. And what is galling is the sheer volume of it." But few in the government shared his outrage. And those few were not in a position to make policy.

While Morgner was quietly building his case file on Bout, the Bush administration had greater and seemingly unrelated concerns: preparing to invade Iraq and topple Saddam Hussein. Morgner had no realization how much the Iraq war would alter his work and the fortunes of the Bout empire.

With a new, major Middle East conflict about to take place, Bout's reputation as the master of chaos was about to be put to the ultimate test. He was either just about to lose his market, or expand it beyond imagination.

CHAPTER 13

Welcome to Baghdad

On his rounds at Baghdad International Airport, U.S. Air National Guard major Christopher Walker had a close-range view of the organized frenzy of the U.S. airlift into Iraq. Landing on the hour in a din of droning propellers and whining jet engines, an armada of civilian cargo planes roared into Baghdad from around the world on a daily mission to replenish America's postwar military supply lines and Iraq's reconstruction.

As many as sixty civilian flights and seventy military aircraft arrived each day from Persian Gulf and Central Asian airports, loaded with deliveries for coalition depots and private contractors' warehouses. At the airport's cargo field, not far from his office inside a dilapidated terminal building, Walker watched as forklifts scuttled by like motorized beetles, skirting into and out of storage bays with pallets and containers loaded with every conceivable cargo: televisions and tents, American-built armored Humvees and Russian-made Kalashnikovs, disassembled oil rigs and massive generators, surgery equipment, electric power poles, frozen food, uniforms, baggage, bulletproof vests, and a ceaseless issue of mail sacks and courier packages. Impatient men hurried everywhere. Teams of American and Iraqi aviation specialists paced into and out of the hangars, bickering over the airport's future. Air force refueling crews struggled with heavy aviation fuel hoses. Armed Gurkhas and American mercenaries patrolled the perimeter fence for insurgents. Anxious pilots readied their planes while their cargo holds were emptied, racing to finish and fly out of Baghdad before a mandatory night curfew left them stranded until dawn.

Walker, a trim, unflappable thirty-seven-year-old Air National Guard veteran from western Maryland, was the point man for the largest U.S. government air cargo operation since the Berlin Airlift of the late 1940s. He had arrived in Baghdad on August 15, 2003, assigned as senior flight clearance officer for the Coalition Provisional Authority (CPA), the American occupation administration. Walker was the final authority on deciding whether each nonmilitary cargo plane could land and depart. He was an air force navigator by trade, and had flown supply missions on C-130 freighters into Afghanistan during the 2002 U.S. invasion. He returned to his wartime mission in spring 2003, guiding the huge cargo carriers on transport sorties into Baghdad, constantly on alert for shoulder-fired missiles. On one night flight, electronic alarms aboard Walker's C-130 suddenly wailed, warning that a manned surface-to-air missile had locked in on the plane's heat trail. The pilot took evasive action, banking steeply, and the missile never neared. As a young Brooklyn high school student enamored of flight, Walker later enrolled in the Air Force Academy to get in on just that kind of action. But when he mentioned to his commander that he wanted to do something more substantial for the postwar effort, Walker was steered to his new job as "airspace guru" on the staff of CPA administrator L. Paul Bremer. Hired in June 2003, Walker arrived in August, shuttling in a beat-up Toyota pickup truck between his window-seat office at Terminal B at the airport and the CPA's complex in the Presidential Palace in downtown Baghdad.

Security at BIAP—aviation industry shorthand for the French-designed field once known as Saddam International Airport—had barely improved by the time Walker took charge. The distant staccato of sniper fire was a reminder of the peril at hand. Several times a week, insurgents outside the five-kilometer perimeter fence lobbed mortar rounds toward the airport. They had the aim of the blind. The shells usually exploded harmlessly wide of the airfield, marked by faint thuds. But the volleys were still close enough to paralyze the airport for several hours. The military side of the divided airport ran like clockwork. Equipped with sophisticated radar, guidance, and evasion systems, the air force's C-130s and other supply planes were well suited to deal with perils from the ground. But on the civilian side, where Walker held sway, few commercial cargo planes had those systems. The constant threat of ground-fired SA-7 and other MANPAD missiles kept delaying the planned return of commercial passenger flights. Skittish U.S. war logistics planners had already forbidden any American commercial air freight firms from participating in the airlift, worried that their sluggish, unprotected planes would be sitting ducks aloft.

Military aircraft such as Walker's C-130 were plentiful, and sufficient to handle the bulk of tactical in-theater supply and transport needs for immediate war operations. But the Department of Defense still required a flotilla of civilian carriers for its strategic long-haul deliveries of everything else—from heavyweight shipments of helicopter gunships to minor everyday items such as boots and blankets. With the American civilian air transport fleet unavailable, Defense contracting officials and major reconstruction firms both moved quickly in spring 2003 to find alternate options. They turned to private air companies that were based in neighboring Middle East airfields and fielded crews experienced at flying into danger zones; more often than not, they hired Russians. Senior logistics officials had already relied on Russian and Ukrainian air firms based in the Persian Gulf and Central Asia to back up American cargo planes after the invasion of Afghanistan. Giant Antonov An-124s had airlifted heavy supplies into Bagram Air Base near Kabul. In July 2002, even as senior military officials were secretly making preparations for the Iraq invasion, air force general John W. Handy, commander in chief of the U.S. Transportation Command, publicly acknowledged that "shortfalls both in airlift and refueling" were forcing planners to rely increasingly on East European aviation firms. The bulk of the capacity was still handled by C-130s. But "the world has changed," Handy told *National Defense* magazine. "The Soviet Union is dead and now we even have contacts with businesses in former Soviet republics."[1]

The first few civilian cargo planes arrived in Baghdad in late April 2003, just weeks after the airport was seized by American troops. Once the crown jewel of Saddam Hussein's grandiose dreams of transforming Baghdad into an international travel and commerce destination, the airport now lay in ruins. Its thirteen-thousand-foot runway was pocked with craters. Looters had stripped furniture and radar equipment from the tower and stolen the facility's fuel trucks. The bullet-riddled main terminal was littered with trash, its gaudy wall tributes to Saddam stripped down. U.S. troops bivouacked in every available building. The earliest flights brought shipments of food, dry milk, medical supplies, and other humanitarian cargoes, and were soon joined by freighters flying for U.S. military contractors. Many of the planes arriving from Dubai, Sharjah, Amman, and other Persian Gulf hubs were familiar staples of Third World aviation—durable, old Ilyushins and Antonovs, their sturdy undercarriages and extra wheels equipped to take the punishment from BIAP's scarred runways.

To oversee the flights, military officials first tapped Army Reserve Sergeant Steve Goldblatt, an Illinois civil affairs expert who had experience in airline industry marketing, to handle flight clearance—the job later taken on by Walker. Goldblatt was never told how the first cargo flights into Baghdad had been chosen or contracted. All he knew was that the flights had been approved at RAMCC (Regional Air Movement Control Center), the U.S. military's centralized air command operation in Qatar. As Goldblatt poked around the devastated airport, he was stunned to find a DHL office already set up and staffed in a bombed-out corner of a vacant building. The DHL agent shrugged when Goldblatt asked how the firm had won permission to operate there. "He told me they got in right after the Third Infantry seized the airport," Goldblatt recalled. Soon afterward, the National Guard sergeant saw arriving DHL flights staffed by Russian crews and planes.

By May, Goldblatt was joined by Captain Mason Sellers, a reserve Civil Affairs officer from Maryland. Sellers toughened clearance procedures at Baghdad, demanding to see copies of Defense contracts and cargo manifests before he would permit new air cargo firms to land. But the first wave of air firms operating in Baghdad were simply grandfathered in—they already had military approval, and as long as their records remained clean, they were not second-guessed. "Planes were just showing up without any proper papers, but you couldn't turn them away because they were carrying critical stuff," Sellers recalled. Besides, Goldblatt concluded, the former Soviet military pilots seemed capable and "pretty fearless." They easily negotiated the difficult corkscrew turns required of aircraft flying into and out of Baghdad to elude missiles and RPG attacks. During long delays, they strung hammocks under their wings and left vodka bottles strewn on the tarmac. "They couldn't care less" about perils of missile attacks or crumbled runways, Goldblatt marveled. "As long as they were being paid, they'd fly."[2]

The Russians were the least of Chris Walker's concerns when he took over Baghdad's flight clearance operation in the fall of 2003. Several fly-by-night air firms had disobeyed landing procedures, and at least one, a Lebanese outfit, was banned outright from Baghdad. The Russians and other East European air crews, adept at seat-of-the-pants flying, blended right in with BIAP's "cowboy environment." They rarely spoke more than a smattering of English, a language barrier that sometimes became a concern during nerve-racking approaches. But their planes were better suited than newer American models for the airport's rugged conditions. "They were cheap and plentiful, old warplanes built for chaos and adverse conditions," Walker said. "They could take bad runways, crash landings, and keep on flying. Airbuses and Boeings were just not built for that kind of wartime stress."

The Russians faded into the background as Walker wrestled with a rash of new problems. Sudden power blackouts were darkening the field and shutting down flight operations several times a week. Looted furniture and equipment still had not been replaced, forcing some airport officials to work on crates. Inexperienced Iraqis had taken over forklift operations, leading to a surge in smashed pallets and punctured aircraft hulls. And in December, a departing German DHL Airbus 300 was struck by a SAM 7 surface-to-air missile. With one wing shredded and an engine aflame, the freighter managed to land safely. The repercussions were immediate: commercial flights were delayed even further. Cargo operations picked up after a brief delay, but with tighter security arrangements. Fearing that skyrocketing air insurance rates would shut down the Baghdad airlift, Walker and another CPA official quietly flew to London to plead with Lloyd's of London to keep carriers' rates low.

By spring 2004, cargo operations had resumed without further incidents, and the airport settled back into its normal high-pitched state of chaos. As the pace of reconstruction work in Iraq quickened, the volume of daily cargo flights rose dramatically, from twenty-five a day in January to more than sixty by April. Overworked air freighters were flying into BIAP in the morning, departing and returning for a second run by day's end. Every day, Walker had to sort through a growing backlog of new e-mails requesting permission to land. And there was the constant intrusion of cold calls from air firm and shipping agents pleading their cases to set up favored new passenger and cargo routes into Baghdad. "Everything was hurry up, we need it now," Walker recalled. "It wasn't when do you want it, it was: Do it now. The fewer questions asked the better."[3]

Then, one morning in mid-May, Walker flicked on his laptop and saw an urgent e-mail relayed from his superior, former marine lieutenant general Jeffrey Oster, Bremer's deputy administrator and the CPA's chief operating officer. Officials in Washington were up in arms about a May 17 news story that had appeared in the *Financial Times* of London. Though its details were sketchy, the newspaper was reporting that Viktor Bout's air transport network was active again: the Russian's air firms appeared to be "delivering goods to U.S. forces in Iraq." At the same time, the newspaper added, French officials were complaining that U.S. and British diplomats were resisting a Security Council proposal to impose an assets freeze on Bout as part of efforts by the United Nations to isolate associates of Liberian dictator Charles Taylor, who had been forced from power in 2003. "U.S. and British officials at the UN deny any knowledge of Mr. Bout's alleged activities in Iraq," the *Times* reported.[4] Oster wanted to know whether the story was accurate. If it was, he wanted Walker's recommendations on how to deal with it. "We need answers," Oster messaged.

Walker had never heard of Viktor Bout. But as Walker began contacting American military contracting officials and scanned aviation and news sites on the Internet in the days that followed, the odd Russian name became depressingly familiar.

Bout had pulled off the ultimate metamorphosis, from hunted international criminal to the U.S. military's secret delivery man. In times of war, his fleet of battered planes had proved again and again that it could move anything into and out of battle zones, no matter how rough the terrain or chaotic the circumstances. It was the global reach of his planes, a rugged transport system that no other private hauler could duplicate, that made Bout's organization such a valued partner across the Third World. Now the same logistical prowess that had alarmed Lee Wolosky because of the access it offered to terrorists and warlords made Bout's network useful to U.S. military planners. When America went to war, repercussions could always be shunted off for later, after the shooting stopped and the supplies were in. Bout got things done, no questions asked. But it quickly became clear in the aftermath of the swift U.S. victory over Saddam Hussein's hapless forces that the shooting would go on and that the urgent need for supplies would not let up. In time, the hiring of Bout's planes in Iraq became a glaring embarrassment for the Bush administration, a textbook case of shoddy postwar planning and bureaucratic blindness.

After only a few hours online, sitting at his desk in the Presidential Palace, Chris Walker realized that the Coalition Provisional Authority and the Defense Department faced an acute public relations problem. As he read up on the Russian's arms trade background and scanned through lists of his suspected air holdings in UN reports and aviation sites, Walker bristled, recognizing the name of Bout's flagship air firm, Irbis. Registered in Kazakhstan, Irbis—Russian for "snow leopard"—based most of its planes in Sharjah. The firm, Walker would learn later, was an alter ego of Bout's Air Bas operation. Walker knew that "Irbis" was listed repeatedly on the RAMCC flight manifests he looked over every day. Irbis planes had been flying into Baghdad even before he arrived in August 2003. And he had never had reason to double-check the firm's background because Irbis had already been approved through RAMCC. As he scrolled further, Walker read about Bout's manipulation of an entire orchestra of air cargo firms—with names often altered to avoid the scrutiny of prying officials like him. That meant that any of the Russian and Eastern bloc air crews who had been the rock-solid linchpins of the Iraq airlift were now suspect. Several dozen East European air cargo firms had been flying into Baghdad since the summer of 2003. Many of the companies were based in the UAE. Their planes had routinely shuttled into and out of BIAP on hundreds of cargo runs. Some of the flights had carried high-security items such as guns, ammunition, and armored vehicles. How many of the firms, Walker wondered, were run by Viktor Bout? Were there security breaches? How did military intelligence agencies fail to flag Bout's flights before they began arriving in Baghdad? Even if Bout's planes did not pose risks, could insurgents similarly exploit the same security gaps and gain access to BIAP and other American air bases in Iraq?

Walker felt sandbagged. He remembered watching idled Irbis crewmen chain-smoking besides their planes while their cargos unloaded. He had even climbed into the cramped cockpit of one of their Antonovs for a random inspection, admiring the 1960s-vintage freighter's antique altimeters and gauges and torn seats patched with duct tape. "Everything was grizzled, even the crew," he recalled. "They looked like guys who needed a buck. They looked like they hadn't shaved in a week."

Now armed with specific tail numbers of Baghdad flights that matched Bout-tied Antonovs and Ilyushins on Internet aviation sites, Walker began contacting American military officials to find out if Irbis was flying with valid government contracts. The officials he spoke to did not volunteer much, but they confirmed the worst. Bout's network was flying for the United States. The officials explained that Irbis had been hired repeatedly as a secondary military subcontractor, delivering tents, frozen food, and other essentials for American firms working for the U.S. Army and the U.S. Marines. The Bout flagship also was a third-tier contractor for the U.S. Air Mobility Command, flying deliveries for Federal Express under an arrangement with Falcon Express Cargo Airlines, a Dubai-based freight forwarder. And Irbis was also flying, Walker learned, under reconstruction contracts with the petrochemical giant Fluor, and with Kellogg, Brown, and Root (KBR), the engineering and construction subsidiary of Halliburton—the influential multinational conglomerate that had been awarded a massive no-bid reconstruction contract in Iraq and that was previously headed by Vice President Dick Cheney. (Even Walker was unaware at the time that Irbis's contract flights for Fluor had been awarded by the agency he worked for—the CPA. Only two weeks earlier, on May 6, an Irbis Antonov An-12 had flown into Baghdad carrying coalition cargo under contract with Fluor.[5])

Walker began preparing a report for Oster, but even as he wrote, calls were coming in from nervous colleagues. Some wanted Bout's firms banned immediately from any participation in the supply pipeline. Walker was just as perturbed as they were. Bout's network had evaded U.S. security checks and flown in and out undetected for months. But at the same time, Walker was reluctant to interrupt the flow of equipment and matériel to American servicemen in Iraq. "I was pretty bummed to learn we had no idea about the extent of this guy's network," Walker recalled. "But I worried for the guys who would lose out on supplies if we shut him down." As he understood the purview of his job, Walker could only bar an air firm for safety or security reasons. Despite Bout's dalliance with the Taliban and his arms work across the Third World, there were no allegations that the Russian's air crews had committed clear security breaches in their Baghdad flights. As he finished his report, Walker hit on what he felt was the right method to shut down the Bout network's involvement in the Iraq airlift: place the responsibility for dealing with Bout's arrangements squarely with the people who hired his organization in the first place—U.S. military contracting officials. "If you're going to ban Viktor Bout, my attitude was to phase him out through the contracting people. They were the people who hired him. That way they could replace his planes with some other company's—quickly, without jeopardizing the supply lines. They would know the schedule of materials that had to come in and they could handle it properly."

Walker's recommendation made sense to Oster. The former marine general had flagged the British newspaper story because of its possible diplomatic repercussions. "Somehow this guy was on the payroll of the U.S. government when he should have been blacklisted," Oster recalled in late 2004. Oster felt the breakdown needed to be investigated, but he also saw Bout's hiring, as Walker did, through the eyes of a combat veteran—in the rush to equip American servicemen, corners are sometimes cut. "We have an old saying in the Marine Corps: If you want it bad, you get it bad." Oster approved Walker's decision. At the same time, concerned that U.S. officials needed to know how they had fouled up, Oster also forwarded the Bout case to Stuart Bowen, the CPA's inspector general.[6]

Oster's decision hardly settled matters. During a teleconference call several days later with U.S. aviation officials at the Baghdad airport, Walker found himself taking heat for allowing Bout planes to continue to fly. Frank Hatfield, a senior Federal Aviation Administration official detailed to Iraq as an adviser to the CPA, wanted Bout barred. Hatfield was already exorcised about the lax customs procedures of Iraqi aviation officials and had complained that cargo manifests were not being toughly scrutinized at the airport. To his reading, the United States was doing business with a known criminal. "This could be an embarrassment, Chris," he told Walker on the open line. Walker held firm. "That may be so, but we've got supply lines to worry about. If you want me to stop him," Walker told the assembled officials, "give me the order." The phone meeting broke up without consensus.[7]

Pressure was also building in Washington to deal with the emerging revelations about Bout. On May 18, the day after the *Financial Times* story broke, Senator Russell Feingold, a maverick second-term Democrat from Wisconsin, waylaid two senior Bush administration officials about the matter during a Senate Foreign Relations Committee hearing on Iraq reconstruction spending. Feingold, the ranking Democrat on the Africa subcommittee, was well aware of Bout's role in inflaming the continent's war zones with his elusive arms pipelines. As Deputy Secretary of Defense Paul Wolfowitz, a key architect of Pentagon war planning, and Deputy Secretary of State Richard Armitage testified about future Iraq costs, Feingold weighed in with barbed questions about Bout's role in the postwar Iraq airlift. He started with Armitage: "Is Viktor Bout or any firm associated with Viktor Bout providing air freight services for coalition forces in Iraq?" Citing the *Financial Times* story, Feingold added: "Has the United States opposed including Bout on an asset-freeze list being compiled by the UN, which targets individuals who are involved with the criminal regime of former Liberian president Charles Taylor? And if so, why?"

"I certainly hope what you suggest is not true," Armitage replied. He described Bout as a "merchant of death," using the well-worn tag line coined by Britain's Peter Hain. "As far as I'm concerned, he ought to be on any asset-freeze list and anything else you can do to him." Wolfowitz appeared equally in the dark. "I share your concern about it," he said, "and I will work with Secretary Armitage to look into it to try to fix the problem if there is one."[8]

State Department officials began moving rapidly in the days afterward to see what could be done to draw the brakes on U.S. contracts with the Bout organization. They also began pulling internal contracting files to see if their own agency had done any work with the Russian's firms in the past. Armitage had an answer back to Feingold in two weeks. Wolfowitz would stay silent for nine months.

The once-promising U.S. campaign to scuttle the Viktor Bout network had devolved into bureaucratic schizophrenia. Plagued by the Clinton administration's inconsistent political will and turf squabbles with international partners before the September 11 attacks, and then left dormant in the months afterward by Bush administration inaction, U.S. policy toward Bout was now lurching in polar-opposite directions. While the State Department remained committed at least in principle to shutting down Bout's global air transport operation, the Defense Department was enriching it with government contracts and American taxpayer funds.

Among the far-flung circle of diplomats and investigators who had worked for years to thwart Bout's aviation empire, the reaction was predictable dismay. Many were already skeptical of American resolve to ground Bout's planes. Now they wondered whether Bout had become a secret partner of the U.S. military, his recent dalliance with Islamic militants conveniently ignored by Bush administration officials eager to launch their postwar airlift into Iraq.

"Oh my, everything is possible nowadays," said a senior Belgian Foreign Ministry official who had been involved in his government's effort to have Bout arrested through Interpol. "Not only does Bout have the protection of the U.S. government, he now works for them. It's incredible, amazing. It has to be the only reason why he is still around and free."[9] Johan Peleman was only slightly more charitable. From his monk's nook in Antwerp, he chuckled derisively: "I have the impression the U.S. government has just been naive," he said. "I don't think they knowingly cooperated with Bout. I think they just didn't clear these companies properly. They should have been careful, given all the articles written and the official reports that are well known. Perhaps they don't read, eh?"[10]

Conspiracy theorists immediately pointed to Richard Chichakli's cryptic claim that Bout had organized post–September 11 flights for the American military into Afghanistan. Although there was no clear evidence that Bout's planes had flown airlifts for the United States, critics suggested that the Russian's organization had been rewarded with new work in Iraq. But even under the more plausible explanation that bungling U. S. military contracting officials had simply failed to do proper background checks in their haste to gear up a massive airlift into Iraq, the effect was largely the same: to the rest of the world, the American government appeared to be run by hypocrites and incompetents.

Through the fall of 2004, a steady drip of revelations dredged up by outraged political bloggers and then by journalists in the United States and Britain revealed the vast dimensions of the Bout organization's Iraq work. Irbis alone accounted for hundreds of flights during 2003 and 2004 that sluiced millions into Bout's coffers. One air transporter with extensive supply work in Baghdad estimated to U.S. Treasury officials that Bout-network affiliated planes made a thousand flights into BIAP and other airfields in Iraq by the end of 2004. That figure could not be confirmed. But official flight records unearthed by reporters suggested the estimate was hardly an exaggeration. RAMCC flight records obtained by the *Los Angeles Times* showed that Irbis planes landed in Baghdad 92 times in the first five months of 2004 alone. And fueling records released by the U.S. Defense Logistics Agency to the *Times* revealed that Irbis planes had refueled at American facilities in Baghdad 142 times between March and August 2004, indicating an almost daily pace of flights into Iraq.[11]

The Bout network's financial take from its work in Iraq was also difficult to assess; in addition to uncertainty over its flight totals, there was enduring silence from Bout himself and from most of the private contractors who hired his planes. When a *Los Angeles Times* staffer phoned Bout's mobile number in Moscow for a response to a story on his Iraq work in December 2004, the Russian was blistering and terse: "You are not dealing with fact, you are dealing with allegations," he snapped. "Don't call me anymore."[12] But others who had been approached for work by agents for Bout firms provided a solid sense of his financial stake. According to a former RAMCC official and a contractor who used Irbis for several flights into Iraq, the Sharjah-based flagship usually charged $60,000 for a single round-trip run into to Baghdad. Keith Chapman, a retired RAF officer who worked as a UN liaison with RAMCC in spring 2003, said that Irbis and other "dubious outfits in Sharjah" aggressively marketed their services, repeatedly calling and e-mailing, and even dispatching agents to "hang around" the UN office in Kuwait, making pitches. The Russians' low-ball offer was well below the $100,000-per-flight cost usually borne by UN humanitarian agencies. Concerned about the firms' "dodgy" claims and the safety of the old Antonovs, "we dismissed them out of hand," Chapman said.[13] Others did not. Dinu Kabiwar, manager of Frames International Travel, a British cargo charter, hired Irbis planes "three or four times" in 2004 at the firm's cut-rate price of $60,000 to fly personnel from Bombay to Baghdad for KEC International, an Indian company hired by the U.S. Army Corps of Engineers to restore electricity in Iraq. Kabiwar considered using British firms but "to fly from here would have been three times the cost."[14] Such were the benefits of sitting atop a massive, inexpensively maintained air fleet. Bout owned his own planes, spent little on their upkeep, paid low wages to pilots and crews, and was able to insure his own planes at low rates. "He just undercuts his way into business," said a rival air firm executive.[15] At $60,000 per flight, Irbis likely raked in a minimum of $5.5 million for its work in the first five months of 2003. And if the estimate of a thousand flights overall is anywhere near accurate, U.S. taxpayers donated as much as $60 million to the Viktor Bout organization.

Irbis planes not only flew into Baghdad, they also landed repeatedly in high-security military bases in Iraq that required additional military clearances. Bout's planes made regular stops at Balad Air

Base in northern Iraq, a hub for F-16 fighter planes and the central depot for distributing matériel to U.S. forces across the country, and at Al Asad, a vital Marine Corps air and helicopter facility. At times Irbis planes landed at all three bases on the same day. In one stretch in early May 2004, for example, a single Irbis Antonov An-24 flying in from Dubai made daily stops at the three airfields with FedEx cargo for two days running, then returned to Baghdad on a third day with deliveries for the CPA.[16] Even as Irbis's role in Iraq drew scrutiny, other UAE-based air firms suspected as Bout affiliates were also flying under lucrative Iraq contracts. Two firms already in the sights of U.S. intelligence officials were Jet Line and Aerocom, Moldovan-registered airlines that shared a single address and phone number at Chisinau Airport in Moldova, and also operated flights from the UAE. Jet Line's general manager, Igor Abadeyev, had acknowledged to *Los Angeles Times* reporters in April 2002 that he was a longtime acquaintance and former partner of Viktor Bout's. And American intelligence officials had concluded in the same year that Jet Line was among the "Victor Butt–associated airlines." At least nine Jet Line planes, including several Ilyushins and Lockheeds, had been linked to the Bout fleet by intelligence officials. Both Jet Line and Aercom had also leased planes back and forth, and one of Aercom's Antonov An-26 freighters traced back to Bout's defunct Centrafricain Airlines.[17]

Aerocom appeared to specialize in heavy-duty arms flights. According to an April 2003 report by a Security Council panel of investigators, the airline had carried arms shipments from Serbia to Liberia in 2002 in violation of a UN arms embargo. U.S. intelligence officials quickly concluded that the firm's sudden appearance in Serbia represented Bout's effort to get back into the air transport business after his planes were temporarily grounded in Sharjah. "Aerocom is obviously dirty," one official said.[18] By 2004 Aerocom had found new opportunities in Iraq. RAMCC flight records documented a January 20, 2004, flight of a mammoth Aerocom Il-76 to Baghdad carrying forty-four tons of ammunition for the American coalition and the Iraqi Ministry of National Security. The plane had picked up the ammunition from Plovdiv, Bulgaria, an arms transshipment point where Bout-orbit planes had often been spotted in the past. By August, accused of safety lapses, Aerocom was stripped of its flying license by Moldovan aviation authorities. The firm flew on illegally. Later that month, Aerocom played a pivotal part in an unsolved mystery of four missing shipments of ninety-nine tons of Kalashnikovs and other used weapons. The arms, seized in the mid-1990s during the Bosnian conflict and controlled by U.S. authorities, disappeared in August 2004, en route from American military storehouses in Bosnia. According to an Amnesty International investigation, the weapons were destined for the Iraqi Ministry of Defense under a deal authorized by U.S. Defense officials. But the Kalashnikovs allegedly never arrived at their destination. An Aerocom Ilyushin supposedly picked up the Bosnian arms during four stopovers at a U.S. military base in Bosnia. But RAMCC officials could provide no record of the plane's arrivals in Baghdad. Amnesty International reported that the Ilyushin had been leased to Aerocom by Jet Line.[19]

Jet Line, Aerocom's twin, was also busy in Iraq in early 2004. The airline flew in telecommunications equipment for Siemens in March and April 2004, and carried oil field equipment for KBR in April. Despite being banned from most European airports because of its deafening Ilyushin engines, the airline was also granted a special noise exemption from Britain's Civil Aviation Authority in March 2004 to fly armored cars into Baghdad and Basra. The airline had been hired by the Department for International Development, Britain's foreign aid agency—a relationship that was suddenly severed the next month when British officials realized Jet Line was tied into the Bout network. The Blair government acknowledged the flights, but gave no explanation about how an arms dealer who had been publicly castigated as a "merchant of death" had managed to land a military contract. Peter Hain, who had been promoted from the Foreign Ministry to Blair's cabinet in 2002 as secretary of state for Wales, was silent. "I was gone by then," he explained recently. He acknowledged that countering Bout's network required a long-term commitment, one that even the most resourceful governments were reluctant to make. "We need to do much better," he said.[20]

Another suspect UAE air cargo firm that pressed hard for U.S. Defense Department contract work in Iraq was Dolphin Airlines, the latest incarnation of Flying Dolphin, the Sharjah-based company that sold Antonovs to the Taliban in concert with Bout's Air

Cess and that was cited for arms embargo violations by UN investigators. Chris Walker almost banned Dolphin from operating anywhere in Iraq after company officials announced in November 2003 that they were inaugurating the first commercial passenger service into the country. "They wanted to bring in a delegation to meet with the Kurdish National government so they put out this release saying they were going to be the new Iraqi airlines," Walker recalled. "It was a dinky little charter, but we had to put out a statement correcting their BS. Dolphin stayed in my sights from them on." But the firm still managed to fly contract runs into Baghdad. By August 2004, Dolphin had joined nearly three dozen air cargo firms on RAMCC's daily e-mail list—an indication that they had finally won prized American flight contracts.[21]

Intelligence officials were also curious about another Sharjah-based airline, British Gulf International. The airline was cleared to fly into Baghdad ninety-two times in early 2004, according to RAMCC files. British Gulf's ties to Bout were more tenuous than the others, and both UN and American intelligence officials were uncertain how closely they coordinated; some doubted that they had any formal relations. But suspicions remained, fanned by information that UN investigators had learned in the late 1990s about frequent money transfers between British Gulf and San Air General Trading, another formerly active Bout airline.[22]

Igor Zhuravlyov, British Gulf's flight manager, said he knew of the Bout brothers, but insisted he had no face-to-face dealings with them. Still, Zhuravlyov admitted his firm had leased planes to Irbis in early 2004 "because they had only one plane. So we carried stuff for them also on U.S. Defense Department contracts to Iraq and to Afghanistan." Irbis and many of the Russian air firms in Sharjah, the flight manager insisted, worked for each other on an informal basis that blurred the Iraq contracting chain and made a mockery of the U.S. military's confidence in its vetting system for contractors and subs. Despite carving out a huge business flying for the American military and its contractors, British Gulf never had a direct U.S. contract. "Sometimes there were three or four companies in the chain which subcontracted to each other," Zhuravylov said, "before they even gave us the cargo to carry to Iraq."[23]

The haphazard American military scrutiny in Baghdad that

allowed Irbis and British Gulf International to fly into and out of Iraq almost at their own initiative also provided the two air cargo firms with unlimited access to American-provided fuel. On their constant routes into and out of Sharjah, the fuel-guzzling Russian planes needed constant replenishment. The only fuel available in Baghdad was stored by the U.S. Air Force. Special fuel permission cards known as "identaplates" were doled out to air firms that flew for the military and private U.S. contractors, but they were supposedly provided only after tough vetting by Defense Department officials.

The fuel cards were absurdly easy to obtain. British Gulf International won its own identaplates after a chance encounter at Balad Air Base in December 2003. After landing on a cargo run, flight manager Zhuravlyov asked an air force fueler if he could buy kerosene for the return flight to Sharjah. "You can't buy it, but you can have it free if you do it the right way," the soldier replied, handing the Russian a blank form. The American explained to Zhuravylov that all he had to do was scrawl basic information on an application and mail it off to the Defense Department. In April 2004, after mailing the form and filling out more correspondence, Zhuravylov received "a plastic card for each of our planes which allowed us to get military fuel."

"This made our business really much more productive," a bemused Zhuravlyov explained later. "It was really so good, all by the mail. No inspectors, nothing like that. Write a letter, fill a form, get a card." [24]

CHAPTER 14

Blacklisted and Still Flying

After Chris Walker's reluctant decision to allow Viktor Bout's planes to keep flying into Baghdad, the Bush administration remained mum about the almost daily procession of Antonovs and Ilyushins that flew among Sharjah, Baghdad, and U.S. air bases across Iraq. On May 18, 2004, in a weekly cable to diplomatic posts around the world, the State Department's public affairs office sent out talking points for diplomats confronted with pesky questions about the Bout plane sightings. The suggested nonanswer was that the United States continued "to support international efforts to end Mr. Bout's illegal activities." A firm "no comment" was advised to address "any alleged connections."[1]

Behind the scenes, officials from Washington to Baghdad struggled to account for Bout's Iraq contracts and contain the damage. Several days after he forwarded his report to Jeffrey Oster, Walker was contacted by a CIA official from headquarters at Langley. The intelligence official messaged that he was seeking to learn anything Walker knew about "airlines/planes associated with Russian arms trafficker Victor Butt." The CIA man said that "interest here" had been whipped up by the exchange between Feingold and Wolfowitz:

"With the above in mind, we are interested in learning the following to better understand the situation there." The CIA official wanted to know who was tracking commercial flights into and out of Baghdad and what information was kept. And he pointedly asked for any evidence that Irbis (or its alter ego Air Bas), Jet Line, and British Gulf planes "are flying to/within the country." Walker responded with a detailed list of the information compiled on the Baghdad-bound air firms and their planes.

Then he vented some bureaucratic spleen. "When it comes to situations like Victor Bout," Walker replied, "we are not given the intel to determine which airlines are run by alleged ne'er-do-wells. That being said, when we were made aware of the Victor Bout situation . . . we immediately looked into it. Apparently the U.S. Army did use the services of Air Bas before, and FedEx is presently using one of the planes allegedly tied to the Bout."

The CIA official responded with a new revelation. Intelligence officials in Washington had sent a "heads up" about possible Iraq flights by Bout's air firms to the agency's Baghdad station in October and November 2003—more than six months before the *Financial Times* report blew the lid on Bout's flights into Iraq. The warning was supposed to have been relayed to CPA officials. But "it would appear," the CIA official wrote, "that it did not make its way to the correct folks."[2]

Walker had heard nothing about the earlier warning. Oster later recalled that he had talked with an unnamed CPA transportation aide who mentioned looking into a suspected Bout flight dating to January 2004. "I recall a little black brief that the shipment in question was not something that the CPA had contracted," Oster said. "It came through Air Mobility Command. There was so much coming and going at that particular time, it could have been any kind of cargo. The issue was whether the airline or plane was owned by or under control of this guy." But Oster said he knew nothing about the 2003 warning and could not explain why it had gone unheeded. "Where it went after that, I honestly don't know," he said.[3] Walker checked through old files to see if the agency's earlier intelligence warning had been buried in his backlog of paperwork but found nothing. He wanted to wash his hands of the entire matter. But he knew he had not heard the last of it.

Within days, there were new reports of Bout contracts—this time from within the government itself. On June 2, the State Department replied officially to Feingold's questions about Bout. Paul V. Kelly, an assistant secretary for legislative affairs, said that a sweep of State contract files had discovered that the department had unwittingly hired Bout planes through freight forwarding firms at least twice in the past, though prior to the Iraq invasion. In response, Kelly said, State vowed to warn overseas posts "to ensure that contracts with freight forwarders preclude any use of entities connected to Bout." Kelly also insisted that the United States still supported the United Nations' plans to freeze Bout's assets as part of Liberia sanctions against Charles Taylor and his associates.

The United States, it turned out, had never tried to remove Bout from the UN sanctions list, as the *Financial Times* reported. Johan Peleman had checked with colleagues on the Liberia panel and learned that the United States and Britain had both sent Bout's name on short lists provided to the UN Secretariat for discussion by the Liberia sanctions committee. "People who had been present in the meetings of the sanctions committee on Liberia assured me that neither the U.K. nor the U.S. had ever raised any questions about Viktor," Peleman said.[4]

The United States had been preparing its own series of sanctions against Bout since March. After gathering investigative string for two years on Bout's holdings, Andreas Morgner saw the United Nations' move against the Russian as a defining international one that provided the United States with an opening to finally take legal action against the Bout network. When he first read the tough sanctions language that the Security Council planned to use to freeze Bout's and Taylor's assets, Morgner grew excited. "It's Taylor-made, excuse the pun, to go after Viktor," he told his superiors at the OFAC. "You could use Liberia as a shoehorn to go after his assets." He was told: "Go for it."

Morgner and a small circle of OFAC attorneys and investigators began building a case against Bout, using the United Nations' research as Treasury's legal spine. As they worked, they meticulously charted the tangled corporate structure of the Bout empire. The detailed UN reports on Bout's role in evading Liberia arms sanctions "got down to specific weapons transactions and that was useful to us as a legal underpinning," a senior Treasury official recalled.[5] Their position was strengthened when a senior State Department attorney ruled that the United States would accept the United Nations' research on Bout in all of the sanctions reports as definitive fact.[6] The "name and shame" campaign doggedly researched by Johan Peleman and his colleagues now buttressed the building U.S. effort to freeze the Bout network's assets.

"We couldn't have replicated what Peleman and the others did, at least not in any reasonable amount of time," Morgner said. "They had summaries, narratives, and source documents. This was golden. The decision to take the UN documents as fact that we were not going to question was vital."

But the rash of reports about the Bout organization's contract flights into Iraq blindsided the Treasury team and slowed its progress. The Bush administration was on high embarrassment alert, and officials were pressed to figure out the extent of Bout's contracts and come up with a way to deal with them without hamstringing the military's supply lines. "There was definite concern about the Iraq stories," Morgner recalled. "There was a lot of confusion over who was using him and how much vulnerability there was. We were all working on it urgently, but the underlying tone was that at bottom, it was DoD's problem." Top Treasury officials felt the OFAC freeze was still the best and cleanest solution to taking on Bout, but were wary of moving ahead until the Iraq mess was under control. "In an emergency situation like a war, it's always a calculus to hire those who can get things done," a senior Treasury official said. "Still," he added carefully, "it would strike me that other airplane contractors could have been used."[7]

The State Department wasted no time making sure its own house was clean. On June 7, State's Office of Logistics Management warned overseas posts and dispatch agents against hiring any Bout network firms. The cable was accompanied by a ninety-day suspension of all known Bout firms and top lieutenants. The list named Bout, three associates, and eight affiliated companies.[8] Several State officials urged the department to go even further. They wanted State to place Bout, his associates, and his known air companies on the federal government's "excluded parties" list. The action would prevent any federal agency from doing business with Bout or the named parties for sixty days. Then, under federal rules, there would be a hearing to determine whether the government could debar Bout permanently from federal contracts.

"We believe Mr. Bout can be suspended pending a hearing, for which he will probably not show," a senior State contracting official wrote. "After not showing at the hearing he can be debarred." The suspension was a temporary measure, but proponents felt it would throw an immediate wrench into Defense contracts with the Russian and prevent him from obtaining any new work. "With the discovery that an apparent Bout company has contracted with a U.S. government agency, there is now an urgent need to ensure that Bout and his associated entities are put on the excluded parties list," one official wrote in a June 15 memo.[9]

"It was the best we could do at the moment to show we backed up our words," a State official explained later. "The idea was if you could ban ten Bout companies, even if you knew there were twenty or thirty out there that couldn't be immediately named, at least we'd have the ten on the federal registry and that would force DoD's hand. You could say these firms are now ineligible and you would advise every government agency to be diligent about even hiring the other unnamed firms."[10] There was another reason to go after Bout's firms by debarment. The United Nations' Liberian assets freeze would only target Bout personally, and even if Morgner's OFAC team followed suit, his interlocking corporate structure and scattered air fleet would remain untouched. There was talk that the UN Liberian sanctions might be toughened further later, but with the United Nations, there were no guarantees.

Still, other State officials preferred to let the OFAC lead the way, warning that any other effort would run into legal thickets. Bout's existing Defense contracts could not be legally terminated by the "excluded parties" suspension, one State skeptic warned, and he would have to be "bought out," perhaps at a cost of millions more. Other departments also weighed in with doubts. Treasury's team did not want to jeopardize their plans to freeze Bout's assets later in the year—they worried aloud that if State moved prematurely, Bout would recognize the government's next step, hide his bank accounts, and further conceal his companies. And intelligence officials raised concerns that a frontal effort to sever Bout's contracts might put a damper on useful business relationships with other figures with questionable backgrounds. "The CIA people were worried about what it might mean for other bad apples they worked with," said one State participant in the discussions. "We'd heard about the rumors of Bout working with our intelligence people, but they didn't allude to that at all. They were simply asking what would be the effect if we did this to him—would it chill future attempts to use bad actors on our side?"[11]

Deputy Secretary of State Lincoln P. Bloomfield Jr. settled the debate on June 29. Bloomfield preferred to stick with the pending Treasury assets freeze on Bout. "OFAC sanctions are the most far reaching and have the broadest effect of any of the possible sanctions that can be taken," he wrote. Treasury planned to expand on its sanctions against Bout by targeting "associated companies" in the late summer of 2004, Bloomfield said. But in the interim, Bloomfield agreed that State would publish a *Federal Register* notice after Bout was personally sanctioned, listing "certain front companies he is suspected of using." Both moves would "prevent American companies and the federal and state governments from contracting with Bout" until the sanctions kicked in, Bloomfield said.[12]

Nearly a month later, on July 22, Andreas Morgner's two years of gathering string finally paid off. Flexing his authority under the International Economic Emergency Powers Act, President Bush signed an OFAC action that officially quarantined Viktor Bout as a "special designated person." The OFAC action against "Viktor Anatolijevitch Bout" branded him as a "businessman, dealer and transporter of weapons and minerals." It listed the usual set of aliases: Butt, Bont, Butte, Boutov, and Vitali Sergitov. Bout and Liberian dictator Charles Taylor were now among twenty-eight associates and relatives facing a permanent assets freeze and a ban on doing business with Americans. Finally, after nearly a decade of intelligence-gathering, ambitious plans, promised action, and repeated setbacks, the United States had finally taken legal steps against Bout. Condemning the arms deals that "perpetuate the Liberian conflict and fuel and exacerbate other conflicts throughout West Africa," Bush directed that "any contribution or provision of funds, goods or services" would be "blocked pursuant to this order."[13]

Yet knowingly or unknowingly, even in the face of a presidential order, the U.S. government continued doing business with Bout's shifting corporate entities. A little more than two weeks later, on August 7, an Aerocom Ilyushin Il-76 was loaded with pallets crammed with Kalashnikovs from storehouses at the U.S. Army's Task Force Eagle base at Tuzla, Bosnia, and then flew southeast, toward Baghdad. The Defense Department would not easily wean itself away from the efficient services provided by the Bout organization.

The military's dependence on the Bout network appeared almost comically hapless, but basic organizational lapses and structural flaws lay at the heart of the Pentagon's continued use of Bout's planes. In the fever-pitch run-up to the Iraq war, the Defense Department's hiring procedures did not provide adequate scrutiny of lower-level subcontractors—and Defense officials had failed to compile a wide-ranging watch list of suspect companies for their military contracting experts.

To former U.S. officials who had been instrumental in pursuing Bout, the Pentagon's heavy use of Bout's supply flights was prime evidence of the Bush administration's paltry postwar planning. When the full dimensions of the military's use of hundreds of Bout flights emerged in a *Los Angeles Times* story in December 2004, Lee Wolosky's voice tightened in outrage. "It befuddles the mind that the Pentagon would continue to work with an organization that both the Clinton and Bush White Houses actively fought to dismantle," he said. The Pentagon's continued use of Bout's planes, Wolosky said, "speaks to the lack of an integrated watch list and the application of that watch list. It speaks to a lack of communication within the government. That a major criminal organization can do this—that means something is wrong." [14]

"It's an obscenity," said former NSC deputy Gayle Smith. "It's contrary to a smart war against terror. Even if you needed a cut-out (to transport supplies) why would you go to the one on the bottom of the pile, with the most blood on his hands? Because he worked fastest and cheapest? What's the trade-off? Where's the morality there? I thought we were in this war to promote democratic ideals? Is that what Viktor Bout represents?"

The Pentagon's contracting officials were hobbled from the start, one knowledgeable State Department official said, because they were only able to rule out from Iraq contracts companies that had been named in the past on the General Service Administration's (GSA's) list of businesses permanently debarred from government work. But even though Bout was sought under an Interpol criminal warrant and other U.S. agencies had built massive files on his arms operations, military contractors had no access to those materials— and at least officially, were obligated to heed only the GSA list.

But the State Department's quick moves in June 2004 to warn its own contractors off from hiring Bout planes showed how far agencies could bend the rules. "This was the big piece of the problem with the DoD hiring process," said the State official. "My office was screaming about DoD, not only about Bout, but with all sorts of shady companies that were coming over the transom. We began seeing cases as soon as the war with Iraq started, but with the press of war, we never got to flag them." [15]

A similar case that also came back to haunt the Pentagon was its 2005 purchase of $29 million in weapons for the Iraqi army from a Chinese-owned company under federal indictment in California for smuggling AK-47s into the United States. Despite checks into the firm's background by the U.S. Army's Tank-Automotive and Armaments Command, the Chinese firm, Poly Technologies, had not been banned from doing business by the GSA. The company was hired, even though federal agents had seized two thousand of the firm's AK-47s in 1996 as they were smuggled into the country— the largest haul of contraband automatic weapons in U.S. history. "We have done everything we can think of to save DoD from itself," the State official said. [16]

Senior military logistics planners defended their vetting system, saying that the hiring of Bout's network was an anomaly, occurring only because the decisions were made so far down in the contracting chain—his firms were unwittingly chosen by private contractors, not the military's own contracting officials. Still, military officials supposedly checked out many of the subcontractors brought on by big reconstructions firms working in Iraq. Former air force general John W. Handy, who headed the U.S. Transportation Command (Transcom) and was senior planner for the military's airlift into Iraq, said that any civilian air cargo firms hired by Transcom were "scrubbed six ways from Sunday."

Most of the contracting decisions that led to the Bout organization's work in Iraq, Handy said, were made separately by U.S. Army, Marine, Army Corps of Engineers, and CPA officials—and most likely involved military contracting officials for each of those services working under the U.S. Central Command. Handy's Air Mobility Command handled its own logistics decisions, providing tactical airlift for the war operations—which relied mostly on the air force's C-130s and other cargo planes and only occasionally hired civilian carriers. "The army corps and other services would likely have each cut their own contracts," Handy said. "It would be a sizable task to run down all the contracts that were let. You'd have to go down a real rabbit hole to find that out." When reports of Bout's contracts surfaced in May 2004, Handy ordered his aides "to send the dogs out" to learn if his command had hired Bout planes. "To my knowledge, we never found a contract."

But the Air Mobility Command (AMC), which operated under Transcom, had indeed hired Irbis as a third-tier subcontractor through FedEx. An AMC spokesman explained the command had an "off the shelf" contract using FedEx's commercial service at a discounted price. FedEx, in turn, hired Falcon Express Cargo Airlines in Dubai. A FedEx official in Dubai explained that Falcon was hired to move military supplies into Iraq and used Irbis and other UAE air firms "either as subcontractors or plane-by-plane leasers." Despite Irbis's normal fee of $60,000, the firm made only $22,000 per round-trip because of FedEx's reduced-fee schedule. But Irbis planes were allowed to fill up with cargoes from other firms if there was still space left over, the FedEx official said—allowing Bout's flagship to boost the profits for many of its FedEx flights. FedEx never received warnings from U.S. officials about Bout's air firms or other UAE companies flying into Iraq. "The U.S. never sent anything to us," the FedEx official said.[17]

Irbis's flights for Federal Express lasted about a year, from August 2003 until late August 2004, when the air force was suddenly informed by Defense logistics officials that there was a problem with their third-tier UAE air contractor. For months, Irbis planes in Baghdad had been refueling with aviation fuel provided by the U.S. Air Force. Using its alter ego Air Bas, Bout's company had secured special cards in March 2004 from the Defense Energy Support

Center (DESC) to fuel up at air force pumps. Through August, DESC spokesman Jack Hooper confirmed, Irbis planes used 494,881 gallons of fuel in Baghdad—until their fuel cards were suddenly suspended. On July 8, the Pentagon's fueling center had contacted Air Bas with a routine request for more information "to clarify which U.S. government agency you have charter agreements with." When the UAE firm did not respond for weeks, the DESC cut off its fuel. Similarly, the air force cut off British Gulf International because of its silence.

Soon after Defense fuel officials revoked Irbis's fuel card, the firm's flights for the air force came under new scrutiny. Armed with details of Treasury's assets freeze against Bout, the air force general counsel's office pressed the Air Mobility Command for information about its dealings with Air Bas, British Gulf, and Falcon Express. On September 14, under prodding from the lawyers, the air force warned FedEx that "it may be in violation of legal prohibitions" for hiring Bout. FedEx wasted no time, moving quickly to terminate its Irbis flights. The air force, a spokesman said, "does not anticipate any future involvement of this nature." [18]

The air force's rapid response contrasted with the sluggish reaction of the U.S. Army and it affiliated commands. Unlike the air force's single third-party contract with Irbis, the Sharjah air firm had been hired to work for the army under numerous separate subcontracts. According to Hooper, there was evidence that Irbis had at least one direct contract with the army. But army officials showed little inclination to look into their relationships with Bout, let alone sever them. Nancy Ray, an army spokeswoman, insisted in December 2004 that "we have no record of any contracts with this company." Ray said it would be pointless to even try to search for the contracts in army records. "We're talking about tens of thousands of contracts," she said. And she dismissed the idea that the army bore any responsibility for its subcontractors. "You contract with your prime and then the prime has responsibility for dealing with subcontractors. That's law, not policy."

But at the ground level, army personnel intimate with contracting decisions complained that the process was rife with chaos. Army Reserve captain Cameron Sellers, who preceded Chris Walker as clearance officer at Baghdad International Airport, also had worked as a civil affairs liaison with army contractors in Iraq. What Sellers saw close up was a "disaster in the making." In case after case, army contractors simply hired large American outfits they were familiar with, but failed to check out the subcontractors that were brought on by the larger firms. Too often, Sellers said, the big contractors relied on local cargo agents and freight forwarders in the Persian Gulf, taking their recommendations on faith. "There would be instances where I would go to these companies and say why did you hire these subcontractors? And over and over, the contractors would say: 'What? I didn't approve these people.' They had no idea who they hired."

Corruption and favoritism also may have swayed American contractors' decisions to award Baghdad routes to Bout-network companies. An executive who worked for one international air chartering operation said his firm had won a competitive bid to staff Baghdad flights for a major American defense contractor in summer 2004, but was suddenly displaced by another global charter firm that regularly hired Bout-network air firms for Iraq work. His company protested to the American corporation's hiring officials and to RAMCC, but to no avail. "I'm not critical of the military. Most of them are above-board," the exasperated executive said. "The Defense contractors at the top of the process were oblivious, I'm sure. But what does it say about the American operation that they're willing to let their contractors pay more to have Bout fly for them?"[19]

The contracting lapses raised questions of internal security as well. At Baghdad International Airport, Sellers said, he ended up operating blindly, deprived of crucial security information, because Defense planners as well as other agencies failed to prepare for the possibility that air firms with criminal backgrounds might attempt to win contracts and gain access to vital American installations. "The interagency people needed to put dedicated personnel on this," Sellers said. "Instead, the military people on the ground got left holding the bag. If we had known who we were doing business with, we would have said right from the start that we're not going to accept any flights coming out of Sharjah. Period."

But if changes needed to be made at the Pentagon, there was only silence at the top. For months after Wisconsin senator Feingold had asked Paul Wolfowitz about Bout's work in Iraq, the assistant defense secretary kept silent. Feingold tried again in November 2004 and again heard nothing. Nine months passed before a letter from the Pentagon finally arrived at Feingold's office.

Finally replying on January 31, 2005, Wolfowitz acknowledged that "both the U.S. Army and the Coalition Provisional Authority did conduct business with companies that, in turn, subcontracted work to second-tier providers who leased aircraft owned by companies associated with Mr. Bout." Wolfowitz wrote that while Defense officials were "aware of a few companies that are connected to Mr. Bout, most notably Air Bas and Jet Line, we suspect that Mr. Bout has other companies or enterprises unknown to the government." Defense officials, he wrote, were complying with the Treasury sanctions and were reviewing "our contracts to ensure that we do not allow Mr. Bout or any other proscribed individual to perform our contracts." But Wolfowitz went on to insist that "we are not aware of any prime contracts or subcontracts with the Department of Defense that involve Mr. Bout."[20]

On February 9, an Irbis flight from Sharjah touched down at the airport in Mosul.

Several times a week through the fall of 2004 and into 2005, Sharjah International Airport's Web-based Flight Information Services board logged the arrivals and departures of Irbis planes as they shuttled between the UAE and Baghdad.

There were more flights to Mosul, as well as runs into Balad carrying KBR personnel. Irbis planes were landing with regularity in Kabul and at Bagram Air Base in Afghanistan, also staffing flights for KBR. On October 26, 2004, the Sharjah board even showed an Irbis flight due to arrive from Fort Leonard Wood, Missouri, where the U.S. Army bases its training academies for army Corps of Engineers, military police, and chemical warfare teams. Plane dispatchers at Fort Leonard Wood/Forney Airport who oversaw civilian flights were puzzled by the Sharjah listing, insisting they had no record of the Irbis plane. But the aircraft could have come and gone as a military flight without their knowledge, one dispatcher admitted.[21]

In Washington, frustrated Treasury officials were bewildered by the military's inability to curb them. "With all of our efforts," a senior Treasury official said acidly, "it would be real helpful to get coop-eration from other countries, let alone from other departments of government."[22]

The Europeans monitoring Bout were also at the end of their rope. Irked by Bout's continued sanctions-busting in Africa and his high-level Russian protection, a small group of intelligence officers was given approval for another try at nabbing him. This operation was to be carried out in March 2004, when the officials knew Bout planned to visit a daughter in Madrid for her birthday party.

But on March 11, an al Qaeda–affiliated terror group set off coordinated bomb attacks on the train system in Madrid, killing 191 people and wounding thousands of others. Bout canceled the trip.

"It was a very good plan, we would have had him," said one operative involved in the planning. "We can't be sure he didn't get wind of it before he came, but we were pretty convinced it was the bombings that scared him off, because of the increased scrutiny at the borders at the time."

Morgner and his Treasury team pressed on. As weeks dragged into months, the effort bogged down with interagency jockeying with State officials and with legal concerns about how many sus-pected Bout companies could be targeted. Treasury officials resisted State's proposal to tie the DoD's hands by listing Bout and some of his companies in the *Federal Register*. There were fears, a State offi-cial admitted, that "we might somehow tip off these parties that OFAC is considering sanctions."[23] Even pinpointing Bout's associ-ates was proving difficult. Treasury officials were considering imposing sanctions on Viktor Lebedev, Air Bas general manager in Sharjah. But Treasury's database disgorged seventeen different Lebedevs, with birth dates ranging from 1934 to 1974, each with a different Russian passport number. "Listing him simply as a Russian residing in a particular city will virtually guarantee a flood of false hits that will endlessly tie up OFAC resources," a Treasury official said.[24]

While Treasury fretted over how to target him, Lebedev was lay-ing plans in Sharjah to bid for a new contract through another UAE firm to deliver general U.S. government cargo into Iraq and Afghanistan. "We expect to provide service from Dubai to Baghdad and Kabul," Lebedev cheerily confided in a telephone interview from Air Bas offices in Novermber 2004. He confirmed Irbis's earlier flights for Federal Express and wondered aloud why "the U.S. government threw us back. They did not give us a reason." He explained that Irbis planes began flying as a U.S. subcontractor "from time to time in 2003. The first flights were difficult because we had to obtain much information and recommendation from civil authorities in Dubai and Sharjah. The situation is better for us now. Now we have obtained some offers and good communications with RAMCC in Baghdad." He boasted of the firm's "good relations" with KBR and told of a run of flights in October 2004 for the firm into Balad. "This was general cargo, which is usually mail, sometimes electric equipment, or military equipment." When asked about his employer, Viktor Bout, Lebedev abruptly turned the receiver over to his sales manager, Oleg Vakushin. "Viktor Bout? I never heard this name," Vakushin snorted before hanging up.[25]

KBR officials acknowledged that they had hired Irbis through Falcon Express Cargo as part of their Restore Iraqi Oil (RIO) contract with the U.S. Army Corps of Engineers starting in 2003. "The service was used to transport RIO personnel into and out of Iraq," said Wendy Hall, a KBR spokeswoman. KBR, Hall emphasized, "manages thousands of first-tier subcontractors in Kuwait and Iraq, and each contractor, in turn, may have additional layers of subcontracts in place to support the mission." But despite overseeing its vast army of suppliers, KBR was also wedded to government contract stipulations that "its subcontractors must operate according to applicable laws." Hall directed further questions to Falcon Express, which never replied. Hall said that "KBR had no knowledge of a relationship between Falcon and Air Bas, and if we had known, we would have terminated the contract." She added that Falcon Express had been terminated in July 2004. Yet Irbis continued flying for KBR as late as October 2004, according to Lebedev and American military officials in Baghdad.[26]

The procession of Irbis flights from Sharjah into Iraq was also followed avidly by journalists and by an obsessed international community of plane spotters. By fall 2004, the Bout network's flights into Iraq had became the repeated targets of newspaper and magazine exposés. The *Los Angeles Times*, *Newsweek*, and *Mother*

Jones all weighed in on the American government's failures, while in the United Kingdom, the *Guardian* and the *Evening Standard* joined the *Financial Times* and the *Times* of London in highlighting the British government's use of the Bout network. But the flights shuttled on, astonishing veteran plane spotters who spent long hours tracking the movements of the elusive Antonovs and could not fathom how intelligence officials with more sophisticated capacities did not stop them.

The most prolific of the spotters was Alexander Harrowell, an activist aviation enthusiast who blogged on the Web from Britain as the Yorkshire Ranter. Harrowell made it his mission to expose the tangled corporate structure of the Bout network and its hidden ties to the American and British war efforts in Iraq. Several times a month, Harrowell dashed off mocking screeds about suspected Bout planes that turned up in Baghdad and elsewhere across the globe. When the devastating tsunami ravaged Indonesia, Sri Lanka and Thailand in December 2004, killing more than a hundred thousand, Harrowell was quick to report that Bout cargo planes had been spotted days later in Phuket and Colombo, carrying humanitarian supplies for the Russian government and unwitting charity organizations.

Even after the United States and the United Nations moved against Bout with assets freezes, Harrowell remained dissatisfied with the pace of their efforts. In a Web lobbying effort he called "Operation Firedump," Harrowell rallied his fellow plane spotters to move against the Bout empire. "It's time to find these aircraft and demand their seizure. All bloggers are invited to mirror this and help land [Bout planes] on the fire dump, which is where most of these planes will end up given their age and general condition," he wrote.[27]

While Irbis and sister Bout-network airlines were busy shuttling into and out of Baghdad, other suspected Bout-orbit aircraft were still plying old routes in Africa. Through the fall of 2004, Johan Peleman tracked weapons flows into the eastern region of the DRC, compiling evidence for a British parliamentary investigative panel. As part of the panel's report, released that December, Peleman traced the May 2004 crash of a Russian-built Mi-8 helicopter owned by the Great Lakes Business Company, a firm headed by Dimitri

Popov, a businessman linked to Bout's network. The crashed heli-copter had previously been registered in Equatorial Guinea by CET Aviation, a firm that Treasury officials were about to include on their banned list of Bout-network companies. The report also cited a July 2004 arms flight into Kongolo Airport of a plane owned by Compagnie Aérienne des Grands Lacs, another link to Bout that the panel concluded "is pertinent and requires further investigation."[28]

Kathi Austin, the American investigator, had been tracking Bout for close to a decade when she accepted a new assignment in 2004 as a weapons expert for a UN panel examining arms embargo viola-tions in the DRC. She had seen enough of Bout's activities over the years to recognize his planes and modus operandi. She found both in the ramshackle Congolese town of Goma, the commercial hub of the DRC's vast northeastern region. Unregistered Russian aircraft lumbered into and out of Goma's airfield all night under the noses of slumbering South African peacekeepers. At night the planes parked on the grass beside a runway pocked with volcanic ash. The Russian crews were driven by minibuses to cheap hotels, where they congregated in bars popular with local hookers.

Austin decided on an audacious tack to find out if the planes were Bout's. She planned a spot inspection with no prior warning. Alerting no other officials in the town, she and her team drove to the airfield just after dawn on November 26, 2004. They roused the dozing UN peacekeepers, while another UN team simultaneously moved in on cargo planes at an airstrip in the Congolese town of Bukavu. When the bleary-eyed Russian crewmen returned to their planes, they were confronted by Austin and her UN team and ordered to produce seven categories of paperwork required by international law. The pilots glared at the UN team in silence. Sev-eral warned that they would search out the families of some of Austin's team. As the day grew hotter, more Russians arrived. In Bukavu, a local military commander terminated the sting. In Goma, several planes took off in the confusion on the tarmac. But Austin and her crew managed to keep most of the aircraft on the ground.[29]

The raids enabled Austin's team to identify several new Bout associates and companies ferrying illicit arms into the region. Almost all of the plane registrations were false, expired, or incom-plete. And many were traced back to Bout's organization. Of the twenty-six aircraft inspected by the two UN groups, only three had valid certificates of registration. Several of the planes carried false documents, including some traced back to the old, outdated registries of Liberia and Equatorial Guinea. Twelve planes did not even have insurance policies.[30]

The UN panel concluded that the aircraft "operated by two companies were linked to the internationally renowned arms broker Viktor Bout through one of his front men, Dimitri Popov." The two firms were the same companies Peleman had turned up, the Great Lakes Business Company and its twin, the Compagnie Aérienne des Grands Lacs. "Both companies," the UN panel wrote, "operate aircraft that had previously been deregistered because of suspicion of involvement in violating the Liberian arms embargo."[31] The panel warned that the DRC's key airports in Goma and Bakuvu "are becoming 'airports of convenience' as well as hubs from which destabilizing operations can be launched."[32]

While the United Nations continued its "name and shame" campaign, the United States finally took concrete action against the Bout empire. After more than eight months of painstaking spadework, the Treasury team was finally ready to file its long-awaited broadside against the Viktor Bout organization. The looming Treasury designation had been bolstered by a secret grand jury investigation of Bout's longtime associate Richard Chichakli. FBI agents and federal prosecutors from the U.S. attorney's counterterrorism unit in Dallas had already spent months probing Chichakli's background and connection to Bout.

On the morning of April 26, Treasury and FBI agents burst into Chichakli's house and accounting and business offices in Richardson, Texas. Chichakli watched, enraged, while the agents seized his computer and documents and took possession of more than $1 million in assets, including diamonds locked in an office safe. While the federal agents trooped through his office, Chichakli took long-distance calls from both Viktor Bout and his brother Sergei. Days later, using frequent-flier miles to purchase his ticket because his bank accounts were frozen, Chichakli quietly left the United States, turning up in Cairo and then in Moscow. He turned his accounting company Web page into a graphics-intensive jeremiad against Treasury and

FBI "Nazis," Johan Peleman, and assorted journalists and bloggers, demanding the return of his frozen assets. "I hereby place an open invitation to the United States government to meet with Victor Bout in Moscow anytime they want, just call my attorney or drop me an e-mail," he wrote. "Victor is ready, so how about you?"[33]

In addition to Chichakli, the OFAC designation targeted Sergei Bout and two associates along with thirty companies; most were dormant, although Irbis, Air Bas, and Transavia Travel were still active. Days after the new sanctions were announced, nearly $3 million in Bout-controlled bank transfers were seized.[34] "I think we finally hurt him psychologically," one Treasury official said. "He couldn't cry that he was an aggrieved businessman any longer. The sanctions raised his profile and took away his shield of legitimacy." The most mysterious of Treasury's targets was Vial, the Delaware holding company that had a role in the cargo plane sales to the Taliban and was cited in the Interpol arrest warrant.

In announcing the OFAC assets seizure, Juan Zarate, assistant secretary of the treasury for terrorist financing and financial crimes, finally acknowledged publicly what U.S. officials had been saying in private since the late 1990s: Bout's network had played a vital role in supplying the Talibs, and indirectly through them, to al Qaeda. Zarate openly cited the Belgian intelligence claim that Bout had provided $50 million in cargo shipments to the Taliban.

In a separate interview with the *Los Angeles Times*, Zarate said Bout had supplied "air services to provide matériel to the Taliban, which was problematic at the time, given their sponsorship of al Qaeda." Well aware of the Pentagon's continuing use of Irbis and other Bout-network air firms, Zarate said the frontal assault on the Russian's business empire would "put the private sector and the DoD and others doing business with these entities on notice that they have to do due diligence to undo any relationships they might have." Zarate said Treasury officials had begun working with the Pentagon to identify Bout firms targeted by the sanctions. "With a business network the size Bout has created there are bound to be these interlocking entities that have to be unwound," Zarate said. But he insisted that Treasury's "dramatic step" would "start to untangle these contracts."[35]

It was like untwining a tight ball of yarn. The strands ran everywhere. In the immediate days after Treasury's move, the OFAC quietly issued a temporary waiver to the U.S. military's Central Command. Centcom had asked for a temporary reprieve to allow Bout's aircraft to continue flying for the military for a final week. Centcom's waiver allowed Bout's freighters to deliver a last flurry of shipments of ammunition and other materials that had been deemed vital to the U.S. war effort—and it ensured that private contractors continued paying Bout's network despite the fact that any other American firm doing the same would have been subject to prosecution.[36]

Even after the waiver period ended, Bout's planes continued to fly into Iraq and Afghanistan on missions for American contractors. On June 24, 2005, two Irbis flights made the rounds into Baghdad. Two days later, they were at Bagram.

Andreas Morgner kept adding to his files as Bout's companies juggled names, locations, registries, and planes. He knew that Bout's network was nimble enough to remain several steps ahead of the small circle of investigators, intelligence officials, activists, and journalists who tried to keep up. He was getting little help. After the media splash about the Bout designations, the OFAC sparred in a protracted debate with State officials over a proposal to extend the Bout network freeze to the United Nations, making the sanctions global rather than affecting only U.S. assets and financial institutions. The delay held off the UN move until December.

One telling vignette spoke volumes about the turf battles that hindered the Bout effort despite pledges of closer cooperation in the wake of September 11. Anxious to expand the rolls of Bout-associated companies on the U.S. and UN designation lists, Morgner had been trying, through normal government channels, to get an internal copy of the FBI interview with Sanjivan Ruprah. Morgner wanted the transcript because it named many of the Russian's companies and described his financial dealings. But the FBI flatly refused to turn the transcript over, even though it was unclassified. Numerous OFAC entreaties for the document were ignored and rebuffed.

But there was another copy of the transcript, in the possession of an Italian court that was overseeing a criminal conspiracy case against Ruprah. The transcript copy had been downloaded by Belgian police from the hard drive of Ruprah's computer.

When Ruprah fled Italy and escaped back to Africa in 2002, the Italian court turned over a copy of his interview to the United Nations–backed Special Court for Sierra Leone. The court was putting together charges of crimes against humanity against Liberia's Charles Taylor and others involved in the West African conflict. The court had requested information from around the world that might be of use, and the Italians felt that the Ruprah interview provided potent evidence.

The court offered to let Morgner go through the files for Bout-related information. In June 2005 Morgner finally had to fly to Freetown, Sierra Leone—a round-trip of almost seven thousand miles and costing several thousand dollars—to retrieve a document that was sitting, unclassified, a few blocks from his office. Morgner also had to gather other documents in Freetown that were unavailable in the United States, including the December 2000 unclassified report issued by the Bureau of Alcohol, Tobacco, and Firearms—a Treasury agency.

Court officials were left shaking their heads at the absurdity of Morgner's trip. "It was a long way to come for stuff that is sitting in the U.S. government files," said one court source. "We enjoyed having Andreas here, but we were wondering why he had to come here instead of taking a taxicab in Washington to get what he needed."

Taking on the quicksilver nature of Bout's corporate structure was much like taking on the narcotics cartels Morgner monitored when he worked at the CIA. It required staying current; keeping in touch with worldwide contacts; watching for new areas of likely exploitation; and most of all, not giving up. "They keep trying new things and you have to adapt," he said.

All through the summer and fall of 2005, Bout's planes flew on for U.S. contractors, relentless, untouchable. In December there was a modicum of progress. Sharjah aviation authorities reported they were on the verge of finally grounding the Air Bas/Irbis fleet. Bout's avionics operation there had already been shuttered.

But Bout's network was already undergoing yet another metamorphosis. Even as Air Bas went dormant, its planes were parceled out to new firms capable of flying from anywhere Bout had airfield connections: Dubai, Fujairah, Ajman, Ras al Kahymah, Chisinau, Almaty.

Chris Walker was not surprised to hear that Bout's fleet was still shuttling into and out of Baghdad. "He sure was persistent as hell. It's a shame the contracting folks weren't as persistent as he was," Walker said. More than a year after he made the reluctant decision that allowed Bout's freighters to keep flying into Iraq, Walker had returned from Iraq, working in a Defense Department annex in Virginia for a military committee making recommendations on whether to build a new cargo aircraft prototype for future American airlifts. Promoted to a lieutenant colonel in the Air National Guard, Walker had shrugged off his frustrating effort to get to the bottom of the military's habitual use of Bout's planes as "a front-row seat on the way the world really works.

"It was dealing with the devil to get what needed to be done and the powers that be approved it, so that's the way it was," he said. "If the government really wanted him bad they could have come up with a pretext and seized his planes. But I guess they looked at Viktor Bout and figured this guy's an asshole, but he's our asshole, so let's keep him in business."

EPILOGUE

After fifteen years of flying weapons for killers and for governments, weathering pursuers and halfhearted sanctions, Viktor Bout's empire endures, now an implacable fact of life on the world stage.

International efforts to hunt him down and scuttle his air operations are mostly abandoned, confined to sporadic efforts by the Treasury Department and the UN Security Council to freeze his assets. The CIA no longer has analysts specifically assigned to monitor his flights and follow his activities. "They're all working on counterterrorism now," a U.S. official said. The Belgian government's money-laundering probe is still active and the worldwide Interpol notice for Bout's arrest warrant remains open, but judicial officials in Brussels have little hope of progress, stymied by Russia's firm refusal to extradite him or even acknowledge his citizenship. Only the British maintain an active intelligence effort to track Bout's movements, and even that operation has been sharply reduced in scope.

Bout has had to adjust to a diminished version of the swaggering, globe-trotting lifestyle he once led. He lives in a luxury apartment complex in Moscow, where he is occasionally spotted eating at the fancy sushi bars he favors. According to Western officials and a

European intelligence source who have followed his activities for several years, Bout is often seen at the Moscow offices of Isotrex, a semiofficial foreign trade firm. The company is directed by a group of deputy ministers for key Russian government agencies tied to the nation's armament manufacturers. At Isotrex, Bout reportedly works closely with an aide who has been known to turn up regularly in countries where he has set up new business operations. European intelligence officials say that the woman, in her late twenties, and whom they have dubbed "Tatyana," is a legal expert who often arranges the Bout firms' initial paperwork and financial infrastructure before returning to her Moscow base. The woman's identity is not known, and officials suggest she may be a composite of two different people. Intelligence officials say Bout himself moves with ease across Russia, Western Europe, and the former Eastern bloc, ranging from his home base to satellite operations in Moldova, Belgium, and Kazakhstan and arms depots in Bulgaria and the Ukraine. Outside Eastern Europe, the UN travel ban forces him to travel mostly by land, relying on disguises and shifting passports. Confirmed and suspected Bout sightings have stretched from Cyprus and Beirut to Moldova and several African nations.

In one recent interview, Bout claimed that he has given up on his air operations. "I'm in construction business in Russia these days," he said.[1] But he still appeared to have vital stakes in several air cargo firms audited by a Canadian aviation consulting group in mid-2005. David Barnes, an air safety expert who heads Beacon Field Corp., traveled to Moldova and Sharjah to inspect several air cargo operations on behalf of KBR, the Halliburton subsidiary that hired Bout's planes for dozens of flights into Iraq and Afghanistan for the U.S. Defense Department. Barnes found numerous questionable air safety and procedural quirks at Jet Line in Moldova, and at several other Bout-linked firms.

Seeking maintenance records for a Jet Line plane that appeared to have previously crashed, Barnes went to the firm's dingy headquarters near the Chisinau airport. But Jet Line officials shrugged him off, producing nothing. One Jet Line staffer warned Barnes to stay away one morning at the Chisinau airport, saying, "It would be better for you if you were not around." Barnes took the advice. "They were probably working on an arms shipment," he concluded.

In Sharjah, curious about Jet Line's use of planes that had previously flown for Aerocom, another Bout-linked firm, Barnes approached a Russian Antonov pilot. "I mentioned it to him and he laughed," Barnes recalled. "He said they changed their company names and aircraft registrations all the time."

Barnes would not detail the recommendations he made to KBR. But he said it was clear that American firms using Bout's flights "have a mission and they need to do it as cheaply as possible. That makes Bout *the* player. He doesn't bring much attention to himself and he's always there with a huge fleet of aircraft. It comes down to how much do you want to spend and what do you want to deliver?" Barnes concluded that Bout remained in business because "the guy's protected. Governments need his services because he's useful. He's not a dumb guy. You have to respect him for what he's done."

In July 2006, just as hostilities erupted in southern Lebanon between Israeli defense forces and Hezbollah fighters, Western intelligence officials learned that Bout had been spotted at a Hezbollah military building. Officials also reported that Bout's longtime associate Richard Chichakli, who had been operating from Moscow after fleeing from Texas following the Treasury Department's seizure of his assets, also traveled to Damascus—where he is now based, according to his American lawyer. The confluence of sightings and the discovery by Israeli intelligence officials that Hezbollah had been armed by late-model Russian antitank weapons and other matériel fanned official suspicions that Bout's network might have played a role in the Hezbollah buildup.

On September 6, 2006, Israel's deputy prime minister Shimon Peres publicly accused Russia of arming Hezbollah with sophisticated armor-piercing Fagot and Kornet antitank missiles during the conflict. He said the weapons had moved to Hezbollah through Syria and Iran. "We saw the weapons, they had certain markings," Peres said in a Russian radio interview. A high-level Israeli delegation was dispatched to Moscow to raise the issue, and by mid-October there were reports that a Russian state weapons official in charge of arms exports had been fired.[2] But officials had not confirmed any direct involvement by the Bout network.

At the same time as the Lebanon crisis, a group of radical Somali militias operating under the banner of United Islamic

Courts seized control of Mogadishu, the battered Somali capital. After several days of pitched combat in late July, the Islamic factions, led by a former lieutenant of Osama bin Laden, quickly consolidated their hold over the city's international airport, a crumbling facility nearly abandoned by foreign aircraft over the past decade. Then, on July 26 and again on July 28, excited residents near the airfield streamed outside after hearing a rumbling from the sky. They watched as a droning Ilyushin Il-76, with the flag of Kazakhstan painted on its tail, descended from the barren horizon and taxied down the airfield's dusty runway. When the plane halted, waiting militiamen clustered around and hurriedly unloaded truckloads of familiar long brown and green boxes used to transport weapons. Journalists were barred from the airport, but several stationed just outside the field managed to snap pictures of the aircraft, using telephoto lenses.[3] The plane's identifying tail number, required by international aviation regulations, had been stripped off, preventing any attempt to learn who was behind the weapons shipments. The Kazakh Foreign Ministry denied any official involvement.[4]

Alarmed at the sudden triumph of an al Qaeda ally on the strategic tip of the Horn of Africa, U.S. military officials ordered an investigation. Within weeks, intelligence officials concluded that the flights were carried out by Bout's air network. The officials grew increasingly dismayed as they continued over the summer to probe into Bout's operations, turning up new disturbing signs that his arms delivery network was active not only with the Islamic militias in Somalia, but also with the faction's allies in neighboring Eritrea. "We have developed a large body of information of what Mr. Bout's organization is doing" in the Horn of Africa, one U.S. intelligence analyst said. "I am alarmed at what he is doing as it undermines Centcom's counterterrorism strategy in the region."

Then, in August, European Union (EU) intelligence officials formally protested to Russia after one of Bout's henchmen, who had been seeking to cut a deal with authorities to exchange information on the Russian's network for immunity and protection, was kidnapped, along with his girlfriend, in Western Europe as he prepared to deliver a large cache of what he claimed were incriminating documents. Suspecting that Bout's organization was behind the

abduction and that he personally may have been traveling clandestinely to Europe to arrange weapons deals, EU officials asked the
Russians to investigate. They received word from Russian officials
that the abduction was a "rogue operation," not an officially sanctioned activity. The Russians did not address the question of
whether Bout had been directly involved in the abduction.

Bout's relations with Russia's intelligence community had
always been suspected but never confirmed, but in November,
reports of a new American criminal investigation into Bout's organization produced the first solid evidence that both networks worked
hand in hand. Federal firearms agents working on a case involving
shotgun sales at a small town Pennsylvania sporting goods store in
July stumbled on documents indicating that the store had provided
more than $240,000 in rifle scopes, optical devices, and other para-
military items to a Russian company that allegedly fronted for the
FSB, the Russian state intelligence agency that had replaced the
KGB. The items had been shipped in spring 2005 to Tactica, Ltd., a
Moscow firm described in an affidavit by ATF investigators as part
of the "'Vympel Group,' which is a known identifier for an elite
counterterrorism unit that is controlled by the Russian Federal
Security Service [formerly the KGB]." The Russian firm's top official
later denied ties to the intelligence branch. The federal agents also
seized foreign wire transfers for the Tactica purchases indicating
that $60,000 had been paid from Rockman EOOD, a Bulgarian
holding company owned by Sergei Bout and sanctioned by Treasury
in 2005 as part of the assets freeze against the Bout network. The
equipment was restricted from foreign export without authoriza-
tion from the State Department, and while the owners of D&R
Sporting Goods, a Nanticoke, Pennsylvania, firm, insisted they had
filed proper documents, federal agents indicated that State had
turned down the firm's request to sell the items. ATF agents invoked
Bout's involvement with Tactica as a compelling reason to continue
the investigation, saying that Bout "and his numerous shell companies around Eastern Europe and the world were also identified as
significant participants in providing weapons to the dictator
Charles Taylor in Liberia, rebel groups in Rwanda and the Taliban,
as well as subsequent war crimes that were committed by those
regimes."[5]

Despite the new flare-ups of interest in Bout's activities, the investigations remained piecemeal, focused only on scattered corners of the world. There was no longer a central U.S. government apparatus that could rapidly transform the new spate of information into coordinated action. Even Centcom, now suddenly anxious about the flood of weapons into East Africa, had been Bout's protector only months earlier, pressuring Treasury officials to hold off on their sanctions while the Russian's cargo planes completed their final deliveries into Baghdad. Despite the uptick in intelligence attention, there remained no concerted American policy to do anything about Bout's continuing activities.

Even as the Bout network faded as a target for Western intelligence and law enforcement agencies, his international mystique grew. Several film scripts emerged from the flurry of media profiles of Bout and his business. The first to appear, the 2005 film *Lord of War*, was loosely based on Bout's gunrunning activities. Nicolas Cage played Yuri Orlov, an amoral Russian American weapons dealer specializing in the delivery of planeloads of weapons to warlords and terrorists in Africa and the Middle East. Just before the film was released in the United States, director Andrew Niccol boasted that an Antonov An-12 used in a pivotal scene had been rented from "one of the most notorious arms traffickers in Africa." Pressed by *Newsweek* reporters, Niccol admitted, "Well, I suppose I can say that it was Viktor Bout's plane. The crew said that plane ran real guns into the Congo the week before we were using it to film fake guns. That plane has since crashed, running something described as suspicious cargo out of Uganda."[6] FBI agents later investigated the film company's use of the plane as a possible violation of the OFAC ban on doing business with Bout, but in the end, no action was taken.

Playing film critic, Bout panned his portrayal. "I'm sorry for Nicolas Cage," he said. "It's a bad movie."[7]

Most of Bout's old nemeses had moved on, despairing of ever seeing him put out of business. Witney Schneidman has a consulting business specializing in African trade. Johan Peleman and Kathi Austin continued to work for the United Nations in missions around the globe that targeted arms trafficking and war crimes allegations. Lee Wolosky was ensconced as a corporate attorney, specializing in international litigation for a New York firm headed by Wall Street legal top gun David Boies. Joining as an adviser for Senator John Kerry during his failed 2004 presidential campaign, Wolosky had hoped that revelations about Bout's flights into Iraq might catch fire as a political issue. But Kerry's inner circle never pressed the matter.

Despite the short-lived promise of the Bout task force that he once headed, Wolosky was convinced that that no American administration was capable of decimating the Russian's organization without fierce political will and clear lines of authority emanating from the White House. "We were doing things a different way," Wolosky mused from his New York office. "We were an ad hoc group that didn't fit into the interagency structure. We were able to bring in State, CIA, FBI, ATF into the White House. Sometimes we had to drag them in. But there was a lot of buy-in once they understood the White House was behind it." In hindsight, Wolosky felt that Bout's global organization was a chilling glimpse of the global logistics capacity that might one day ferry a nuclear weapon—exactly the sort of airlift that was used by militant Pakistani physicist A. Q. Kahn in smuggling dangerous nuclear materiel to Libya, Iran, and North Korea in the late 1990s. "We were beginning to see and understand how people were conducting business in the seams of the international economy," Wolosky said. "But we were trying to herd international cats."

Only Andreas Morgner remained on the case, still lobbying for action against Bout inside the OFAC. Government working groups dealing with Bout and weapons trafficking had long been disbanded, but Morgner kept on as time permitted. He enjoyed some small successes. An executive order signed by President Bush on October 31, 2006, redesignated Bout under a new set of sanctions targeting arms traffickers who had allegedly violated a UN weapons embargo imposed on the Democratic Republic of the Congo. Bout's years of deliveries into the DRC constituted an "unusual and extraordinary threat to the foreign policy of the United States," the order stated.[8] Similar to the assets freeze related to Bout's activities in Liberia, the new sanctions authorized the OFAC to seize all Bout's U.S. accounts and prohibited any American person or company from doing business with him. The sanctions list also included several of Bout's well-known associates in the DRC: Sanjivan Ruprah, Dimitri Popov, and Douglas Mpano. Popov and Mpano were the managers of two Bout-related air freight companies, which were also designated: Great Lakes Business Company and the Compagnie Aérienne des Grands Lacs.

Bout emerged from seclusion to scoff at the latest American slap. Appearing on the Russian Today television network, he stuck to his old lines. "Every time it is the same story, the same repetition. I can even call it a witch hunt," he said. "They are accusing me since 1998 of all kinds of illegal arms trade in Africa. But even with all the power of the American administration, the CIA, the FBI, and all their means, like satellites, they are still not able to come with certain proof."[9]

Indeed, the new assets freeze was more symbolic than practical. Most of the limited funds that were within reach of authorities had already been seized in the earlier Liberian sanctions. At best, it was a way to keep up the pressure, to let Bout know that he could not operate with complete impunity, and that someone inside the U.S. government was still watching. But the sanctions had limited real value, amounting to small-bore nuisances at best compared to the dashed international manhunt that preceded them. The new efforts were ghost pains, nagging reminders of both the brief promise of the now-abandoned Bout chase and the United States' unsavory dalliance with Bout's network in Iraq. They were paper threats postured by a paper tiger.

"They don't stop him. They only make him mad," sighed a European intelligence official who once specialized in Bout's operation but now had less and less time and latitude to keep tabs on the network's constant metamorphoses. "These actions are only reminders that he is out there, still doing his deadly business."

In the end, international hypocrisy and the collapse of the post–Cold War order had allowed Bout's empire to thrive and sustain itself. Like the bleakly amoral characters that populate Graham Greene's novels and John le Carré's thrillers, Bout deftly surfed the upheaval of the 1990s, playing to the shifting desires of nations uncertain of their own way in the rapidly changing world. Bout intuitively understood the business potential of catering to rebel armies and criminal regimes that controlled access to lucrative natural resources and were willing to barter for weapons. Reaching far into remote lawless regions and failed states, he had become the master of weapons delivery to all corners of the globe, redefining the logistics of twenty-first-century warfare.

His nimble, shape-shifting network consistently outpaced the hidebound and often contradictory responses of the nations that pursued him. Nowhere was this policy schizophrenia more apparent than in the Bush administration's eagerness to use his planes in Iraq while pestering his network with limited sanctions. The United States was hardly alone in its clashing impulses: Britain, Belgium, South Africa, and the United Nations targeted the Bout empire, yet they all had employed his network or benefited from his operations—and dozens of smaller countries, from the UAE to Liberia, unabashedly courted Bout's business and welcomed his planes.

Institutional blindness, incompetence, corruption, and lack of sustained efforts often paved the rise of Bout's global network. From the rapacious greed of the Eastern bloc's newly liberated armaments industry to the flimsy contracting methods of the U.S. military, officials had consistently looked the other way, either unwittingly or purposely, allowing Bout's planes to keep on delivering their long, green crates. The shortsighted official paralysis that some cynics described as "superpower attention deficit disorder" seemed sadly fitting in a world that had made scant progress in instituting clear, strongly enforced international standards governing the global movement of weapons.

Only the all-too-brief momentum shown by the American and European efforts to curtail Bout's operation in early 2000 and 2001 held out the promise of what might be accomplished if nations were to set aside their provincial interests and join in common efforts against the contraband arms trade. The idealistic, single-minded determination of officials such as Wolosky, Schneidman, Morgner, and Hain and activists such as Peleman and Austin provide determined models for those who would confront the vast arms flows that continue to fuel violent conflicts around the world.

Still, for all their failings, governments have at worst been only Bout's enablers. It is Bout and his associates who ultimately bear the blame for the lethal wares they deliver. But guilt is not in Bout's lexicon. He clings perpetually to his denials, complaining always that he has been unfairly persecuted for being a successful business-man. His prosperity is indeed remarkable, owing much to the vision, ambition, guile, and discretion of one exceptional, enterpris-ing man. But over the course of his audacious career, Bout reaped his brimming fortune at the expense of the nameless thousands who were victimized by the wars he stoked.

NOTES

All the material collected for this book, unless otherwise noted, was obtained by the authors in interviews with the people involved.

Prologue

1. Human Rights Watch World Report, 2000, and press accounts.
2. Authors' interview with Bout associate, March 13, 2006.
3. Notes of Chichakli interview provided by Andre Verloy.

Chapter 1: The Delivery Man

1. This account is based on interviews and the writings of Belgian journalist Dirk Draulans, the only journalist to spend time with Bout in the African bush. His writings include "De Criminele Verhalen van de Brave Soldaat Bout," *Knack*, May 16, 2001.
2. Christian Dietrich, "Diamonds and the Central African Republic: Trading, Valuing and Laundering," Diamond and Human Security Project, Occasional Paper 8, Partnership Africa Canada, January 2003.
3. Lora Lumpe, ed., *Running Guns: The Global Black Market in Small Arms* (London: Zed Books, 2000), p. 2.
4. Intelligence reports obtained by the authors; interviews with U.S. Treasury officials and press release, "Treasury Designates Viktor Bout's International Arms Trafficking Network," April 26, 2005; Stephen Braun, Judy Pasternak, and T. Christian Miller, "Blacklisted Russian Tied to Iraq Deals," *Los Angeles Times*, December 14, 2004. Intelligence reports that touted the Bout network's $50 million take from the Tal-

iban have been questioned by some arms trade experts, but in 2006, Treasury officials backed the estimate. One official later explained that the $50 million amount included both arms and noncontraband cargoes. In Iraq, U.S. flight and fuel service records obtained by the *Los Angeles Times* documented at least 142 flights between March and August 2004, and several contractors verified that Bout-orbit firms were charging as much as $60,000 for each flight. Hundreds more flights are estimated between mid-2003 and the present, and hard estimates of as many as a thousand flights in that period may have netted the Bout network as much as $60 million.

5. Intelligence reports obtained by the authors; Interpol warrant for Bout's arrest, February 18, 2002. The Interpol warrant, based on a Belgian charging document, alleged that from 1994 to 1996, some 860 million in Belgian francs were moved from a Liberian firm and the Angolan air force and Angolan armed forces into the Belgian accounts of a Bout-controlled firm. From 1996 onward, another 150 million in Belgian francs were "systematically transferred" to two other Bout-operated companies. The total amount of Belgian francs equaled U.S. $32.5 million.

6. Paul Salopek, "Shadowy Men Run Guns, Feed Fires of War," *Chicago Tribune*, December 24, 2001, p. 1.

7. James Boxell, "The Kalashnikov, the World's Most Prolific Killing Machine, Stands the Test of Time," *Financial Times* of London, June 7, 2006, p. 5.

8. "RPG-7/RPG-7V/RPG-7VR Rocket-Propelled Grenade Launcher Multipurpose Weapon, Manufacturer: Basalt Russia, Defense Update," *International Online Defense Magazine*, 2004, issue 1.

9. Authors' interview with Bout associate, March 13, 2006.

10. *Frontline* interviews with Johan Peleman, October–December 2001.

11. Special Court for Sierra Leone, *Prosecutor v. Charles Ghankay Taylor*, Case SCSL-2003-01-1, March 7, 2003.

12. "Hague Referral for African Pair," BBC, April 14, 2005, accessed at http://news.bbc.co.uk/2/hi/africa/4908938.stm.

13. John Prendergast, "Angola's Deadly War: Dealing with Savimbi's Hell on Earth," United States Institute of Peace, October 12, 1999.

14. Air crash incidents gathered from news accounts, international air registries, and from AirDisaster.com, a Web archive of aviation accident histories. Plane crashes linked to the Bout organization include an Ilyushin Il-18 in the DRC in 1998 and an Antonov An-32 the same year; two Yakovlevs damaged in Kenya and the Central African Republic in the late 1990s; and an Antonov An-12 that crashed in Yemen in 2005.

15. *Los Angeles Times* interviews with Russian aviation executives, March 2002.

16. Authors' interviews and Thomas M. Callghy, "Life and Death in the Congo," *Foreign Affairs*, September/October 2001.

17. Center for Public Integrity, *Making a Killing: The Business of War* (Washington, D.C.: Public Integrity Books, 2003), p. 145.

18. Peter Landesman, "Arms and the Man," *New York Times Magazine*, August 17, 2003.

19. Authors' e-mail interview with Sanjivan Ruprah, May 18, 2006.

20. John Daniszewski, Stephen Braun, Judy Pasternak, Maura Reynolds, and Sergei L. Loiko, "On the Trail of a Man behind Taliban's Air Fleet," *Los Angeles Times*, May 19, 2002.

21. *Los Angeles Times* interview with Alexander Sidorenko, March 25, 2002.

22. *Los Angeles Times* interview with Sergei Mannkhayev, April 2002.

23. *Los Angeles Times* interviews with Russian aviation executives and U.S. officials, April 2002.

24. *Los Angeles Times* interview with Vladimir Sharpatov, March 27, 2002.

25. *Los Angeles Times* interview with Igor Abdayev, April 2002.

26. Translated transcript of Viktor Bout interview with Radio Echo Moskvy, February 28, 2002. The authors requested an interview with Bout and also offered to relay questions by e-mail, but neither Bout or his Russian lawyer responded.

27. *Los Angeles Times* telephone interview with Sergei Bout, March 2002.

Chapter 2: Planes, Guns, and Money

1. FBIS, trans., "Viktor Bout Interviewed on Western Press Allegations," *Moscow Komsosmolskaya Pravda*, March 5, 2002.

2. Passport copy from U.S. Department of Treasury, Bureau of Alcohol, Tobacco, and Firearms, "Intelligence Brief: Victor But, Transnational Criminal Activities," December 2000. Bout gave his place of birth in a February 28, 2002, interview with Radio Echo Moskvy. Interpol Red Notice, February 18, 2002.

3. Intelligence documents obtained by the authors.

4. Peter Landesman, "Arms and the Man," *New York Times Magazine*, August 17, 2003.

5. Intelligence documents obtained by the authors.

6. *Los Angeles Times* interview with Alexander Sidorenko, March 25, 2002.

7. Authors' interview with British intelligence analyst, June 2006.

8. Translated transcript of Viktor Bout interview with Radio Echo Moskvy, February 28, 2002.

9. Dirk Draulans, "The Criminal Stories of the Good Soldier Bout," *Knack* 20, May 16, 2001.

10. *Los Angeles Times* interview with Alexander Sidorenko, March 25, 2002.

11. British intelligence analyst, op. cit..

12. Landesman, "Arms and the Man."

13. Authors' interview with Bout associate, April 2006.

14. A European intelligence source who tracked Bout for several years said that he came to be protected by, and work for, a semiofficial Russian company called Isotrex, whose board is largely made up of deputy ministers of different key government agencies tied to the weapons trade. An indication of how much backing Bout had, according to European intelligence sources, was his reported involvement in the founding in 1992 of a small private Swiss bank in Geneva. The chief financial officer was Olivier Piret, whom Bout would later take to South Africa to handle his financial affairs. The Swiss shut the bank down in 1997 because of questionable financial practicies, according to European and intelligence reports.

15. *Los Angeles Times* interview with Sergei Mankhayev, April 2002. The identities of most of Bout's military contacts and other prominent Russian backers remain shrouded. One name that repeatedly surfaced was Major General Vladimir Marchenko, reportedly a longtime Bout business associate. Marchenko was a senior veteran of the Federal Security Bureau, the counterintelligence agency once headed by Russian Federation president Vladimir Putin. Marchenko was selected by Putin in May 1998 to head the Internal Security Directorate, Russia's leading antiterror unit. Said to be a specialist in ethnic organized crime, Marchenko held that official position until 2002. A South African intelligence document said the intelligence veteran headed a crime syndicate known as the "Marchenko organization." According to intelligence documents, Marchenko ordered Bout to return to Russia in 1998 after the Angola government canceled its business with him, discovering that he had supplied both sides in the nation's civil war. Richard Chichakli, Bout's Syrian American partner, told Andre Verloy that "Bout cannot be recalled by anyone, because he works for no one." Still, Chichakli acknowledged, Marchenko was a "business acquaintance" of Bout's.

16. Andre Verloy, unpublished notes of interview with Richard Chichakli, February 21, 2002.

17. *Los Angeles Times* interview with Valery Spurnov, April 2002.

18. *Los Angeles Times* interview with Russian aviation executive, March 2002.

19. *Los Angeles Times* interview with KAS official, April 3, 2002.

20. *Los Angeles Times* interviews with Spurnov and Russian aviation executive.

21. Authors' interview with British intelligence analyst, June 2006

22. Authors' interview with Bout associate, March 16, 2006.

23. John Daniszewski, Stephen Braun, Judy Pasternak, Maura Reynolds, and Sergei L. Loiko, "On the Trail of a Man behind Taliban's Air Fleet," *Los Angeles Times*, May 19, 2002.

24. "Gunrunners," *Frontline*, PBS, March 2002, accessed at www.pbs.org/frontlineworld/stories/sierraleone/bout.html.

25. Stephen Braun and Judy Pasternak, "Long before Sept. 11, Bin Laden's Aircraft Flew under the Radar," *Los Angeles Times*, November 18, 2001.

26. Graham H. Turbiville Jr., "Mafia in Uniform: The Criminalization of the Russian Armed Forces," U.S. Army, Foreign Military Studies Office.

27. Intelligence documents obtained by the authors.

28. *Los Angeles Times* interview with U.S. and UN officials, April 2002; letter dated April 19, 2002, from the chairman of the Security Council Committee established pursuant to Resolution 1343 (2001) concerning Liberia addressed to the president of the Security Council, paras. 65–66; investigative Journalist Assn. (Bulgaria), "The Business with Death and the Yuroembargo," December 22, 2003.

29. R. W. Dellow, repr., 1992 speech by General Petr Stepanovich Deynekin. Sandhurst, U.K.: Conflict Studies Research Centre, Royal Military Academy, June 1993.

30. Authors' interview with British intelligence analyst, op cit.

31. Authors' interview with U.S. Treasury official, May 23, 2006.

32. Report of the Panel of Experts in Relation to Sierra Leone to the Secretary-General, United Nations, December 2000, paragraph 221. From 1996 through 1998, Bout associates Michael Harridine and Ronald De Smet conducted business in the United Kingdom on behalf of the Liberian Aircraft Register. This presented no logistical problems, since the aircraft did not need to be physically present to receive certificates of airworthiness. The certificates allowed Bout's planes to make international flights. The involvement of the two Bout associates was documented by the UN's Final Report of the Monitoring Mechanism on Angola Sanctions to the Secretary-General, December 21, 2000, paras. 142–144.

33. United Nations Final Report of the Monitoring Mechanism on Angola Sanctions to the Secretary-General, December 21, 2000, paras. 142–144.

34. Landesman, "Arms and the Man."
35. Ibid.
36. Author interviews with intelligence officials and Bout associates.
37. *Los Angeles Times* interview with Sidorenko.

Chapter 3: A Dangerous Business

1. *Los Angeles Times* interviews with former Afghan deputy defense ministers Ahmet Muslem Hayat and Abdul Latif and with former Afghan deputy civil aviation minister Mohammed Eshaq, March 2002. All three men said Bout's planes started flying for the Rabbani government in 1992 after the collapse of the government of Mohammed Najibullah, and continued until Taliban forces seized power in September 1996.
2. Peter Landesman, "Arms and the Man," *New York Times Magazine*, August 17, 2003.
3 Authors' interview with Bout associate, March 6, 2006. According to the associate, the blossoming ties between Bout and the Afghans had origins in the Russian's Tajik birthplace. Both Massoud and Rabbani were ethnic Tajiks, whose customs and language Bout knew well. The Russian's first Afghan connection was a Tajik warlord named Salam, who operated in the Pamir district of Afghanistan. Bout also had fixers, the associate said, in Russia's 201st Army Division, then based in Tajikistan.
4. John Daniszewski, Stephen Braun, Judy Pasternak, Maura Reynolds, and Sergei L. Loiko, "On the Trail of a Man behind Taliban's Air Fleet," *Los Angeles Times*, May 19, 2002; also the *Los Angeles Times* interviews with Hayat, Latif, and Eshaq.
5. Daniszewski et al., "On the Trail"; *Los Angeles Times* interview with Hayat, March 2002; James Risen, "Russians Are Back in Afghanistan," *New York Times*, July 27, 1996: "Massoud has said in interviews that he receives much of his equipment from the Russian mafia, not the Russian government."
6. John C. Holzman, diplomatic cable from U.S. embassy, Islamabad, April 17, 1995, provided by National Security Archive, George Washington University; Robin Bhatty and David Hoffman, "Afghanistan: Crisis of Impunity," Human Rights Watch, July 2001; Robert Fisk, "Circling over a Broken, Ruined State," *Independent* (London), July 14, 1996: In a classified cable sent to Washington in April 1995, Holzman, deputy chief of mission at the U.S. embassy in Pakistan, said that Russia's public stance against the involvement of private arms dealers profiteers only increased "the price to a point where other

suppliers may become more attractive." But as Massoud's forces battled other Afghan warlord factions and contended with the rise of the
Taliban, Russian officials looked the other way while Bout and other
arms suppliers kept weapons flowing. Some weapons shipments
arrived through overland routes across the Tajik border "with the
active collusion of the Russian government," Holzman wrote.

7. *Los Angeles Times* interview with Vladimir Sharpatov, March 27, 2002.

8. Agence France Presse, August 11, 1995; Antonov and Ilyushin model
histories, Russian Aircraft Museum, Aeromarket.ru.

9. Daniszewski et al., "On the Trail"; *Los Angeles Times* interview with
Sharpatov.

10. Peter Andreas, "The Clandestine Political Economy of War and Peace
in Bosnia," *International Studies Quarterly* 48 (2004): p. 33.

11. For a more complete look at the role of al Qaeda in Bosnia see Evan F.
Kholmann, *Al Qaida's Jihad in Europe: The Afghan-Bosnian Network*
(New York: Berg, 2004).

12. Founded in 1987 in Vienna, Austria, the TWRA was run by Elfatih
Hassanein, a Sudanese with a diplomatic passport accrediting him as
a cultural attaché in Vienna, enabling him to travel unhindered
around the region without being subject to customs or immigration
checks. When the war broke out Hassanein, who had studied medi-
cine in Belgrade in the 1970s, quickly turned the TWRA agency into
an unofficial arm of the Bosnian government and its president, Alija
Izetbegovic. The TWRA's chief contact in the new Bosnian government was Hasan Cengic, a well-known radical Islamic Bosnian official
who was primarily responsible for acquiring weapons for the Muslim
forces and breaking the weapons embargo. Cengic, an imam frequently described as an Iranian intelligence agent, later served as
Bosnia's deputy defense minister. The United States would eventually
place Cengic on the Treasury Department's list of banned individuals
because of his ties to Iranian intelligence and efforts to disrupt the
Balkans peace process. For the most extensive research on TWRA see
John Pomfret, "Bosnia's Muslims Dodged Embargo," *Washington Post*,
September 22, 1996, p. A1. For designation reference see Office of
Foreign Assets Control, "List of Designated and Blocked Individuals,"
p. 65.

Bout continued dealing with Cengic long after the Maribor shipments, as the imam guided TWRA and its successor agencies in the
acquisition of weapons and aircraft. Over time Bout sold or donated
several aircraft to Cengic and his air company, BIO Air. According to
2004 Bosnian intelligence reports, Bout, with the help of Cengic loy-

alists and family members, sent four aircraft to Bosnia after the Maribor shipments were discovered. The aircraft were not registered with the government customs office as having been legally imported. Two of those aircraft were then leased back to Bout from BIO Air. The report says that the intelligence services "suspect that Victor Bout in collaboration with Hasan Cengic is transporting weapons to Chechnya via Air Bosna pilots. Weapons are originating from a Bulgarian weapons plant."

13. According to Pomfret and others, another major donor was Wael Julaedan, a Saudi companion of bin Laden who was later designated a terrorist financier by the U.S. Treasury Department and the United Nations. One of those in frequent contact with TWRA and Hassanein was Sheikh Omar Abdul Rahman, the blind Egyptian cleric now serving a life sentence for planning a series of terrorist attacks in New York. The 1993 plot, dubbed "Day of Terror," was to be simultaneous strikes on the UN headquarters, the Holland and Lincoln tunnels, the George Washington Bridge, and other landmarks. Intelligence services had tapes of Rahman calling TWRA offices to discuss selling tapes of his sermons there.

14. Pomfret et al., ibid.

15. Author interviews with Western intelligence officials in the former Yugoslavia at the time of the transaction and Andreas, "Clandestine Political Economy."

16. "Joint Study of the Muslim Brotherhood," November 15, 2005, p. 12, in possession of the authors. That pipeline was short-lived but vital. Due to internal political maneuvering, Croatia in October suddenly closed the smuggling routes through its territory after just four flights. A shipment of 10,000 assault rifles and 750,000 rounds of ammunition, rockets, and explosives, valued at $10 million, was left in a warehouse in Maribor and paid for by TWRA until Slovenian officials revealed the contents a year later. Cengic then publicly admitted that "we paid the Slovenian police in cash and with no records" kept for the weapons transfers through Maribor. Soon other pipelines, principally via Iran, were opened, and Slovenia continued to serve as a primary supplier of the Bosnian cause. At the same time Bout was dealing with Cengic, Cengic was dealing with envoys of bin Laden, who was helping to channel millions of dollars to TWRA.

17. A likely link is Nicolas Oman, a Slovenian weapons merchant who would give Bout at least a preview of the possibilities of the riches to be had selling weapons in Africa. He was also a pioneer in playing several different sides in a conflict. Oman, at the start of the Bosnian

war, traveled to Liberia. At the time Liberia was under the rule of an illiterate sergeant named Samuel Doe. Oman talked or bribed his way into obtaining a Liberian diplomatic passport based on being named honorary Liberian consul in Slovenia, even though the countries did not have even minimal commercial or political ties. But Oman's real business was the weapons-for-diamonds trade that Bout would later perfect. With a diplomatic passport, Oman was free to travel unhindered with millions of dollars in diamonds, arrange weapons deals, and inspect weapons around Europe. He often did business from an ancient castle on the outskirts of Bled, where he entertained Russian mobsters and ultranationalists, intelligence officials from different countries, and arms dealers. The history of Oman's involvement is contained in the Italian investigation known as the "Cheque-to-Cheque Affair," as well as numerous other intelligence and media reports in possession of the authors. In addition to his help in arming the Bosnian Muslims, Oman was involved in trying to procure, for $60 million, a "vacuum bomb" on behalf of Radovan Karadzic, a Serbian war criminal responsible for the massacre of thousands of Muslims through "ethnic cleansing" campaigns. The bomb was supposed to suck the oxygen out of the air, killing everyone. The bomb was never built and may not even have existed, but Oman appears to have cheated Karadzic out of $8 million in the deal. According to Oman associates and European intelligence officials Bout's relationship with Oman endured for more than a decade. When Bout began flying weapons and ammunition into Iraq for the U.S. military in 2003, Oman was one of the providers.

18. Pomfret et al., note 13.
19. Ibid.
20. Translated copy of Transavia Travel Agency license provided to the *Los Angeles Times*. The license was registered with the UAE Ministry of Justice on March 3, 1993, and renewed on July 11, 1998.
21. *Los Angeles Times* interview with Richard Chichakli, January 2002.
22. The "Transavia Network" was designated by the Treasury Department's Office of Foreign Assets Control on April 26, 2005. The designated companies include NVtrans Aviation Network, aka TAN Group; aka Trans Aviation; aka Transavia Travel Agency; aka Transavia Travel Cargo. Transavia planes were still flying as late as May 2005, when the firm was chartered by the British Ministry of Defence to fly troops and armored vehicles from the United Kingdom to Baghdad.
23. *Los Angeles Times* interview with Alexander Sidorenko, March 25, 2002.

24. *Los Angeles Times* interview with U.S. diplomat, December 2001.
25. *Los Angeles Times* notes for October 20, 2001, story on UAE.
26. Andre Verloy, unpublished notes of interviews with Richard Chichakli, 2002.
27. Andre Verloy, "Viktor Bout's American Connection," Center for Public Integrity, November 20, 2002. According to Verloy, Chickakli claimed to be a nephew of a former president of Syria. But Chichakli later denied that family connection. Also, Verloy notes of Chichakli interviews, ibid.
28. *Los Angeles Times*, Chichakli interview.
29. Verloy notes of Chichakli interviews. Chichakli later claimed in a fax to Treasury officials that he did not meet Bout in 1993 and that he only worked for the free-trade zone in 1995 and 1996. Chichakli has disavowed many of his earlier statements made in interviews. He turned down a request from the authors for a new interview.
30. Office of Foreign Assets Control, "List of Specially Designated Individuals," April 26, 2005.
31. Verloy notes of Chichakli interviews.
32. Group Audit Middle East, "Fraud Investigation Report: Saeed al Jabri (SAJ), Sharjah Branch, UAE," December 1999, in possession of the authors. See also Glenn R. Simpson and Erik Portanger, "U.A.E. Banks Had Suspect Transfers," *Wall Street Journal*, September 17, 2003, p. A1.
33. Group Audit Middle East, p. 10.
34. Ibid.
35. *Los Angeles Times* interviews with Belgian and U.S. officials, April 2002; also open-access files of CleanOstend, a Belgian antiarms-trafficking group.
36. Dirk Draulans, "De Criminele Verhalen van de Brave Soldaat Bout," *Knack*, May 16, 2001.
37. *Los Angeles Times* interview with Ronny Lauwereins, March 2002.
38. Richard Newell, "Mujahadin Victory: The Islamic Republic of Afghanistan," Federal Research Division, Library of Congress, 1997; Agence France Presse news accounts.
39. *Los Angeles Times*, Sharpatov interview; Agence France Presse news accounts; confidential cable from U.S. embassy in Islamabad, August 6, 1995, provided by National Security Archive, George Washington University.
40. *Los Angeles Times*, Sharpatov interview.
41. Holzman, diplomatic cable from U.S. embassy, Islamabad.
42. Daniszewski et al., "On the Trail."
43. *Los Angeles Times* interview with Zamir Kabulov, April 13, 2002.

44. Ibid.
45. *Los Angeles Times*, Sharpatov interview.
46. *Los Angeles Times* interviews with Sergei Mankhayev, March 2002.
47. *Los Angeles Times*, Kabulov interview.
48. Daniszewski et al., "On the Trail." Agence France Presse news accounts.
49. *Los Angeles Times* interview with Russian aviation executive, March 2002.
50. Landesman, "Arms and the Man."

Chapter 4: Continental Collapse

1. Lynne Duke, *Mandela, Mobutu, and Me: A Newswoman's Africa Journey* (New York: Doubleday, 2003), p. 124.
2. Thomas M. Callaghy, "Life and Death in the Congo," *Foreign Affairs*, Spring 2002, accessed at: www.foreignaffairs.org/20010901fare viewessay5576/thomas-m-callaghy/life-and-death-in-the-congo.html.
3. This account is based on interviews with the official involved, who cannot be identified by name because of his ongoing work in the intelligence community.
4. Peleman interview that appeared in "Gunrunners," *Frontline/World*, PBS, May 2002, accessed at www.pbs.org/frontlineworld/stories/sierraleone/bout.html.
5. John Reader, *Africa: A Biography of a Continent* (New York: Vintage Books, 1999), p. 686.
6. Richard H. Shultz, Douglas Farah, and Itamara V. Lochard, "Armed Groups: A Tier-One Security Priority," Institute for National Security Studies, U.S. Air Force Academy, Occasional Paper 57, 2004.
7. Jeffrey Boutwell and Michael Klare, "Small Arms and Light Weapons: Controlling the Real Weapons of War," *Arms Control Today*, August/September 1998.
8. "Arms and Conflict in Africa," U.S. Department of State Fact Sheet, Bureau of Intelligence and Research, July 1, 2001.
9. William D. Hartung and Bridget Moix, "Deadly Legacy: U.S. Arms to Africa and the Congo War," Arms Trade Resource Center, January 2000; Boutwell and Klare, "Small Arms."
10. Oxfam International, "Up in Arms: Controlling the International Trade in Small Arms," July 2001.
11. Stephen Ellis, *The Mask of Anarchy: The Destruction of Liberia and the Religious Dimension of an African Civil War*, (New York: New York University Press, 2001), p. 72.
12. European intelligence sources and report seen by authors; confidential government list of Bout planes provided to the authors; *Los Angeles Times* interview with U.S. official, April 2002.

13. State Department fact sheet on Osama bin Laden, August 14, 1996.
14. NATO working paper, "NDL and USA Joint Paper on the Muslim Brotherhood," November 15, 2005.
15. Eric Reeves, "Regime Change in Sudan," *Washington Post*, August 23, 2004, p. A23.
16. Written reply to the South African National Assembly by the Ministry of Home Affairs, October 4, 2002.
17. Ofcansky interview that appeared in "Gunrunners," *Frontline/World*, PBS, May 2002.
18. On June 8, 2006, Gus Kouwenhoven, a Dutch national who supplied weapons to Taylor in Liberia in exchange for timber concessions, was sentenced in a Netherlands court to eight years in prison. See Africa Governance Monitoring and Advocacy Project, June 8, 2006, accessed at www.afrimap.org/newsarticle.php?id=504.
19. UN Panel of Experts, UN Report on Sierra Leone, December 2000, para. 293.
20. "Final Report of the Monitoring Mechanism on Angola," S/2000/1225, December 21, 2000, para. 36; Interpol red notice for Victor Bout, February 28, 2002.
21. "Final Report of the Monitoring Mechanism on Angola," para. 37.
22. Ibid., paras. 32–38.
23. Ibid., para. 119.
24. Peleman interview, "Gunrunners."
25. Ibid.
26. European intelligence reports in possession of the authors.
27. Interpol red notice for Victor Bout, February 28, 2002.
28. This account is based on the following: Susan Schmidt and James V. Grimaldi, "The Rapid Rise and Steep Fall of Jack Abramoff," *Washington Post*, December 29, 2005, p. A1; Wikipedia entry: en.wikipedia.org/wiki/Jonas_Savimbi; Danny Schechter, "Jack Abramoff's White Man's Burden," Common Dreams News Center, February 16, 2006 (www.commondreams.org/views06/0216-21.htm).
29. "The Final Report of the UN Panel of Experts on Violations of Security Council Sanctions against UNITA," S/2000/203, March 10, 2000; author interviews with weapons dealers. The timing of Bout's arrival on the scene in Angola and Zaire was fortuitous. For several years Savimbi had relied on a South African arms dealer, Ronnie De Decker, who went by the alias "Watson," to provide his war matériel. However, by 1994 De Decker was having difficulty procuring the types of weapons Savimbi wanted, including sophisticated surface-to-air missile systems. Savimbi was gearing up for a major offensive, and was

desperate to acquire weapons that would allow him to defend his diamond-rich enclave against government jets and tanks. Bout had both the access to weapons and the airlift capacity to undercut the prices of the competition.

30. "Final Report . . . UNITA," paras. 33–34.
31. "Addendum to the Final Report of the Monitoring Mechanism on Angola," UN Security Council, S/2001/363, paras. 22–32.
32. Bout's use of EUCs from Ivory Coast and Burkina Faso is detailed in several of the UN Panel of Experts' reports on Liberia and Sierra Leone, including Report of the Panel of Experts concerning Liberia, S/2001/1015, October 26, 2001, and Report of the Panel of Experts in Relation to Sierra Leone, December 2000, paras. 204–206.

Chapter 5: At a Crossroads

1. Banele Ginindza, "Couriers Air Cess Sets Up Shop in Swaziland," *Business Day*, October 9, 1997.
2. *Los Angeles Times* interview with Johan Peleman, March 2002. During his travels in Africa in 2001, Peleman said, Bout was often accompanied by a Russian who owned Stealth Telecom, a telecommunications firm in Sharjah. According to Peleman, the firm provided satellite phones for mobile use and also for offices and hangars. A Belgian Senate report issued on February 20, 2003, asserted that Stealth Telecom provided communications equipment to Bout and his associates and also to Bemba and his forces.
3. A 2001 South African secret intelligence profile of Viktor Bout, "Profile of Victor Butt," marked "Secret," NIA, February 5, 2001, noted another interesting link: Ward was the ex-wife of a man named Peter Farquar, who owned another airline, Metavia Airlines. Farquar, the report said, "has a long history of smuggling from Mozambique and was also a supporter of UNITA." In August 1997 Farquar presented a proposal to sell Metavia Airlines to Bout and Ward, and Bout accepted. Through Ward he bought all of Metavia Airlines Pty, changed its name to Metro D Pty., and used it under the name Norse Aircharter.
4. This account is based on European and South African intelligence reports in possession of the authors; International Consortium of Investigative Journalists, *Making a Killing: The Business of War*, (Washington, D.C.: Public Integrity Books, 2003), pp. 150–151.
5. *Los Angeles Times* interview with Richard Chichakli, May 2002.
6. "Final Report of the Monitoring Mechanism on Angola," S/2000/1225, December 21, 2000, paras. 127–128.

7. "Victor Bout in South Africa," European intelligence analysis in possession of the authors.

8. "Profile of Victor Butt."

9. Andre Verloy interview with Chichakli, February 21, 2002.

10. Andre Verloy notes.

11. European intelligence summary in possession of the authors; International Consortium of Investigative Journalists, *Making a Killing*, p. 143.

12. Ibid.

13. "Victor Bout in South Africa,"

14. Andre Verloy notes; "The Secret Empire," *Seattle Times*, February 28, 2002.

15. "Intelligence Brief: Victor But Transnational Criminal Activities," U.S. Department of the Treasury, Bureau of Alcohol Tobacco and Firearms, Intelligence Division, December 2000.

16. "Final Report of the Monitoring Mechanism on Angola," para. 134.

17. Ibid., paras. 129–135.

18. "Profile of Victor Butt."

Chapter 6: The Chase Begins

1. "Report of the Panel of Experts in Relation to Sierra Leone," United Nations, December 2000, para. 254.

2. Authors' interview with CIA official, December 2000.

3. John L. Hirsch, "War in Sierra Leone," *Survival* (Autumn 2001): 153.

4. *Los Angeles Times* interview with U.S. official, April 2002.

5. Authors' interview with former U.S. official, June 2006.

6. *Los Angeles Times* interview with U.S. official, March 2002; authors' interview with British intelligence analyst, June 2006.

7. E-mail communication with the authors, September 26, 2006.

8. *Los Angeles Times* interview with Alex Vines, April 2002.

9. *Los Angeles Times* interviews with Devos Bart and Ronny Lauwereins, March 2002.

10. *Los Angeles Times* interview with Johan Peleman, March 2002; also *Moscow Times* interview with Peleman, October 8, 2002.

11. *Frontline* interview with Peleman, May 2002.

12. This account is based on interviews with Austin, Peleman, Winer, and U.S. officials.

13. Text of President Clinton's inaugural speech, January 20, 1993.

14. Authors' interviews with former Clinton administration officials; 9/11 Commission Report, pp. 100–101; Steve Coll, *Ghost Wars: The Secret History of the CIA, Afghanistan, and Bin Laden, from the Soviet*

Invasion to September 10, 2001 (New York: Penguin, 2004), pp. 386–391.

15. Winer interview; Mark Bowden, *Killing Pablo: The Hunt for the World's Greatest Outlaw* (New York: Atlantic Monthly Press, 2001), p. 219. According to former U.S. officials quoted in Bowden's book, Clarke intervened with senior DoD officials in 1993 to allow Delta Force soldiers to secretly accompany Colombian troops on drug raids.

16. Text of President Clinton's speech to the UN General Assembly, October 22, 1995.

17. Text of Arms Export Control Act of 1968, amended to outlaw unlicensed brokering, 22 USC 2778.

18. *Los Angeles Times* interview with U.S. official, March 21, 2002.

19. *Los Angeles Times* interview with Alex Vines, April 2002.

20. *Los Angeles Times* interview with U.S. official, March 21, 2002.

21. Winer interview; authors' interviews with U.S. official, May 2006.

22. Authors' interview with former U.S. official, June 2006.

23. Text of National Security Act of 1947 amended in 1966, 50 USC (402)I; also, Richard A. Best Jr., "Intelligence and Law Enforcement: Countering Transnational Threats to the U.S.," Congressional Research Service report, December 3, 2001, p. 23.

24. White House press secretary's announcement of National Security Council staff realignment, July 30, 1998.

25. *Los Angeles Times* interview with Peleman, March 2002, and with former U.S. State Department official, April 2002.

26. *Los Angeles Times* interview with Peleman; *De Standaard* interview with Peleman, January 5, 2002.

27. Authors' interview with Graham Allison, July 31, 2006.

28. *New York Times*, November 10, 2003; BBC News profile, June 16, 2004. In October 2003, Khodorkovsky was charged by Russian prosecutors with tax evasion. He was sentenced in 2005 to a nine-year jail term and sent to a prison in Krasnokamensk.

29. Lee Wolosky, "Putin's Plutocrat Problem," *Foreign Affairs*, March/April 2000.

30. Authors' interviews with former Clinton administration officials; Strobe Talbott letter to Anne Applebaum, *Slate*, June 10, 2002.

Chapter 7: The Taliban Connection

1. John Daniszewski, Stephen Braun, Judy Pasternak, Maura Reynolds, and Sergei L. Loiko, "On the Trail of a Man behind Taliban's Air Fleet," *Los Angeles Times*, May 19, 2002; also Robin Bhatty and David Hoffman, "Afghanistan: Crisis of Impunity," Human Rights Watch, July 2001.

2. Daniszewski et al., "On the Trail"; also, *Los Angeles Times* interviews with Russian and UAE airport executives and workers, March and April 2002.

3. *Los Angeles Times* interview with Sherin, April 2002.

4. Bhatty and Hoffman, "Afghanistan;" Afghan and U.S. officials and the Human Rights Watch report all described bin Laden as a key "source of funds for the Taliban," paying for a four-hundred-man unit of non-Afghan fighters—the 055 brigade—at the Rishikor base south of Kabul.

5. Bhatty and Hoffman, "Afghanistan;" Bhatty and Hoffman described "buying teams in Hong Kong and Dubai" that worked for Pakistani-based firms to supply the Taliban. The firms reportedly moved military supplies by truck and by sea.

6. *Los Angeles Times* interview with U.S. officials, April and May 2002.

7. *Los Angeles Times* interview with senior Afghan official, March 2002.

8. *Los Angeles Times* interview with Samir Zeidan, December 19, 2001.

9. *Los Angeles Times* interview with Richard Chichakli, January 2002. Asked if Farid had attempted to move arms shipments from Sharjah, Chichakli did not rule it out: "Is it possible? Maybe. I'm not aware of something sticking to him, though." Chichakli insisted that "officially, Ariana never operated in Sharjah," and added that "most of the flights that went into Afghanistan were chartered on other companies." He did not name them.

10. *Los Angeles Times* interviews with former Ariana executive, January, March, and April 2002. Iran's official IRNA News Agency reported that Mansour was killed in southeastern Afghanistan on October 7, 2001, during air strikes by U.S. and British jets. Taliban spokesmen denied the account, and Mansour's name remains on official U.S. lists of wanted Taliban officials.

11. Stephen Braun and Judy Pasternak, "Long before Sept. 11, Bin Laden's Aircraft Flew under the Radar," *Los Angeles Times*, November 18, 2001. UAE and other gulf state sheikhs frequently flew in the late 1990s to a landing strip south of Kandahar that had been refurbished by the Taliban at bin Laden's expense. Afghan air controllers reported that both the late Sheikh al Nahyan and Sheikh Maktoum visited several times during the late 1990s. The presence of a hunting party of UAE sheikhs in winter or spring 1998 dashed U.S. hopes of a commando raid to capture bin Laden, who also reportedly attended. That tale and an account of the UAE royalty's enthusiasm for bustard-hunting with the Taliban are detailed in Steve Coll, *Ghost Wars: The Secret History of the CIA, Afghanistan, and Bin Laden, from the Soviet*

Invasion to September 10, 2001 (New York: Penguin, 2004), pp. 445–450.

12. *Los Angeles Times* interviews with former Ariana executive, January and April 2002. Mansour told the executive that the UAE had waived landing fees for all Afghan flights at Sheikh Maktoum's request. The move saved the Taliban more than $1,000 a week. The elder Sheikh al Nahyan died in November 2004, replaced by his older son, Sheikh Khalifa bin Zayid al Nahyan. In January 2006 Sheikh Maktoum was elevated to the position of UAE vice president and prime minister.

13. Ibid.; *Los Angeles Times* interviews with UAE officials, April and May 2002. Ghanem al-Hajiri, director-general of the Sharjah Airport Authority, insisted in an April 2002 interview that no weapons had moved illegally from Sharjah to Afghanistan, only "general cargo." There were no international sanctions against the flights at the time because a UN arms embargo against the Taliban was not imposed until December 2000. Other UAE officials conceded that weapons shipments from Sharjah during that period were a known problem. A senior official of the UAE's federal government said "we did manage to stop all the flights from the UAE to Afghanistan" after the UN flight embargo was imposed in 2000. But "prior to that," the official acknowledged, "they were able to smuggle anything."

14. *Los Angeles Times* interviews with Russian and UAE executives and workers, March and April 2002; also, *Los Angeles Times* interview with former Ariana flight engineer Abdul Shakur Arefee, January 2002.

15. *Los Angeles Times* interview with Inchuk, April 2002.

16. Daniszewski et al., "On the Trail."

17. Judy Pasternak and Stephen Braun, "Emirates Looked the Other Way while al Qaeda Funds Flowed," *Los Angeles Times*, January 20, 2002. Ahmed told the Ariana official that the arms originated in East Germany, Czechoslovakia, and other East European sites.

18. Translated transcript of Viktor Bout interview with Radio Echo Moskvy, February 28, 2002. Bout statement provided to the Center for Public Integrity, 2002.

19. U.S. State Department fact sheet, "African Arms Transfers, Trafficking," July 9, 2001.

20. Text of European Union Council of Ministers' embargo on the Taliban, December 1996

21. Ibid.; *Los Angeles Times* interview with Vladimir I. Sharpatov, April 2002.

22. State Department cable, U.S. embassy, Islamabad, September 29, 1996. Obtained by National Security Archive, George Washington

University. The cable relayed worried Russian reaction to the Taliban victory and recounted remarks from Taliban Mullah Abdul Jallil that relations with Russia were "tense."

23. State Department cable, April 17, 1995, assessing the arming of the Taliban, Rabbani government, and other Afghan factions. Obtained by National Security Archive, George Washington University. Also, interview with consultant who studied aid to various Afghan groups in the late 1990s.

24. Bout interview with Radio Echo Moskvy, February 28, 2002.

25. James Risen, "Russians Are Back in Afghanistan," *New York Times*, July 27, 1998.

26. Ibid.

27. Authors' interview with Bout associate, March 6, 2006.

28. Daniszewski et al., "On the Trail." *Los Angeles Times* correspondent John Daniszewski noted the contents of Taliban files with permission of Afghan officials in late March 2002.

29. UN panel reports on Sierra Leone and Angola; also, *Los Angeles Times* interview with former UN investigator Johan Peleman.

30. *Los Angeles Times* interviews with Sheikh Adbdullah bin Zayed al Saqr al Nahyan, January and April 2002.

31. *Los Angeles Times* interviews with Lakhiyalov and with Afghan government officials and review of Taliban documents, late March 2002; also interview with an official of KAS of Kyrgyzstan, April 3, 2002. According to Afghan aviation registries made available to the *Times*, the Taliban air force registered seven planes from Bout-orbit firms: on January 23, 1998, two Antonov An-12 planes bought from Flying Dolphin and Santa Cruz Imperial; on June 2, 1998, two An-32s bought from Vial; on September 18, 1998, an An-12 bought from Flying Dolphin; and on January 5, 1999, two An-12s bought from Air Cess. All of the military planes were given false registries as civilian Ariana aircraft by Taliban officials. Ariana also registered five planes purchased from suspected Bout-orbit firms: in November 1998, an An-24 bought from Flying Dolphin; on January 16, 1999, an An-24 bought from Air Cess; on March 25, 1999, an An-24 bought from Santa Cuz Imperial; on July 20, 1999, the An-24 bought from Aerovista; and on April 1, 2001, an An-24 that was bought from an unknown source but later suspected by Afghan officials as also originating with the Bout network.

32. Bout associate; authors' interview with Dirk Draulans, May 1, 2006.

33. *Los Angeles Times* interview with senior Afghan officials, March 2002.

34. *Los Angeles Times*, April 26, 2005. In late 2001, soon after the September

11 attacks, an intelligence document surfaced with a brief but tantalizing entry linking Bout to Taliban arms sales. One translation reported that "Victor previously made in the region of $50 million in Afghanistan, selling heavy ordnance of former Soviet stock to the Taliban." A January 2002 account for the Center for Public Integrity by Phillip van Niekerk and Andre Verloy dated the document to a period prior to the attacks and added that "Bout ran guns for the Taliban 'on behalf of the Pakistan government.'" Dubious about Bout's relationship with the Talibs, Johan Peleman questioned the reliability of the report, which he said came from South African sources but likely originated with Belgian intelligence. Despite his skepticism, Treasury officials publicly cited the report as the agency's Office of Foreign Assets Control ordered sanctions against "Viktor Bout's International Arms Trafficking Network." A Treasury official later reconfirmed the estimate and said it had been authenticated by American analysis, adding that the $50 million figure included both weaponry and other cargoes delivered to the Taliban.

35. Daniszewski et al., "On the Trail."
36. *Los Angeles Times* interviews with Russian aviation executives, Sharjah, April 2002.
37. Daniszewski et al., "On the Trail."
38. *Los Angeles Times* interview with U.S. diplomat, April 2002; translated copy of Sharjah Municipality trade license between Victor Butt and Sultan Hamad Said Nassir al Suwaidi, registered with UAE Ministry of Justice on March 3, 1993, and renewed on July 11, 1998.
39. *Los Angeles Times* interview with U.S. diplomat, April 2002; authors' interview with U.S. diplomat.
40. *Los Angeles Times* interviews with Valery Spurnov and other Russian air cargo executives, April 2002; "Afghanistan: Crisis of Impunity," Human Rights Watch, July 2001.
41. *Los Angeles Times* interview with Russian air executive, April 2002.
42. *Los Angeles Times*, Ariana records, and interview with Valery Spurnov, April 2002; A cache of Ariana waybills, flight records, and financial documents that surfaced in early 2003 provided a glimpse of the airline's activity between 1998 and 2000. The material—which was authenticated by a former Ariana official—includes Farid Ahmed's ANZ Sharjah bank records and utility bills, Ariana flight schedules, manifests, and crew lists, and more than thirty pages of waybills for flights to Kabul and Kandahar.
43. *Los Angeles Times* interview with Igor Abdayev, April 2002. Jet Line was later linked to Bout's orbit by CIA officials.

44. *Los Angeles Times* interviews with Spurnov and other Russian air executives, April 2002.
45. Daniszewski et al., "On the Trail."
46. *Los Angeles Times* interview with Richard Chichakli, January 2002; *Los Angeles Times* interview with U.S. official, April 2002.
47. Daniszewski et al., "On the Trail."
48. *Los Angeles Times* interview with Mankhayev, April 2002.
49. *Los Angeles Times* interview with former Ariana executive, April 2002.
50. Daniszewski et al., "On the Trail."

Chapter 8: Black Charters

1. *Los Angeles Times* interview with Jakkie Potgeiter, April 2002.
2. John Daniszewski, Stephen Braun, Judy Pasternak, Maura Reynolds, and Sergei L. Loiko, "On the Trail of a Man behind Taliban's Air Fleet," *Los Angeles Times*, May 19, 2002.
3. Afghan Ariana Airways flight and financial documents obtained by the authors; *Los Angeles Times* interview with Arefee, March 2002. Wardak was one of four Taliban air force pilots whose false Ariana identities were found in Taliban aviation files.
4. "Testimony of Detainees before the Combatant Status Review Tribunal," released March 3, 2006, by the Department of Defense, Set 29, 2001–2047.
5. *Los Angeles Times* interviews with former Ariana pilot and former Ariana executive, April 2002.
6. "Bin Laden Bodyguard Details al-Qaeda's Time in Sudan, Move to Afghanistan," *al-Quds al-Arabi*, March 21, 2005; also related by former FBI counterterror agent Jack Cloonan in Lawrence Wright, *The Looming Tower: Al-Qaeda and the Road to 9/11* (New York: Alfred A. Knopf, 2006), p. 223.
7. *Los Angeles Times* interview with former U.S. official, April 2002.
8. UN Office for Drug Control and Crime Prevention report, 1998; U.S. State Department 2000 Narcotics Control report. Total Afghan opium production jumped from twenty-five hundred tons in 1998 to forty-six hundred tons in 1999.
9. *Los Angeles Times* interviews with Dr. Ravan Farhadi, December 2001, and with U.S. officials, April 2002.
10. Stephen Braun and Judy Pasternak, "Long before Sept. 11, Bin Laden's Aircraft Flew under the Radar," *Los Angeles Times*, November 18, 2001.
11. *Los Angeles Times* interview with Julie Sirrs, November 2001.
12. 9/11 Commission report, p. 124.

13. Reuters, August 23, 1999.
14. Published minutes of meeting of UN Security Council, October 22, 1999.
15. "Consolidated List of Taliban Aircraft Issued by the Secuity Council Committee Established by Resolution 1267" (1999). The aircraft, banned from all international flights, included an Ariana Antonov An-24 previously owned by Flying Dolphin and a second Ariana An-24 of unknown origin, but suspected by Afghan officials as a Bout-network plane. A third An-24, previously owned by Aerovista and KAS, also was on the list.
16. UN list of banned Afghan planes, December 2000
17. *Los Angeles Times* interviews with Sheikh Abdullah bin Zayed al Saqr al Nahyan, January and April, 2002.
18. *Los Angeles Times* interview with former U.S. official, April 2002.
19. *Los Angeles Times* interview with Sheikh Abdullah bin Zayed al Saqr al Nahyan, January and April 2002.
20. "Report of the Committee of Experts to the UN Security Council Regarding the Arms Embargo against the Taliban," May 22, 2001.
21. *Los Angeles Times* interviews with Ariana officials, April 2002.
22. Daniszewski et al., "On the Trail"; *Los Angeles Times* interview with Farid Ahmed, April 2002.
23. *Los Angeles Times* interview with Potgeiter, April 2002; Texas state incorporation records obtained by the authors.
24. During a tour of Kabul International Airport on April 10, 2002, *Los Angeles Times* correspondent John Daniszewski found the ruins of three Taliban Antonovs. One, on the civilian side of the airport, bore the tail number, YA-DAI, of an An-24 that Taliban records indicated had been sold to the militant government from Bout's Air Cess operation and then placed with Ariana. A flight load data chart inside the plane indicated it had last flown on January 28, 2001, with forty-two passengers from Kabul to Konduz, near the front lines in the long conflict with the Northern Alliance.

Chapter 9: Gunships and Titanium

1. This account is based on the recollections of two eyewitnesses present at the meeting and who separately related the same essential elements of the story. One is Cindor Reeves, who is in a witness protection program of the United Nations–backed Special Court for Sierra Leone, where he is expected to testify against Taylor in his crimes against humanity trial in The Hague. The other source cannot be named for fear of reprisals by Bout.

2. "Final Report of the Panel of Experts on the Illegal Exploitation of Natural Resources and Other Forms of Wealth in the Democratic Republic of the Congo," S/2002/1146, United Nations, October 15, 2002, paras. 72–74.

3. Paul Salopek, "Shadowy Men Run Guns, Feed Fires of War," *Chicago Tribune*, December 24, 2001, p. A1.

4. "Final Report . . . Illegal Exploitation," para. 107.

5. This was documented in the film documentary *Darwin's Nightmare*, written and directed by Hubert Sauper, distributed by Mille et Une Productions, Coop 99 and Saga Film, 2004.

6. U.S. Department of State, notes on Sierra Leone, accessed at www.state.gov/r/pa/ei/bgn/5475.htm.

7. Authors' interviews with Cindor Reeves and second source indicated in note 1 for this chapter.

8. Authors' interviews with two sources with direct knowledge of events.

9. For a full discussion of Bah's ties to al Qaeda and other terrorist organizations see Douglas Farah, *Blood from Stones: The Secret Financial Network of Terror* (New York: Broadway Books, 2004).

10. Author interview with Cindor Reeves, Bah's aide-de-camp, November 2001.

11. *Los Angeles Times* interview with Simi Ruprah, sister of Sanjivan Ruprah, Brussels, March 2002.

12. "Executive Outcome," Federation of American Scientists, April 2002, accessed at www.fas.org/irp/world/para/executive_outcomes.htm.

13. UN Panel of Experts, UN Report on Sierra Leone, December 2000, para. 225.

14. "Final Report . . . Illegal Exploitation," paras. 72–73.

15. Ruprah interview with the FBI, January 25, 2002, transcript obtained by the authors; also, e-mails between Ruprah and Farah, summer 2006.

16. Ruprah e-mail to author, May 18, 2006.

17. "Final Report . . . Illegal Exploitation," paras. 72–73.

18. Lansana Gbrie, "War and Peace in Sierra Leone: Diamonds, Corruption, and the Lebanese Connection." Diamond and Human Security Project, Occasional Paper 6. Ottawa: Partnership Africa Canada, January 2003.

19. "Report of the Panel of Experts in Relation to Sierra Leone," United Nations, December 2000, para. 227.

20. Ruprah interview with FBI and e-mails to the authors, 2006.

21. Ibid. Ruprah's direct boss in maritime affairs was Benoni Urey, an Israeli Liberian who also was a Taylor confidant. A short, beefy man,

Urey was an avid member of the Rotary Club who was a holdover from previous regimes, retained by Taylor because he knew how to make money. Because government ministers often had to pay Taylor a high commission on any transactions within Liberia, Ruprah was told that he would pay 30 percent of the profits he reaped from his mining concessions to Taylor. The money was to be paid to Urey. In an illuminating exchange with the FBI agents, Ruprah was asked if the money he paid went to government coffers. "I don't believe so," Ruprah responded. "Rather, they went to private coffers." The FBI agent asked incredulously, "But Urey represented the government, right?" "He represented Taylor," Ruprah answered, stressing the crucial difference.

22. "Report of the Panel of Experts in Relation to Sierra Leone," para. 226.
23. Ruprah e-mail to the authors, May 18, 2006.
24. Ibid., August 1, 2006.
25. "Final Report of the Monitoring Mechanism on Angola," United Nations, S/2000/1225, December 21, 2000, paras. 142–143.
26. "Report of the Panel of Experts in Relation to Sierra Leone," para. 229.
27. Kathi Austin was the first to discover the tie between the aircraft used for the FARC weapons drops and Bout's aircraft empire.
28. Peruvian and Colombian judicial documents provided by Kathi Austin to the authors; Sean Federico-O'Murchi, "Peru Confirms Drugs-for-Guns Ring," MSNBC, August 25, 2000, accessed at www.msnbc.msn.com/id/3340855/print/1/displaymode/1098/; An Vrankckx, "European Arms Exports to Latin America: An Inventory," IPIS Background Report, March 2005, pp. 33–40.
29. Federico-O'Murchi, "Peru Confirms."
30. U.S. Department of the Treasury, Bureau of Alcohol, Tobacco, and Firearms, "Intelligence Brief: Victor But, Transnational Criminal Activities," December 2000, p. 9.
31. Ibid.
32. Ruprah interview with FBI, Washington, D.C., January 25, 2002.
33. Ibid.
34. "Report of the Panel of Experts concerning Liberia," United Nations, October 26, 2001; Belgian 2003 intelligence report on Viktor Bout, in possession of the authors.
35. "Report of the Panel of Experts concerning Liberia," October 26, 2001, para. 207.
36. Ibid., para. 257. One of the certificates from Guinea was dated September 25, 1998, almost two years older than the actual date when the weapons were actually purchased. The Guinean official who signed the original document had left the government several years before.

37. "Report of the Panel of Experts in Relation to Sierra Leone," paras. 232–234.
38. Ibid., para. 234.
39. Ibid., para. 233.
40. "Report of the Panel of Experts concerning Liberia," para. 52.
41. Ibid., para. 416. After the first two transfers, the LISCR officials refused to make further payments in that way, so Urey changed his strategy. On September 13, 2000, Urey authorized a payment of $174,000, and a week later another transfer for the same amount from the Maritime Affairs account at Ecobank in Monrovia "for onward transmission to the San Air General Trading Account in Sharjah, via the account of S. Ruprah." Further payments were made in coming months, through Ruprah to Bout and San Air General.
42. Documents in possession of the authors. The documentation from Ruprah's computer is extensive and explicit. For example, on August 24, 2000, Ruprah sent a fax of an "account statement" on what was owed to Bout by Taylor. It noted the delivery of the first helicopter on July 4, and that it cost $525,000, which had been paid in full. It listed the delivery of a second helicopter on July 27 at the same price, but that only $500,000 had been paid. It noted that "Statement 1" for weapons totaling $640,000 remained unpaid, as did "Statement 2" for weapons totaling $650,500. "Statement 2" notes "Items Delivered 23-08-00," including 4 Strela antiaircraft launchers; 16 missiles for Strela launchers; 40 100-kilogram bombs for an Mi-8 helicopter; 250,800 rounds of ammunition; and 1,016 missiles for an Mi-8 helicopter. Airfreight for the deliveries cost $125,000. In total, the "account statement" showed that Bout had been paid $1.55 million and was owed an additional $1.11 million. An undated fax sent after the first account statements was addressed "To: V" "From: SR." It noted payments made in the previous fax and other payments made for other, miscellaneous weapons-related activities. A separate document, called "Statement 3," lists the weapons scheduled for delivery on August 31, 2000, with a total value of $1,305,500. The statement lists the quantity and cost of each item on the list. The 1,000 AK-47 assault rifles were $195 each; the 100 RPG launchers cost $2,100 each; the 20 60-millimeter mortars coast $5,250 each; and the 2,000 60mm mortar bombs cost $69 each.
43. "Report of the Panel of Experts concerning Liberia," paras. 282–290.
44. Ibid., para. 288. Authors' interviews with Johan Peleman, member of the UN panel of experts on Liberia.
45. "Report of the Panel of Experts concerning Liberia," para. 290.

46. Authors' interview reporting during the crisis, and interviews with U.S. and British intelligence officials and RUF commanders.

47. On March 7, 2003, the United Nations-backed Special Court for Sierra Leone indicted Sankoh, Taylor, and Bockarie for crimes against humanity. Sankoh died in prison on July 29, 2003. Fearing Bockarie planned to turn himself in and cut a deal, Taylor reportedly ordered the execution of the commander he had publicly called his son. On May 6, 2003, Bockarie was gunned down by forces of the Liberian Special Security Service. The soldiers then proceeded to Bockarie's compound and shot down his wife and at least three children. The next month, the UN tribunal indicted Taylor himself for war crimes. It was only the second time that the sitting president of a country had been accused of crimes against humanity. Taylor was charged with creating and backing the RUF in its long spree of atrocities and use of child soldiers. Taylor also was accused of harboring members of al Qaeda sought in connection with the 1998 bombings of U.S. embassies in Kenya and Tanzania. Under mounting pressure to resign, Taylor agreed in August 2003 to go into exile in Nigeria. He remained there for three years as the prosecutor's noose tightened and UN authorities froze his assets and targeted his inner circle, including his old friend and arms connection Bout. In March 2006 Liberia's newly elected president, Ellen Johnson-Sirleaf, formally asked Nigeria to extradite Taylor to face the war crimes charges. Taylor tried to flee to Cameroon but was captured and now waits in a jail cell in The Hague for his trial.

Chapter 10: "Get Me a Warrant"

1. Human Rights Watch World Report, 2000; Agence France-Presse and Reuters accounts and weekly news roundups by the United Nations' Integrated Regional Information Network for West Africa, 2000.

2. Agence France-Presse and Reuters accounts and Human Rights Watch, World Report, 2001.

3. "Final Report of the UN Panel of Experts on Violations of Security Council Sanctions against UNITA," S/2000/203, March 10, 2000, fn. 7.

4. *Los Angeles Times* interview with Johan Peleman, January 2002.

5. Authors' interview with British intelligence analyst, June 2006.

6. House of Commons, Hansard debates, January 18, 2000.

7. Agence France-Presse and Reuters accounts and Sierra Leone government Information Services Archives, May 1–31, 2000; authors' interview with British intelligence analyst.

8. *Los Angeles Times* interview with former U.S. official, April 2002; Peter

Landesman, "Arms and the Man," *New York Times Magazine*, August 17, 2003.

9. House of Commons, Hansard debates, November 7, 2000.
10. *Los Angeles Times* interview with Peleman.
11. John Daniszewski, Stephen Braun, Judy Pasternak, Maura Reynolds, and Sergei L. Loiko, "On the Trail of a Man behind the Taliban's Air Fleet," *Los Angeles Times*, May 19, 2002.
12. *Los Angeles Times* interview with Johan Peleman, March 2002.
13. Authors' interviews with former U.S. officials; Daniszewski et al., "On the Trail."
14. Authors' interviews with former U.S. officials.
15. Texas Secretary of State Limited Liability Company Record, San Air General Trading, LLC. Registered agent: Richard A. Chichakli. Charter number: 0706956223. Filing date: 6/6/2000. Also U.S. Treasury, Office of Foreign Assets Control, Specially Designated Nationals List, April 26, 2005, San Air General Trading FZE (aka San Air General Trading LLC), P.O. Box 932-20C, Ajman, United Arab Emirates; P.O. Box 2190, Ajman, United Arab Emirates; 811 S. Central Expwy, Ste. 210, Richardson, TX 75080. In 2005, Treasury Department officials targeted both Chichakli and the Texas branch of San Air for assets freezes. In a June 2, 2005, letter to Treasury (posted on Chichakli's Web site) demanding the return of his assets, Chichakli insisted that "Treasury had no proof, nor have presented any evidence to support that business relations existed between Richard Chichakli and Victor Bout."
16. Daniszewski et al., "On the Trail."
17. *Los Angeles Times* interview with former U.S. official.
18. *Los Angeles Times* interview with Jerry Dobby, April 2002; Air Cess incorporation records, Florida Department of State, Division of Corporations, document 97000081214, filed 9/18/1997, dissolved 9/21/2001.
19. *Los Angeles Times* interview with former U.S. official.

Chapter 11: Now or Never

1. This account of the briefing was based on conversations with a participant in the meeting and a person who was briefed on the session immediately after it took place.
2. "Final Report on the Monitoring Mechanism on Angola Sanctions," S/2000/1225, para. 136. "Another company apparently involved in the Air Cess network is the Liberian registered air company Santa Cruz Imperial, a subsidiary of the Flying Dolphin, owned by United Arab Emirates. Although it is registered in Liberia, it lists its operations office as Dubai, United Arab Emirates, but the actual base for the

aircraft seems to be in Sharjah. In the past, one of its aircraft, EL-ALE, was noted as supplying UNITA forces

3. *Los Angeles Times* interview with senior Belgian Foreign Ministry official, February 2002.
4. Peter Landesman, "Arms and the Man," *New York Times Magazine,* August 17, 2003, p. 57.
5. *Los Angeles Times* interview with Jan D'Olivera, April 2002.
6. "Report of the Panel of Experts pursuant to Security Council resolution 1343 concerning Liberia," S/20001/1015, October 26, 2001, para. 19.
7. Ibid., pp. 51–52.
8. Ibid., para. 19.
9. This account is based on the account of one person who attended the party. Other sources confirmed that the party took place but declined to provide details.
10. Douglas Farah, "Arrest Aides Pursuit of Weapons Network," *Washington Post,* February 26, 2002, p. A1; authors' interviews with U.S. officials.
11. "United Nations List of Individuals Affected by the Travel Ban," Resolution 1323 (2001).
12. Copy of invoice in possession of the authors.
13. Ibid.
14. Authors' interviews with European intelligence sources; review of intelligence documents by author.
15. Excerpt of Sanjivan Ruprah e-mail obtained by the *Los Angeles Times* from Belgian attorney Luc de Temmerman, former lawyer for Ruprah.
16. Copy of the proposal in possession of the authors. The correspondence was first made public by the International Peace Information Service of Belgium on October 13, 2003. The documents were found on the hard drive of Ruprah's computer following his arrest in Italy in August 2002, after his skipping bail in Belgium.
17. *Los Angeles Times* interview with Johan Peleman, March 2002.
18. Ibid., *Los Angeles Times* interview with Luc de Temmerman, March 2002.
19. Copy of the proposal in possession of the authors, note 16.
20. Ibid.
21. Farah, "Arrest Aides Pursuit"; Stephen Braun, Judy Pasternak, and Sebastian Rotella, "Al Qaeda Linked to Russian Arms Dealer," *Los Angeles Times,* February 16, 2002.
22. Copy of the proposal in possession of the authors. Its existence was first made public by the International Peace Information Service of Belgium on October 13, 2003.

23. Excerpt of Ruprah e-mail obtained by the *Los Angeles Times*.
24. Authors' interview with European intelligence official.
25. Andre Verloy, "Victor Bout's American Connection," Center for Public Integrity, June 7, 2004.
26. Authors' interview with private contractor, May 10, 2006
27. *Los Angeles Times* interview with U.S. Defense official, May 2002.
28. First report of the Monitoring Group on Afghanistan, UN Security Council, January 15, 2002, S/2002/65, para. 22.
29. Transcript, including time and date of interview, in possession of the authors.
30. Eddy Surmont, "Justice System: Four Bulgarians Arrested: Arms Trafficking from Ostend," *Le Soir*, February 9, 2002, trans. FBIS.
31. Press release, by Luc de Temmerman, Brussels, February 18, 2002.
32. Ibid.
33. Copy of the letter in possession of the authors. The letter confirms that Ruprah's lawyers had told him his telephone had been tapped, confirmed to the authors by Belgian officials.
34. *London Sunday Telegraph* and Australian Associated Press, February 17, 2002
35. Authors' interviews with two sources with direct knowledge of the operation.

Chapter 12: "We Are Very Limited in What We Can Do"

1. With Peter Hain's public attacks on Bout, the British press, led by the *Financial Times*, the *Sunday Times*, and the *Guardian*, had published accounts of Bout's activities. The Belgian reporter Dirk Draulans did groundbreaking work by reporting on his travels with Bout in the DRC bush. The first American to profile Bout was the *Chicago Tribune*'s Paul Salopek, a two-time Pulitzer Prize winner who detailed the Bout network's activities in the DRC and elsewhere in Africa. The articles, which ran in December 2001, included an extensive interview with Richard Chichakli, who at the time was hardly shy about identifying himself as a Bout associate. In late January 2002 a new cluster of accounts raised the first public hints about the Bout organization's clandestine dealings with Islamic militants in Afghanistan. The first was an article that appeared in the *Washington Monthly* by investigative reporter Ken Silverstein. The piece told briefly of the Bout operation's shift from the Northern Alliance to the Taliban and quoted Lee Wolosky, who had returned to a private law practice in New York. Within days, Andre Verloy and Philippe van Niekirk of the International Consortium of Investigative Journalists cited secret Belgian and

South African intelligence reports that reported the Bout network's alleged $50 million earnings from Taliban weapons sales. After a Novermber 2001 story chronicling the secret use by the Taliban and al Qaeda of Ariana Airways flights to ship in arms, transfer cash and narcotics, and move terror operatives, Judy Pasternak and Stephen Braun of the *Los Angeles Times* followed up with a January 2002 story describing the Sharjah meeting between Mullah Farid Ahmed and agents for Bout-orbit air firms. The *Washington Post*'s Douglas Farah followed with several stories following the trail of contraband diamonds, gold, and other commodities that had been exploited by both Islamic militants and Bout's operation. A *Los Angeles Times* team that included Braun and Pasternak and Moscow staffers John Daniszewski, Maura Reynolds, and Sergei L. Loiko responded in mid-May with a detailed report on the secret scheme that enabled the Taliban to amass a fleet of cargo planes sold by Bout-linked companies. The story also provided the first full account of efforts by U.S. and international officials to arrest Bout. Finally, in August 2003, the *New York Times Magazine* carried a lengthy profile based on a extensive interview with Bout by freelancer Peter Landesman.

2. Translated transcript of Viktor Bout interview with Radio Echo Moskvy, February 28, 2002.
3. Ibid.
4. "Gunrunners," *Frontline*, PBS, May 2002, accessed at www.pbs.org/frontlineworld/stories/sierraleone/bout.html.
5. Ibid.
6. "In Response to the Recent Published Reports concerning Victor Bout," posted by the ICIJ at www.publicintegrity.org/report.aspx?aid=244&sid=100.
7. Ibid.
8. Ibid.
9. Viktor Baranetsm and Igor Chernyak, "Interview with Viktor But," *Moscow Komsomlskaya Pravda*, March 5, 2002, trans. FBIS.
10. Ibid.
11. *Los Angeles Times* interview with U.S. national security official, May 2002.
12. "Report of the Panel of Experts on Liberia," October 25, 2002, paras. 62–82.
13. Ibid., p. 18.
14. Nicholas Woods, "New Yugoslav-Iraqi Ties Alleged: U.S. Says Defense Firms Developing Cruise Missile for Baghdad," *Washington Post*, October 27, 2002, p. A1.

15. "Report of the Panel of Experts on Liberia," para. 18. For a look at the impact of the fishing on Lake Victoria and the presence of Russian pilots there after delivering weapons elsewhere, see the film documentary *Darwin's Nightmare*, written and directed by Hubert Sauper, distributed by Mille et Une Productions, Coop 99 and Saga Film, 2004.
16. Douglas Farah, "Al Qaeda Gold Moved to Sudan," *Washington Post*, September 3, 2002, p. A1.
17. Translation of Osama bin Laden's audio message of May 6, 2004, provided to the authors by Rohan Gunaratna.
18. Farah, "Al Qaeda Gold."
19. "Belize: Country Brief 2003," Intelligence Division, Drug Enforcement Administration, March 2004, p. 5.
20. Authors' interviews with Belgian officials and review of intelligence reports.
21. *Los Angeles Times* interview with Joseph M. Meyers, October 2004.
22. William F. Wechsler and Lee S. Wolosky, "Moscow Should Hand Over Fugitive Weapons Trafficker," *Los Angeles Times*, July 23, 2002.
23. *Airway*, August 2001, pp. 15–16.
24. Authors' interviews with senior U.S. Treasury official, May 23, 2006.

Chapter 13: Welcome to Baghdad

1. *National Defense*, July 2002. In a May 2006 interview with the authors, Handy, now retired from the air force, added that U.S. military planners went with Russian and Ukrainian air firms in Afghanistan and later in Iraq because their planes had reliable, heavy-duty lift capacity and "they were already flying in the area." Handy added that West European carriers, for example, rarely won cargo contracts because "we never had an offer."
2. *Los Angeles Times* interviews with Sergeant Steve Goldblatt and Captain Mason Sellers, November 2004.
3. Ibid.; RAMCC flight records obtained by the *Los Angeles Times*.
4. Mark Turner, Mark Huband, and Andrew Parker, "UK Snubs France over Arms Trafficker," *Financial Times*, May 17, 2004.
5. Ibid.; RAMCC flight records.
6. Stephen Braun, Judy Pasternak, and T. Christian Miller, "Blacklisted Russian Tied to Iraq Deals," *Los Angeles Times*, December 14, 2004.
7. *Los Angeles Times* interview with U.S. officials, November, 2004.
8. *Washington Post*, May 18, 2004.
9. *Los Angeles Times* interview with Belgian Foreign Ministry official, November 2004.

10. *Los Angeles Times* interview with Johan Peleman, October 2004.

11. RAMCC and Sharjah International Airport flight records, and Defense Logistics Agency records obtained by the *Los Angeles Times*; also, authors' interview with air transport firm executive, July 16, 2005.

12. Braun, Pasternak, and Miller, "Blacklisted Russian."

13. *Los Angeles Times* interview with Keith Chapman, November 2004.

14. *Los Angeles Times* interview with Dinu Kabiwar, November 2004.

15. Authors' interview with air cargo executive, April 18, 2006.

16. RAMCC flight records

17. *Los Angeles Times* interviews with Igor Abadeyev, April 2002, and with U.S. officials, April 2002. An intelligence document provided to the *Times* showed that nine Jet Line planes were positively identified as Bout assets: three BAC One-Elevens, two Ilyushin Il-76s, two Lockheed L-1329s, an Ilyushin Il-62, and an Antonov An-72. Aerocom's and Jet Line's shared address and phone appeared in Moldovan air cargo directories and was confirmed by U.S. officials.

18. UN panel of experts' report on Liberia arms embargo violations, April 2003; *Los Angeles Times* interview with U.S. official, November 2004.

19. RAMCC flight records; Amnesty International report, "Dead on Time," May 10, 2006; *Guardian*, May 10, 2006.

20. RAMCC flight records; *Los Angeles Times* interview with Shavia Ejav of the British Department for International Development, December 13, 2004.

21. Walker; RAMCC e-mails

22. RAMCC files; *Los Angeles Times* interview with former UN investigator, November 2004. The information about British Gulf's bank activities with San Air emerged from a 2001 inquiry by a UN Security Council panel of experts into Liberia's violations of a UN arms embargo.

23. *Los Angeles Times* interview with Igor Zhuravylov, November 2004.

24. Braun, Pasternak, and Miller, "Blacklisted Russian."

Chapter 14: Blacklisted and Still Flying

1. State Department diplomatic cable obtained by the *Los Angeles Times*.

2. E-mails obtained by the *Los Angeles Times*.

3. *Los Angeles Times* interview with Jeffrey Oster, November, 2004.

4. Letter from Assistant Secretary of State Paul V. Kelly to Senator Russell Feingold, June 2, 2004; *Los Angeles Times* interview with Johan Peleman, November 15, 2004.

5. Authors' interviews with U.S. Treasury officials, May 23, 2006.

6. Ibid.
7. *Los Angeles Times* interview with senior Treasury official, November 2004.
8. State Department Office of Logistics Management order, June 7, 2004. Named on the ninety-day suspension list were Viktor Bout (along with eight aliases), his brother Sergei, and associates Richard Chichakli and Victor Lebedev. Sanctioned firms included Irbis, Air Bas, Air Cess, Air Pass, San Air General Trade FZE, San Air General LLC, Central African Airways, and Transavia Travel Agency.
9. State Department internal memo, June 15, 2004.
10. Authors' interview with State Department official, May 12, 2006.
11. Ibid.
12. Memo from Deputy Secretary of State Lincoln P. Bloomfield Jr., June 29, 2004.
13. Presidential Executive Order 13348, OFAC Liberia sanctions
14. Stephen Braun, Judy Pasternak, and T. Christian Miller, "Blacklisted Russian Tied to Iraq Deals," *Los Angeles Times*, December 14, 2004. Account of Bout network's flights for the U.S. military and private contractors in Iraq.
15. Authors' interview with State Department official, May 2006.
16. Ibid.; Jonathan S. Landay, Knight Ridder Newspapers, April 28, 2005
17. *Los Angeles Times* interview with Federal Express official in Dubai, November 2004.
18. *Los Angeles Times* interview with Air Mobility Command spokesman, December 8, 2004.
19. Authors' interview with private contractor, May 10, 2006
20. Letter from Deputy Secretary of Defense Paul Wolfowitz to Senator Russell Feingold, January 31, 2005.
21. *Los Angeles Times* interviews with Fort Leonard Wood/Forney officials, November 2004.
22. Authors' interview with Treasury official, May 23, 2004.
23. Internal State Department memo, July 2004, provided to the authors.
24. Internal State Department memo, September 2004, provided to the authors.
25. *Los Angeles Times* interviews with Victor Lebedev and Oleg Vakushin, November 2004.
26. *Los Angeles Times* interview with KBR spokeswoman Wendy Hall, December 13, 2004; also Lebedev and military officials, December 2004.
27. Alexander Harrowell, Yorkshire Ranter blog, December 9, 2005.

28. "Arms Flows in Eastern DR Congo," All Party Parliamentary Group on the Great Lakes Region, pp. 21–22.

29. Douglas Farah and Kathi Austin, "Air America: Viktor Bout and the Pentagon," *New Republic*, January 23, 2006, p. 11.

30. "United Nations Group of Experts Report on the Democratic Republic of Congo," January 25, 2005, paras. 81–83.

31. Ibid., paras. 66–67.

32. Ibid., para. 76.

33. OFAC designation, "Viktor Bout's International Arms Trafficking Network," April 26, 2004; authors' interviews with U.S. government officials; Richard Chichakli Web site.

34. Authors' interview with U.S. official.

35. Ibid.; OFAC designation, April 26, 2006. The Treasury action targeted Sergei Bout, Richard Chichakli, Sergeuei Dennisenko, Valeriy Naydo, and twenty-nine companies: Abidjan Freight (Liberia); Air Bas (Sharjah); Air Cess (Equatorial Guinea); Air Zory (Bulgaria); ATC, Ltd. (Gibraltar); Bakuvu Aviation Transport (Liberia); Business Air Services (Liberia); Centrafricain Airlines (Central African Republic); Central African Development Fund (Richardson, Texas); CET Aviation Enterprise (Ajman, UAE); Chichakli and Associates (Richardson, Texas); Richard A. Chichakli, PC (Richardson, Texas); Continue Professional Education, Inc. (Richardson, Texas); DHH Enterprises Inc. (Richardson, Texas); Gambia New Millenium Air, Inc. (Gambia); IB of America Holdings, Inc. (Richardson, Texas); Irbis Air Company (Kazakhstan); Moldtransavia SRL (Moldavia); Nordic, Ltd. (Bulgaria); Odessa Air (Uganda); Orient Star Corp. (Richardson, Texas); Rockman, Ltd. (Bulgaria); San Air General Trading, FZE (Ajman, UAE); Santa Cruz Imperial (Sharjah, UAE); Southbound, Ltd. (Gibraltar); Trans Aviation Global Group (Richardson, Texas); Transavia Network (Sharjah); Vial Company (Delaware); and Westbound, Ltd. (Gibraltar).

36. May 12, 2005, document obtained by authors.

Epilogue

1. "Russian Businessman Denies His Involvement in Arms Deliveries to the Congo," MosNews, November 3, 2006.

2. "Peres: Hizbullah Used Russian-Made Weapons," Associated Press, September 6, 2006; "Russia Fires Arms Export Official after Israeli Complaints," *Jerusalem Post*, October 5, 2006.

3. "Air Company 'Sayaht' Opens Inner Investigation on Supposed Arms

Traffic to Somalia," accessed at http://intelligence-summit.blogspot .com/2006/08/air-company-sayahat-opens-inner.html.

4. Ibid.; The Kazakh Foreign Ministry declared: "With reference to information published by a number of media about illegal exports of military freights by an airplane Il-76, supposedly with Kazakhstan symbols, to Mogadishu, Somalia, the Ministry of Foreign Affairs of Kazakhstan is authorized to declare that the Republic of Kazakhstan has nothing to do with this fact and that it has never exported any arms to that country."

5. Application and affidavit for search warrant sworn out by U.S. Alcohol, Tobacco, and Firearms special agents Mitchell A. Worley and Michael A. Culp and approved by U.S. magistrate Thomas M. Blewitt, November 7, 2006; Stephen Braun, "Arms Transport Probe Zeros in on Pennsylvania Store," *Los Angeles Times*, November 24, 2006

6. Tom Masland and Andrew Cohen, "Deal with the Devil: Writer-Director Andrew Niccol on What It Took to Make *Lord of War*," *Newsweek* Web exclusive, September 23, 2005, accessed at www.msnbc .msn.com/id/9442606/site/newsweek/.

7. "Russian Businessman Denies His Involvement."

8. "Executive Order Blocking the Property of Certain Persons Contributing to the Conflict in the Democratic Republic of Congo," October 31, 2006, accessed at www.whitehouse.gov/news/releases/2006/ 10/20061031-2.html

9. "Russian Businessman Denies His Involvement."

INDEX

www.ingramcontent.com/pod-product-compliance
Lightning Source LLC
Jackson TN
JSHW080856211224
75817JS00003B/86